Researching Transitions in Lifelong Learning

In today's society, people and organisations are increasingly undergoing processes of transition. This affects all areas of life: our jobs, our relationships, our status, our communities, our engagement in civil society, our lifestyles, even understandings of our own identity. Each person must expect and make ready for transitions, engaging in learning as a fundamental strategy for handling change. This is where lifelong learning steps in. From career guidance to third-age programmes, from 'learning to learn' in kindergarten to MBA, from Mozart for babies to gender reassignment counselling, people face a crowded world of learning activities designed to help them through transitions.

Researching Transitions in Lifelong Learning presents new research from Britain, Australia and North America. The authors include leading scholars with established international reputations – such as Kathryn Ecclestone, Sue Webb, Gert Biesta, W. Norton Grubb, Nicky Solomon and David Boud – as well as emerging researchers with fresh and sometimes challenging perspectives. While emphasising the complexity and variety of people's experiences of learning transitions, as well as acknowledging the ways in which they are embedded in the specific contexts of everyday life, the authors share a common interest in understanding the lived experiences of change from the learner's perspective. This volume therefore provides an opportunity to take stock of recent research into transitions, seen in the context of lifelong learning, and outlines important messages for future policy and practice. It will also appeal to researchers worldwide in education and industrial sociology, as well as students on courses in post-compulsory education.

John Field is Professor of Lifelong Learning at the University of Stirling and co-director of the Centre of Research in Lifelong Learning, Glasgow Caledonian University. He is author of *Social Capital* (Routledge, 2003) and co-editor of *Lifelong Learning: Education across the lifespan* (Routledge, 2000).

Jim Gallacher is Emeritus Professor of Lifelong Learning, Centre for Research in Lifelong Learning, Glasgow Caledonian University. He is author of *Researching Widening Access to Lifelong Learning: Issues and approaches in international research* (Routledge, 2004) and *Learning Outside the Academy* (Routledge, 2006).

Robert Ingram is a Research Fellow at the Centre for Research in Lifelong Learning, Glasgow Caledonian University. He is a political scientist who has worked on a number of studies in lifelong learning policy, and he has published a number of research papers.

Researching Transitions in Lifelong Learning

Edited by John Field, Jim Gallacher and Robert Ingram

Routledge
Taylor & Francis Group

LONDON AND NEW YORK

First published 2009
by Routledge
2 Park Square, Milton Park, Abingdon, Oxon OX14 4RN

Simultaneously published in the USA and Canada
by Routledge
270 Madison Ave, New York, NY 10016

Routledge is an imprint of the Taylor & Francis Group, an informa business

© 2009 Selection and editorial matter, John Field, Jim Gallacher
and Robert Ingram; individual chapters, the contributors

Typeset in Garamond by Wearset Ltd, Boldon, Tyne and Wear
Printed and bound in Great Britain by TJ International Ltd,
Padstow, Cornwall

British Library Cataloguing in Publication Data
A catalogue record for this book is available from the British
Library

Library of Congress Cataloging- in-Publication Data
Researching transitions in lifelong learning / edited by John Field,
Jim Gallacher, and Robert Ingram.
p. cm.
1. Continuing education. 2. Adult education. I. Field, John, 1949–
II. Gallacher, Jim, 1946– III. Ingram, Robert, Dr.
LC5215.R45 2009
374—dc22

2008055166

ISBN10: 0-415-49598-9 (hbk)
ISBN10: 0-415-49599-7 (pbk)
ISBN10: 0-203-87517-6 (ebk)

ISBN13: 978-0-415-49598-1 (hbk)
ISBN13: 978-0-415-49599-8 (pbk)
ISBN13: 978-0-203-87517-9 (ebk)

Contents

Contributors

Barbara Allan is Senior Lecturer in the Business School at the University of Hull, UK.

Ann-Marie Bathmaker is Professor in the School of Education at University of the West of England, Bristol, UK.

Gert Biesta is Professor of Education at the Stirling Institute of Education, UK, and Visiting Professor for Education and Democratic Citizenship at Örebro University and Mälardalen University, Sweden.

David Boud is Professor of Adult Education in the Department of Education, University of Technology Sydney, Australia.

Clive Chappell is Associate Dean at the Department of Education, University of Technology Sydney, Australia.

Kim Diment is Associate Research Fellow in the School of Education and Lifelong Learning, University of Exeter, UK.

Kathryn Ecclestone is Professor of Post-Compulsory Education, Oxford Brookes University, UK.

John Field is Professor in the Stirling Institute of Education and Co-Director of the Centre for Research in Lifelong Learning, University of Stirling, UK.

Jim Gallacher is Emeritus Professor in the Centre for Research in Lifelong Learning, Glasgow Caledonian University, UK.

Barry Golding is Associate Professor in the School of Education at the University of Ballarat, Australia.

André P. Grace is Professor in the Department of Educational Policy Studies, University of Alberta, Canada.

Garnet Grosjean is Lecturer in the Department of Educational Studies, and Senior Research Fellow at the Centre for Policy Studies in Higher Education and Training, University of British Columbia, Canada.

W. Norton Grubb holds the David Gardner Chair in Higher Education at the University of California, Berkeley, USA.

Muir Houston is Lecturer in the Department of Adult and Continuing Education, University of Glasgow, UK.

Robert Ingram is Research Fellow in the Centre for Research in Lifelong Learning, Glasgow Caledonian University, UK.

Art Kube is President of the Council of Senior Citizens Organizations of British Columbia, Canada.

Jill Lawrence is Senior Lecturer in the School of Humanities and Communication and Associate Dean in the Faculty of Arts at the University of Southern Queensland, Australia.

Robert Lawy is Senior Lecturer in the School of Education and Lifelong Learning, University of Exeter, UK.

Yann Lebeau is Lecturer in the School of Education and Lifelong Learning, University of East Anglia, UK.

Dina Lewis is Head of the Centre for Lifelong Learning at the University of Hull, UK.

Sylvia MacLeay is Vice-President of the Council of Senior Citizens Organizations of British Columbia, Canada.

Gavin Moodie is Principal Policy Advisor to the Vice Chancellor, Griffith University, Australia.

Uma Patel is Lecturer in the Department of Education and Lifelong Learning, City University London, UK.

Sheila Pither is Treasurer of the Council of Senior Citizens Organizations of British Columbia, Canada.

Jocey Quinn is Professor in the Institute for Policy Studies in Education, London Metropolitan University, UK.

Donna Rooney is Lecturer in the Department of Education, University of Technology Sydney, Australia.

Hermine Scheeres is Associate Professor in the Department of Education, University of Technology Sydney, Australia.

Laurence Solkin is Head of the Centre for Adult Education, Department of Education and Lifelong Learning, City University London, UK.

Nicky Solomon is Professor in the Faculty of Education at University of Technology Sydney, Australia.

Michael Tedder is Research Fellow in the School of Education and Lifelong Learning, University of Exeter, UK.

Will Thomas is Senior Research Associate at University Campus Suffolk, UK.

Simon Warren is Lecturer in Critical Policy Studies, School of Education, University of Sheffield, UK.

Ruth Watkins is Lecturer in the Stirling Institute of Education, University of Stirling, UK.

Sue Webb is Professor of Continuing Education and Director of the Institute of Lifelong Learning, School of Education, University of Sheffield, UK.

Leesa Wheelahan is Senior Lecturer in the School of Education and Professional Studies, Griffith University, Australia.

Chapter 1

Learning transitions

Research, policy, practice

Robert Ingram, John Field and Jim Gallacher

Transitions in a liquid age

References to constant change are something of a cliché, but are none the less apt. Well over a decade ago, in the early days of the current policy pre-occupation with lifelong learning, Richard Edwards drew attention to the ways in which the language of change had become a pervasive theme of our times (Edwards 1997). Familiar suspects parade before us as the drivers of change: globalisation, new technologies, science-based innovation, organisa-tional restructuring and the search for competitive advantage (for a detailed analysis at transnational level see Schemmann 2007). To these we might add cultural and social factors, such as the continuing rise in the aspirations of – and expectations from – women, the apparently inexorable growth in average life expectancy and (perhaps more controversially) a tendency towards indi-vidualisation of values and lifestyles.

Little wonder, then, that life transitions have become such a focus of atten-tion among researchers. Surrounded by a wall-to-wall discourse of change, people have had to adjust their expectations; constantly told that 'A job is not for life any more', they have learned to expect uncertainty, regardless of whether things are actually changing or not. And for many people, life is bringing new challenges and experiences, which are certainly experienced subjectively as being unprecedented in their scale and speed. This is not simply to suggest that there has been a quantitative growth in the number of transitions that any individual might make in the course of their life, though there are compelling reasons for supposing this to be the case, including the plain fact that people who live longer than previous generations are likely to survive through more changes as a result. The public discourse of change ensures that people are sensitised to the possibility and the experience of transition, and this in turn helps create a ready market for educational mater-ials such as self-help texts that purport to help individuals navigate their way through the choppy waters of life today (Chappell *et al.* 2003). And even when you do not really expect something to change, you are aware that other people's decisions might affect you at any time – in your job, in your family, in your home or in your leisure activities – and you may conclude that it is prudent to adopt the old Boy Scout motto, and be prepared.

Transition is a fundamental feature of life in late modernity. It is at the heart of much contemporary social theory, a point illustrated particularly clearly by Zygmunt Bauman's torrent of writings on 'liquid life' (Bauman 2000, 2005). For Bauman, each social routine or institution, every relationship and practice, is fluid and open to change; there are no fixed points on today's social compass. And flexible citizens need to dip in and out of education and training, constantly seeking insurance against the risks and uncertainties of tomorrow (Bauman 2001). Anthony Giddens, whose theories of institutionalised reflexivity similarly reflect a preoccupation with change and its implications, has also concluded that lifelong learning is the main educational consequence, and built it into his conception of 'Third Way' policies (Giddens 2000).

Lifelong learning and active citizens

Third Way policies envisage a renegotiation of the contract between citizen and the state. In seeking to 'activate' the citizen, so that individuals and businesses plan ahead for their future well-being and success and assume the lion's share of responsibility for investing in future skills and knowledge, Third Way thinking shares a very similar outlook to much centrist political thinking on the future of welfare (see for example Rosanvallon 1995). For Edwards (2007), the discourse of lifelong learning has served a legitimating function, constructing notions of the learning citizen as a way of engaging people in planning for their own learning, as well as underpinning a pronounced vocational tack in funding and structures. Andreas Fejes (2006) detects similar processes at work in his analysis of Swedish policies on lifelong learning.

These ideas place the individual in the spotlight, where each person must expect and make ready for transitions and engage in learning as a fundamental strategy for handling change. And citizen-workers who dip in and out of education and training will also be engaging in almost permanent transitions in their learning as well as using learning to prepare for and cope with other transitions. In turn, each individual faces increasingly differentiated trajectories through their lives resulting from the particular constellations of transitions, and their various outcomes, that they experience. And these individualising tendencies reinforce the absence of a prescribed script for many of the transitions; habit and routine no longer provide a reliable guide to decision making (Giddens 1990). People's trajectories are partly shaped by their own capacities for exercising control over their lives, capacities that include different degrees of reflexivity and levels of human capital; but as well as this agency, people's trajectories are embedded in a lived context of external factors, which structure the opportunities that people face (Biesta and Tedder 2007).

So how has the life course fared in liquid modernity? Have postmodern conditions thrown the life course into a chaos of endless choice? Are transitions experienced as coercion, a kind of eviction of the self, or do they represent people – either as individuals or as groups – achieving what they desire? From a broadly postmodern perspective, it has been argued that the life cycle has become increasingly elective and fragmented. Thus Glastra, Hake and Schedler recently suggested that:

> As is now well established, the standard biography has been replaced by the 'elective biography'.... This development has two corollaries. One is that in certain periods of life, many different tasks must be combined.... The second is that given the individualization of life courses, coordination of life and work on an aggregate social level becomes problematic.
>
> (2004: 295)

While arguably this is an exaggerated claim, it does point to some aspects of non-linearity that seem to be characteristic of late modernity. Institutionalisation has been accompanied by individualisation, in a wider context where there are strong economic and cultural pressures favouring greater flexibility; these are experienced by a variety of actors as deeply contradictory tendencies, and they increasingly form the focus for a rather heated public debate over issues such as retirement age and pensions reform (Kohli 2003: 536).

Transitions may therefore be seen as personal troubles and public issues, but contemporary conditions have tended to individualise them and emphasise the individual's responsibility for their own life planning. And this is where lifelong learning steps in. From career guidance to third-age programmes, from 'learning to learn' in kindergarten to MBA, from Mozart for babies to gender reassignment counselling, people face a crowded world of learning activities designed to help them through transitions. The 'silent explosion' of adult learning (Field 2006) that has been experienced in many western countries includes much that might be described as 'transitional learning', or in Alheit's words, as 'biographical learning', in which the capacity to learn for and from one's own life is an increasingly significant resource (1994).

Researching transitions

This book presents selected papers from the fourth biennial international conference of the Centre for Research in Lifelong Learning (CRLL). A joint initiative of Glasgow Caledonian University and the University of Stirling, CRLL was established in 1999 with a view to promoting research and debate over lifelong learning in post-compulsory education and training. The volume therefore provides an opportunity for taking stock of recent research into transitions, seen in the context of lifelong learning. This introductory chapter seeks to place the papers against the background of earlier work on this theme, and notes what appear to be some general trends among scholars working in the area.

First, it should be said that when it comes to adult life, research on transitions is still relatively underdeveloped. There is a comparatively mature literature on transitions among young people, and particularly on the transition from youth to adulthood and from school to work, but this has yet to make a significant impact on studies of adult transitions; and this work has not yet stretched out to encompass continuing transitions through the life course. Recent youth transitions research should be of considerable interest to anyone interested in transitions and lifelong learning, linking an understanding of youth agency with recognition of structures and constraints, informed by wider theoretical understandings of learning lives in late modernity – sometimes conceptualised, following Ulrich Beck, as 'risk society' (see for example Walther *et al.* 2006).

Second, much adult education literature on transitions has tended to focus on movements into particular forms of learning. By far the largest body of work has concerned movement into higher education, with far less attention even within this sub-field being given to what happens next to the adults who enter university.

While participation research has developed incrementally since the 1960s, research into access developed relatively rapidly as a response to policy concerns that first emerged in the late 1970s. Peter Scott (2007: 23) has suggested that most access research falls into three broad types: macro-level studies of the evolution of higher education systems, analyses of particular policy initiatives aimed at broadening or increasing access and detailed studies, often conducted by practitioners, of student experience. Effectively, though, the study of access has until recently generally meant the study of recruitment, with a particular focus on constraints – often described as barriers – to recruitment. Osborne and Gallacher (2007: 11) correctly note that there is increasing interest in the outcomes of study, particularly in higher education where the costs of expansion have generated a wider policy debate about who benefits (and who should pay), but this is a comparatively recent development.

Third, the adult education literature sometimes tends to paint transitions as difficult, troubling, even unpleasant. The dominant view is that people must set out to remedy deficits, such as poor literacy skills, weak employability or a lack of cultural capital. They must then negotiate the various barriers that deny them access to learning opportunities, and then navigate the middle-class values and procedures of the providing institution and its staff. Even once they have joined a learning programme, people need access to emotional support in the form of counselling and informational support in the form of guidance, to help them make sense of the confusing and alien world that they have entered (Ecclestone 2004). Ideas of collective learning and social purpose, it is claimed, are being subordinated to the imperatives of social policy and social control (Martin 2003). Instead of bonding together in solidarity, uncovering the causes of oppression and learning how to create a new world, learners plod fearfully down individualised pathways through a hostile and threatening terrain.

Nevertheless, as these papers show, there is an emerging body of research on transitions in adult life that is promising to make a major contribution to our understanding of lifelong learning. This can be seen as part of a wider set of developments in social science research into adult learning. First, the wider biographical turn in adult education research has focused attention on the interplay of learning with other spheres of adults' lives, as these processes work out across the life course (West *et al.* 2007). Second, from a rather different methodological perspective, the study of transitions has also been encouraged by the application of new quantitative techniques to longitudinal data sets, which enable researchers to trace the wider impact of changes on people's lives over time (see Bynner and Joshi 2007). This work is at a relatively early stage, however, and while it has shed considerable light on some of the wider benefits of adult learning (Schuller *et al.* 2004), it has yet to be applied systematically to experiences of learning transitions. Third, wider theoretical preoccupations with the centrality of change and flexibility in contemporary social life have also helped to focus attention on the meaning and nature of transitions for adults across the life course.

So, to return to the agenda for researchers, this leaves us with some remarkably challenging and demanding tasks. The chapters in this volume are presented in this spirit, as contributions to an ongoing debate over the ways in which people learn for, from and through transitions across the course of their lives. While emphasising the complexity and variety of people's experiences of learning transitions, as well as acknowledging the ways in which they are embedded in the specific contexts of everyday life, the authors share a common interest in understanding the lived experiences of change from the learners' perspective. While much remains to be done, and significant gaps remain (with respect to migration, ethnicity and nationality in the context of globalised transitions, simply to take one example), the chapters confirm the fruitfulness of this agenda for continuing research. They also contain important messages for policy and practice.

References

Alheit, P. (1994) 'The "biographical question" as a challenge to adult education', *International Review of Education* 40, 283–298.

Bauman, Z. (2000) *Liquid Modernity*, Cambridge: Polity.

Bauman, Z. (2001) *The Individualized Society*, Cambridge: Polity.

Bauman, Z. (2005) *Liquid Life*, Cambridge: Polity.

Biesta, G. and Tedder, M. (2007) 'Agency and learning in the lifecourse: Towards an ecological perspective', *Studies in the Education of Adults* 39, 132–149.

Bynner, J. and Joshi, H. (2007) 'Building the evidence base from longitudinal data: The aims, content and achievements of the British birth cohort studies', *Innovation: The European Journal of Social Science Research* 20, 159–179.

Chappell, C., Rhodes, C., Solomon, N., Tennant, M. and Yates, L. (2003) *Reconstructing the Lifelong Learner: Pedagogy and identity in individual, organisational and social change*, London: Routledge.

Ecclestone, K. (2004) 'Learning or therapy? The demoralisation of education', *British Journal of Educational Studies* 52, 112–137.

Edwards, R. (1997) *Changing Places: Flexibility, lifelong learning and a learning society*, London: Routledge.

Fejes, A. (2006) 'The planetspeak discourse of lifelong learning in Sweden: what is an educable adult?' *Journal of Education Policy* 21, 697–716.

Field, J. (2006) *Lifelong Learning and the New Educational Order*, Stoke on Trent: Trentham.

Giddens, A. (1990) *The Consequences of Modernity*, Cambridge: Polity.

Giddens, A. (2000) *The Third Way and its Critics*, Cambridge: Polity.

Glastra, F., Hake, B. and Schedler, P. (2004) 'Lifelong learning as transitional learning', *Adult Education Quarterly* 54, 291–307.

Kohli, M. (2003) 'Der institutionalisierte Lebenslauf: ein Blick zurück und nach vorn', in J. Allmendinger (ed.), *Entstaatlichung und soziale Sicherheit*, Opladen: Leske & Budrich, pp. 525–545.

Martin, I. (2003) 'Adult education, lifelong learning and citizenship: Some ifs and buts', *International Journal of Lifelong Education* 22, 566–579.

Osborne, M. and Gallacher, J. (2007) 'An international perspective on researching widening access', in M. Osborne, J. Gallacher and B. Crossan (eds), *Researching Widening Access to Lifelong Learning: Issues and approaches in international research*, London: Routledge, pp. 3–15.

Rosanvallon, P. (1995) *La nouvelle question sociale: Repenser l'État-providence*, Paris: Editions du Seuil.

Schemmann, M. (2007) *International Weiterbildungspolitik und Globalisierung: Orientierungen und Aktivitäten von OECD, EU, UNESCO und Weltbank*, Bielefeld: W. Bertelsmann Verlag.

Schuller, T., Preston, J., Hammond, C., Brassett-Grundy, A. and Bynner, J. (2004) *The Benefits of Learning: The impact of education on health, family life and social capital*, London: Routledge.

Scott, P. (2007) 'Researching widening access: An overview', in M. Osborne, J. Gallacher and B. Crossan (eds), *Researching Widening Access to Lifelong Learning: Issues and approaches in international research*, London: Routledge, pp. 17–28.

Walther, A., du Bois-Reymond, M. and Biggart, A. (2006) *Participation in Transition: Motivation of young adults in Europe for learning and working*, Frankfurt-am-Main: Peter Lang.

West, L., Alheit, P., Andersen, A.S. and Merrill, B. (2007) *Using Biographical and Life History Approaches in the Study of Adult and Lifelong Learning*, Frankfurt-am-Main: Peter Lang.

Part I

Themes, methods and concepts

Chapter 2

Lost and found in transition

Educational implications of concerns about 'identity', 'agency' and 'structure'

Kathryn Ecclestone

Managing educational transitions effectively has become a focus for policy, practice and research in the UK, leading to growing numbers of interventions throughout the education system. These tend to be rooted in assumptions that transitions are problematic for certain groups and individuals and therefore need to be managed more effectively.

In order to evaluate the implications of different meanings and assumptions about transitions for educational goals and practices, this chapter draws on a seminar series 'Transitions through the life-course' in the Economic and Social Research Council's (ESRC) Teaching and Learning Research Programme (TLRP). It explores how concepts of identity, agency and structure appear in political, academic and practical concerns about transitions. It asks whether current emphasis on identity and agency over structure leads to practices that present transitions as inherently difficult and threatening, remove risk and challenge, formalise support and create the 'self' as a new subject with a curriculum, pedagogy and forms of assessment.

Introduction

Supporting and managing transitions has become a concern amongst policy makers, professionals and academic researchers across the education system in the UK. From early years to widening participation initiatives in higher education, to continuing professional development and workplace learning, a dominant theme in policy texts, practical strategies and research reports is that transitions are problematic and need 'support', particularly for children, young people and adults deemed to be vulnerable, disaffected or 'at risk'.

A plethora of initiatives and associated research activities have grown around this idea. The establishment of peer mentoring and buddy schemes runs alongside calls for closer alignment between home, school and life knowledge and learning, and between different institutional and assessment systems, curriculum content, pedagogy and between the norms and expectations of different learning cultures. Notions of 'bridging' and 'blurring' divisions and differences between these aspects of educational experience are now commonplace in debates around transitions. It is important to note at the outset that a great deal of concern and the subsequent calls for easing, smoothing and supporting transitions arise from the idea that they are inherently unsettling, daunting and risky.

This chapter draws on the work of a seminar series on 'transitions through the life-course' as part of the TLRP and papers presented at an international conference on transitions at the University of Stirling in June 2007 (see www.trlp.org/transitions; Ecclestone *et al.* 2009; www.stirling.ac.uk/CRLL). It explores how policy texts and research studies of transitions employ, implicitly or explicitly, ideas about people's sense of self (identity), their capacity for autonomous, empowered action (agency) and the effects of structural factors (class, gender, race and economic and material conditions) on the processes and outcomes of transitions. It evaluates the ways in which considerations of identity, agency and structure in different types of transition lead to contrasting views about what a transition is, what challenges it presents to individuals or groups and how it might best be managed.

First, the chapter summarises the rise of political interest in transitions. Second, it discusses different meanings of transitions and shows that concepts of agency, identity and structure illuminate and challenge different aspects of transitions. Third, it highlights some examples of how studies discussed in the second part of this chapter offer very different views about the best way to manage transitions through assessment, support structures, curriculum and pedagogy. Finally, it challenges normative assumptions in different meanings of transitions and evaluates their implications for educational goals and practices and for further work around the theme of transitions.

Political interest in transitions

In some respects, political interest in transitions is not new. The 1959 Crowther Report, for example, analysed the nature of risk, change and opportunity for 15–18 year olds. Since 1997, a growing number of initiatives to deal with transitions across the education system reflect political concerns to ease transitions between educational sites, different phases and requirements, from education to other social sites, such as welfare, health and social work, and to minimise the difficulties that they cause for students. Particular concerns focus on the transition from nursery to primary school, the dip in achievement and motivation in the move to secondary school, a drop in retention in further/tertiary education at 17, and rising rates of dropout in higher education.

Political attempts to manage transitions more effectively emerge, in part, from the de-standardisation and increasing non-linearity of youth transitions, together with the individualisation and complexity of many life-course transitions for adults. Initiatives to deal with transitions also arise from other policies, such as targets for participation, achievement and engagement, proposals to raise the compulsory school-leaving age to 18 and the creation of a new formal transition at 14. Policy therefore both stimulates concerns about success, failure and dropout and the role of transitions in these outcomes and creates normative expectations about appropriate processes, outcomes and dispositions.

Attempts to manage transitions are reinforced by pressures across Europe to deal with the ways in which globalisation is bringing about the deregulation of labour markets, privatisation, technological advances, changing employment patterns, changing organisational forms and structures, demographic and labour market changes, new tensions between work and non-work life, lack of job security, and changes in educational goals and systems for assessing them (see, for example, OECD 2004). Concerns about social exclusion and disadvantage caused by the inability to move easily through education and labour markets are also evident in OECD analysis.

Similar concerns and responses also feature in the UK, embellished by a view that better management of specific social, educational and career transitions is crucial for breaking cycles of social and economic disadvantage. This view, first presented in 'Bridging the Gap' by the Social Exclusion Unit in 1999 is reinforced through 'Every Child Matters' (ECM), which promotes outcomes for health and well-being, leisure, and economic and educational achievement and requires different agencies to work together to achieve them (DfES 2004; SEU 1999). It also features in policies to raise achievement and increase participation for 'non-traditional' groups where better management of transitions into higher education for working-class young people is supposed to realise benefits of social cohesion and the creation of 'engaged citizens' (see DfES 2006; HEFCE 2005; Quinn *et al.* 2005; Colley 2003).

Meanings of transition

Navigating pathways, structures and systems

Researchers agree that transition is not the same as 'movement' or 'transfer', although it involves both. Instead, transition depicts change and shifts in identity and agency as people progress through the education system. For example, Lam and Pollard analyse the transition of children from home to nursery school and differentiate between transition as the movement from one institutional setting or from one activity to another, namely as a change of context. They differentiate further between horizontal transitions as 'movement between various settings, that a child and his/her family may encounter within the same time frame' while vertical transitions refer to 'movement among education/care programmes, health and social services across time' (2006: 124). From this perspective, transition is a change process but also a shift from one identity to another:

> [transition is] the process of change that is experienced when children (and their families) move from one setting to another ... to when the child is more fully established as a member of the new setting. It is usually a time of intense and accelerated development demands that are socially regulated.

> (ibid.: 125)

This depiction means that managing transitions requires more than facilitating changes in context or easing transfer between them: effective transitions require a better understanding of how people progress cognitively, emotionally and socially between different subjects at different stages of their learning, and how they navigate the complex demands of different contexts. A number of studies examine the psychological and socio-cultural factors that affect how children manage, influence and adapt to, the transition from home to nursery, home to primary school, primary school to secondary or from national settings for compulsory schooling to institutions in other countries (Lam and Pollard 2006; Pollard and Filer 1999; Osborn *et al.* 2006; Fabian and Dunlop 2002; Fabian 2006).

Strands of life-course research reinforce an institutional or context-specific image of transitions, suggesting that 'individuals generally work out their own life-course in relation to institutionalized pathways and normative patterns' (Elder *et al.* 2003: 8). This meaning presents transitions both as the product of social institutions and the outcomes produced by social expectations. It also differentiates between institutionalised pathways, which are about transitions as 'changes in state or role' that 'often involve changes in status and identity, both personally and socially, and thus open up opportunities for behavioural change' (ibid.: 8) and normative patterns.

The notion of transitions as the navigation of institutionalised pathways or systems is supported by research on career by Pallas who describes transitions as attributes of social systems rather than as attributes of an individual's life course. He depicts pathways as attributes of a social system that comprise well-travelled sequences of transitions shaped by cultural and social forces that are shaped by cultural and structural forces. From this perspective, educational attainment is determined by movement through a predictable sequence of educational transitions that have normative expectations embedded in them (Pallas 1993).

'Becoming somebody'

Some research from the fields of careers, guidance and life transitions, challenges the depiction of transition as change brought about through navigating institutional norms and procedures, focusing instead on processes of 'being' and 'becoming'. A number of studies illuminate the ways in which people make social and cultural transitions, individually and collectively, in response to a broader context of structural change, such as opportunities in the labour market or changes in work structures and organisation. Gallacher and Cleary define transition as 'personal transition between two states of "being" – the before and after of specified learning experiences' (2007). Blair defines it as a 'discontinuity in a person's life-space' (2007). One influential strand of thinking on transitions as a process of becoming has been the work on pupil and learning 'career' and 'careership' (see Pollard and Filer 1999; Bloomer and Hodkinson 2000; Hodkinson *et al.* 1996).

A body of work aims to show how transitions combine turning points, milestones or life events with subtle, complex processes of 'becoming some-body' personally, educationally and occupationally. Such processes are some-times a response to particular events, and sometimes events arise out of shifts and developments in identity and agency. For example, the evolution of a professional or occupational identity in a particular field, navigating uncer-tain labour and educational systems, changes in cultural identity for asylum seekers or migrants taking up educational opportunities in a new culture or for women returning to education after time at home might trigger a turning point or life event, or arise from one.

Such transitions also involve setbacks or processes of 'unbecoming' over time, are located and enacted within specific fields rather than emerging from a fixed series of rational decisions and they emerge through periods of routine and stability, as well as from change. They are influenced by ele-ments of a person's whole life, rather than merely through their involvement with education systems. Transitions are therefore not always discernible events or processes and a transition may happen long after subtle, subcon-scious changes in feelings and attitudes (see, for example, Banks *et al.* 1992; Ball *et al.* 2000; Reay *et al.* 2005; Hodkinson *et al.* 1996, 2007; Evans 2002; Hughes 2002; Fuller 2006; Colley 2006).

Life-as-transition

Postmodern and some feminist perspectives challenge transition depicted as rites of passage, movement through life stages, bridges that connect old and new, 'crisis events' or 'critical incidents' and life change rooted in theories of discernible processes of 'typical' adult maturation. In contrast to movements from one life stage to another, bounded by periods of stability, many women argue that they have been psychologically in transit almost all their adoles-cent and adult lives (Hughes 2002).

From this perspective, many depictions of transition ignore the particular distinctiveness of women's transitional experiences and use, instead, andro-centric lenses that overlook how certain transitions create emotional conflict that is crucial to their outcomes and management, whilst also reproducing inequalities of class and gender (see Hughes 2002; Colley 2006). Such per-spectives illuminate transition as something much more ephemeral and fluid, where the whole of life is a form of transition, a permanent state of 'becom-ing' and 'unbecoming', much of which is unconscious, contradictory and iterative.

This work not only challenges notions of linearity, chronology, time and change (see Colley 2009), it also questions the assumption that there is a coherent 'identity' around which people can generate a coherent narrative about themselves. According to Quinn's study of working-class students leaving higher education early, individuals construct multiple identities that draw on 'many interlocking cultural narratives and these are often classed and gendered'. She shows how working-class young men combined narra-tives of masculinity, nostalgia for extinct employment opportunities and hedonism as reasons to leave university (Quinn 2009). A feminist perspective therefore undermines assumptions that:

> 'becoming somebody' involves a unified subject capable of being transformed: 'a subject is not an "entity" or thing, or a relation between mind (interior) and body (exterior). Instead, it must be understood as a series of flows, energies and movements and capacities, a series of fragments or segments capable of being linked together in ways other than those that congeal it into an identity.'
>
> (Grosz, quoted by Quinn 2009)

From this standpoint, 'we are always lost in transition, not just in the sense of moving from one task or context to another, but as a condition of our subjectivity' (Quinn 2009).

The lenses of identity, agency and structure

Perspectives on transition, summarised above, show that political, academic and practical interests in transition are underpinned both explicitly and implicitly by different views about the extent to which people's identity and agency and the effects of structure affect assumptions about the processes and outcomes of different types of transition in the education system, and the best ways to deal with them. While the three concepts are inextricably connected, researchers explore transitions in different ways, depending on the emphasis they place on each or all of the concepts.

Identity

Broadly, identity can be defined as the ways in which the self is represented and understood in dynamic, multidimensional and evolving ways. Stuart Hall defines identity as 'the unstable point at which the unspeakable stories of subjectivity meet the narratives of history and of a culture' (Hall, quoted by Wetherall 2005). Contemporary studies of identity explore the ways in which the social, personal and cultural meet, the subsequent ways in which people are 'stitched into' social relations, how identities are made within this psycho-social nexus and the possible actions that flow from understanding one's place in a system of social relations (Wetherall 2005; also 2006). Identity is therefore constructed through complex interactions between different forms of capital (cultural, social, economic and emotional), broader social and economic conditions, interactions and relationships in various contexts, and cognitive and psychological strategies.

Successful creation of a viable identity in navigating transitions into school and between home and school is a central theme in the Home/School Knowledge Transfer Project in the TLRP. This develops insights from longitudinal, ethnographic studies of children and young people's learning/ schooling careers through primary and secondary education and post-education careers (Pollard and Filer 1999). This work depicts identity as having a narrative structure that enables children to tell viable, coherent stories about themselves and their lives in order to achieve a viable way of 'being' in a particular context. Brookes argues that:

> Individual learners are active agents constructing understanding and 'making sense' of new experiences and challenges by drawing on various cultural resources at their disposal. In the case of transition, pupils' relationships with their parents, siblings, teachers and peers will affect the types of support received as new learning challenges are encountered.
>
> (2005: 5)

From this perspective, transitions become problematic if a viable identity in one context does not transfer to another. Having to reconstruct an identity narrative can disrupt a viable way of being in a context, making transitions demotivating and stressful and learning ineffective (see Pollard and Filer 1999; Lam and Pollard 2006; Osborn *et al.* 2006).

The TLRP's 'Transforming Learning Cultures in Further Education' project also explored identity but linked it to questions about agency and structure as part of Bourdieu's notions of 'habitus' and 'field'. The project showed that transition by students and their teachers through the demands of a learning programme and the evolution of an acceptable occupational identity was a gradual process of orientation, navigated between the tensions of idealised and realised identities in different vocational cultures (see Colley *et al.* 2003). Identity and habitus embody and enact past and current dispositions and horizons for action within specific fields. These interact in complex and subtle ways with the practices, expectations, norms and relationships of specific learning cultures. The unpredictable and idiosyncratic features of this interaction in different learning cultures shape identity and habitus and create new practices (see James and Biesta 2007).

Some researchers argue that the socially constructed components of identity should be of special interest:

> Such constructions [of identity] happen in relation to horizons of interpretation opened by the society and by interaction with significant others. They involve configurations of the past, perceptions of the present and imagined futures. 'Ideal identity' is part of such projections of the individual in the future and there might be a mismatch between the ideal identity as harboured by an individual and the externally imposed models received as pressures from school, family or peers.
>
> (Hayward *et al.* 2005b: 116)

Agency

People's capacity to interact with others and with material conditions in order to shape their own destinies, both individually and collectively, requires self-direction, self-efficacy, opportunities to exercise autonomy and perhaps a desire to shape a specific field or context. The idea that eduation can, and should, help people develop their capacities for agentic and autonomous action has been a long-standing tradition in western societies since the Enlightenment. Yet the rhetoric of agency often elides 'choice', 'action' and 'autonomy' in confusing ways.

Life-course research presents agency as the ways in which 'individuals construct their own life-course through the choices and actions they take within the opportunities and constraints of history and social circumstance' (Elder *et al.* 2003: 11). In a paper from the TLRP 'Learning Lives' project, Biesta and Tedder explore the relationship between the development and enactment of agency and different types of learning through the life course. They define agency as:

> the temporally constructed engagement by actors of different structural environments – the temporal-relational contexts of action – which, through the interplay of habit, imagination and judgement, both reproduces and transforms those structures in interactive responses to the problems caused by changing historical situations.
>
> (Embirbayer and Mische, quoted in Biesta and Tedder 2007: 33)

From this perspective, understanding agency in different contexts and times requires a focus on 'the dynamic interplay' between influences from the past, engagement with the present and orientations towards the future. Agency builds on past achievements, understandings and patterns of action and is not something that people possess as an attribute but something they do in different contexts (Biesta and Tedder 2007).

Combining identity, agency and structure

In contrast to Biesta and Tedder, other researchers see agency inextricably linked to the effects of structural factors of class, race and gender, economic and occupational conditions. Many researchers argue that it is not possible to understand agency and identity without an account of how they are shaped, constrained and sometimes determined by the material conditions and normative expectations of different structural factors (see also Collin and Young 2000; Watts *et al.* 1996; Watts and Sultana 2004).

For example, studies of working-class participation and 'dropout' from higher education show the extent to which agency is affected by the ways in which working-class and middle-class young people and adults are attracted to, and have access to, very different courses and 'types' of institution. In addition, the apparent exercise of agency in deciding to drop out is often presented by careers and other agencies as confirming 'helpless failure': 'drop out [becomes] a self perpetuating narrative and this discourse [is] more important than individual choice or even structure' (Quinn 2009; Ball *et al.* 2005).

From this perspective, agency cannot be divorced from structural factors since different access to economic, social and symbolic forms of capital arises from key social divisions, such as class, race and gender, that frame possibilities and restrict social mobility (see, for example, Reay *et al.* 2005; Ball *et al.* 2005; Colley 2006, 2009).

Considerations of structure also reveal the day-to-day interactions between habitus, adaptation and progression through specific transitions that shape identity and agency in both exploitative and transforming ways. In her analysis of vocational habitus of young women learning to become nursery nurses, Colley explores how gendered notions of caring for others and the deployment of emotional labour are crucial to the development of that habitus:

> as students talked about what they have learned as they participated in their work placements, their narratives centred on coping with the emotional demands of the job, and revealed a vocational culture of detachment in the workplace which contrasts somewhat with the nurturing ideal that is officially promoted.
>
> (Colley 2006: 15; see also Bates 1994)

Conflict between the 'nurturing ideal' formalised in the childcare curriculum and the 'vocational detachment of the job' produces coping strategies, but also frictions as students move between the two contexts, particularly in relation to the cultivation of 'acceptable' forms of emotional labour as part of becoming 'respectable' young women. This emotional element of the transitional process, as students move into and out of different settings is not only problematic emotionally for some students but it reinforces class and gendered exploitation. Yet, it is also a means of escape from what young people and their tutors see as the 'mass of the non-respectable' (Colley 2006).

While some researchers do not separate the effects of structural conditions from the construction and shaping of identities and agency, the seminar series revealed very different views about the respective emphasis that should be given to identity, agency or structure in understanding transitions. And, although it is commonplace to acknowledge the importance of 'context' (history, socio-economic conditions, institutional ethos, subject discipline, etc.), many studies do not engage closely with the effect of structural conditions on the forced or chosen nature of transitions, or their negative and positive effects. 'Structural environment' ('temporal-relational contexts of action'), 'resources', 'context' and 'social circumstance' are not therefore synonymous with structure.

Instead, Evans argues that combining insights about identity, agency and structure illuminates the lived social reality within policy discourses relating to transitions. In particular: 'If policies and interventions are to be made effective, we need to sharpen our awareness of the interplay of structural forces and individual's attempts to control their lives' (2002: 265). In a similar vein, the authors of the Nuffield Review of 14–19 education advocate combining structure, agency and identity:

Young people interpret the incentives and disincentives to participate and progress in the 14–19 phase differently, depending on a variety of historical, social and cultural factors. They actively construct the decision 'field' and their position within it using a variety of locally, historically and culturally situated resources to imagine their futures, interpret the opportunities available to them and develop their aspirations and motivations. Some young people are able to make choices and to succeed against the odds.

(Hayward *et al*. 2005b: 112)

The Review is the latest in a series of studies exploring how young people in different local and transnational labour and education markets approach adulthood, the kinds of adult they become, the influences that mould their choices and the dilemmas they have to resolve (Hayward *et al*. 2005a, 2005b). An earlier study illuminated normative and structural influences on transitions, including puberty, school and peer influences, parental and teacher influences, other structural factors (gender, class and race), background, self and identity and people's capacity for agency within structural constraints (Banks *et al*. 1992).

Building on this earlier work, a study of 900 18–25 year olds in Derby, Hannover and Leipzig investigated transitions in higher education, employment and unemployment and analysed the relationships between structure and agency. As 'social actors in a social landscape', young people showed little evidence of fatalism, trying actively to gain control of their lives, and therefore were struggling and frustrated rather than passively alienated. This suggested the notion of 'bounded agency' as an alternative to a more deterministic view of the ways in which young people manage transitions in an interplay between cultural context, institutional systems, their own attitudes and actions in labour and education markets and associated 'transition systems' (Evans 2002).

A four-year study of the choices, pathways and transitions of young people leaving school in London shows the inequalities and different outcomes of different groups of young people, and the individuals within those groups, within the habitus of families with access to very different cultural capital. Choices were classed, raced and gendered but also affected strongly by institutional cultures and expectations, differential access to 'hot' and 'cold' information about opportunities within a local area and peer and family expectations. Transition was therefore a slow, subtle process of 'becoming somebody' within imagined and realised identities in specific contexts (Ball *et al*. 2000).

Managing transitions

The respective emphasis given to the role of identity, agency and structure in transitions is a matter of disagreement and conceptual fragmentation. Depictions about what transitions are, why they are problematic and the links between agency, identity and structure lead to different perspectives on the best way to manage transitions.

Easing and supporting the navigation of transitions

Transitions presented in policy are discernible events, experienced in a linear sequence of progression through funding, institutional and achievement structures and designed to raise levels of participation, retention and achievement of formal qualifications. In turn, this creates normative expectations that people must be motivated to make successful transitions through the pathways, structures and expectations framed by policy and achieve measurable outcomes: eliminating the dip in achievement between primary and secondary school; enrolling on further courses; reducing dropout levels; gaining higher levels of achievement through qualifications and certificates. Linked to funding and quality assurance, the attainment of targets narrows what it means to make a successful transition.

In various guises, assessment dominates transitions into, through and out of, the formal system. Successful transitions require formal procedures for initial diagnostic assessment and guidance, the setting, reviewing and tracking of goals and targets through Individual Learning Plans, informal and formal mentoring schemes, and the increasing use of detailed coaching and feedback on tasks broken into manageable parts. These assessments aim to ease students' transition through the requirements of summative assessments as painlessly as possible (see Torrance *et al.* 2005; Ecclestone 2007a). In turn, artefacts and procedures of assessment create normative expectations and associated rituals and 'rites of passage' (see, for example, Hamilton 2009).

Each meaning of transition suggests a desire on the part of researchers and sometimes practitioners to ease transitions, either through formal systems for doing so or by helping people understand their own transitions better, and sometimes by doing both. The insertion of interest in identity, agency and structure affects perceptions of how that should be done and subsequent activities. Nevertheless, easing transitions creates new roles for education professionals working alongside other people working informally and formally as 'mediators of learning' or, perhaps more accurately, as 'transition workers'. These include parents, siblings and also a large and growing number of children, young people and adults who are being trained in counselling to act as 'buddies' to peers, new or younger students in order to manage both the emotional aspects of formal transitions as well as simplifying the logistics of new structures and systems. 'Support' for transitions is being increasingly formalised and expected at all levels of the education system, leading to a growth industry in coaching and mentoring (see, for example, Colley 2003; Cullingford 2006).

Although there are differences in perspective between policy imperatives to formalise transitions and to set up systems of support, and calls for a better understanding of changes in identity and the strategies and narratives that people use to navigate them, both notions lead to 'support'. For example, studies discussed in the second part of this chapter of the ways in which children navigate the different demands of home and school suggest that paying more attention to the artefacts, activities and knowledge that children use at school and home can help children, parents and carers and peers evolve a constructive learning identity that is congruent between the two contexts. Crucially, this has to be in the children's own terms (see Osborn *et al.* 2006; Hughes 2006). Lam and Pollard argue that understanding what children encounter during the transition from home to kindergarten, and knowing what makes a positive experience for them can be achieved by 'transition policies' and 'transition practices' for a 'smooth' transition (2006). In a similar vein, some researchers argue that 'non-traditional' entrants to higher education need 'functional capabilities' in order to construct and manage a viable 'learning identity' (see, for example, Walker 2006).

Interest in how learners construct a learning identity and engage with the relationships, norms and expectations of a particular learning community of practice leads other researchers to advocate support through closer alignment between the learning cultures of different educational contexts. For example, a study of adults in community-based further education illuminates how adults who have had negative experiences of formal education, and who experience profound emotional and practical difficulties caused by class and gender, need and then come to expect particular types of relationships and approaches to teaching. Drawing on Bourdieu's notions of habitus, the study argues that adults bring particular dispositions that both create and reinforce expectations and activities in a new habitus. This is a barrier in the transition to mainstream further education. Yet, the study also acknowledges that reinforcing the learning cultures of community education can create comfort zones, expectations of 'acceptable' behaviour on the part of both teachers and students and exclusion for those who do not fit (Gallacher *et al.* 2007).

Such ideas resonate with current practice. In an article about primary to secondary school transition, the focus was entirely on the risks, threats, fears and anxieties of children. One response is to make secondary schools more like primary ones. A school in Manchester has the same teacher for 11–14 year olds

> for every lesson, every day, just as they are at primary ... the teacher will have a shepherding role ... they [*sic*] will have intimate knowledge of their class from their circumstances at home to what their special needs are.... Specialists will join the regular teacher for certain subjects.
>
> (Frankel 2007: 18)

Some researchers argue that such strategies may be appropriate for other major transitions in the education system (see, for example, Dixon and Alcock 2007; see also Ecclestone and Hayes 2008, chapter 2).

Developing self-awareness about transitions

Researchers interested in identity and agency go further in what they regard as support. Instead of general technical support, they advocate a deeper understanding of 'typical' learning identities or 'typical' problems that particular learners face. One perspective is to argue for research to help people both to understand and then change their own responses to problematic situations: according to Biesta and Tedder, for example, this requires learning about the composition of one's agentic orientations and how they 'play out' in one's life. On the other hand, it requires learning about how one might change the composition of one's 'responsiveness' (2007). Research methods of life history and biography elevate the validity and authenticity of self-reports and are seen to enable people to learn about their 'agentic orientations', where telling stories about our lives and sharing these stories with others is a particular kind of learning that helps people to be agentic (ibid.). In a similar vein, but with a different peda-gogy, other researchers argue that formal modules in personal develop-ment, reflection and developing skills for lifelong learning offer learners a 'means of exploring and connecting learning identities, working identities and personal identities' (Buckley and Fielding 2007).

These notions resonate powerfully with therapeutic approaches advocated by some adult educators as a pedagogy that helps people understand patterns of action and reasons for them (see, for example, Hunt and West 2006). An important question here is whether research interest in biographical approaches, reflection on the self or in more overtly therapeutic applications of psychoanalysis or counselling as pedagogy, leads to calls for learners and various transition workers around them to draw out individuals' agentic ori-entations, or perceptions of identity in order to develop better strategies. An alternative view is that the outcomes of such research offer important insights and practical strategies for policy makers, institutions and teachers rather than direct interventions in people's feelings about identity and agency.

The question becomes more salient because research interest in raising awareness about identities and/or agency in transition resonates with con-temporary cultural expectations that we should be self-aware, able to disclose and to be coherent in our accounts of ourselves. For example, there is a growing alignment between educational policy and practice and cultural narratives around emotional well-being. This, in turn, relates to interest in the reflexive self, where, according to Giddens, 'reflexive self-awareness' on the part of the public and policy makers alike is a positive trend. He argues that psychoanaly-sis and therapy flowing from a quest for self-awareness provides a setting and a

> rich fund of theoretical and conceptual resources for the creation of a reflexively ordered narrative of self. In a therapeutic situation, whether of the classical psychoanalytical type or not, individuals are able (in principle) to bring their past into line with the exigencies of the present, consolidating a story-line with which they feel relatively content.
>
> (Giddens 1991: 31; see also Ecclestone 2007b)

Broader cultural interest in self-awareness therefore makes it important to consider the links between biographical learning and life history approaches in relation to identity and agency in research and a strong therapeutic turn in policy and pedagogy across the system (see Ecclestone and Hayes 2008).

Critical pedagogy

A different, more radical notion of 'support' for transitions comes from a long-standing tradition in post-compulsory education that aims to help people to understand how structural factors of class, race and gender shape agency and identity in particular ways. This requires incorporating questions about structure in discussions about identity and agency. For example, in relation to young women learning emotional labour, Colley argues that curriculum content and teaching should enable students to see how 'structure and agency combine to produce and reproduce social inequalities' (2006: 25). In relation to the creation and exploitation of emotional labour, she draws on Reay to argue:

> the concept of gendered habitus holds powerful structural influences within its frame. Gendered habitus includes a set of complex, diverse predispositions. It involves understandings of identity based on familial legacy and early childhood socialisation. As such, it is primarily a dynamic concept, a rich interfacing of past and present, interiorized and permeating both body and psyche.
>
> (ibid.: 26)

This argument leads to two different interpretations of critical pedagogy rooted in the notion that 'the personal is political': one is a psycho-social analysis of how gendered habitus has evolved in individuals and groups; a form of critical therapy, advocated by well-known feminist psychotherapists such as Susie Orbach, for example. The other is a less overtly therapeutic goal that challenges students to 'ask critical questions about what [those] destinies both offer and demand; and to ask why their education contributes so often to the reproduction of social inequality' (Colley 2006: 27). Following this argument, Colley argues that curriculum designers, awarding bodies and employers also need to support better the emotional skills demanded of young women in caring occupations and to consider the content of the care curriculum.

Challenges and critical questions

Despite different meanings of transition summarised in this chapter, the navigation of the processes, outcomes and normative expectations of social institutions, and associated shifts in identity and agency, dominate policy images of transition and much research, both inside and outside the TLRP. Transition as processes of 'becoming somebody' with turning points, rites of passage, periods of routine are also evident in the TLRP and other areas of research. More fluid, ephemeral notions of life-as-transition remain at the margins of research on transitions in the TLRP, as do those that see structure as central to the shaping of identity and agency (see Colley 2006).

Yet, I would argue that, albeit in different ways, the three perspectives on transitions summarised in this chapter not only risk pathologising transitions by depicting them as unsettling, disruptive, daunting, anxiety inducing and risky but also create normative assumptions about how best to manage them. Political creation and management of transitions undoubtedly narrows what transition means, depicts those refusing or unable to make them as 'demotivated', 'disaffected' or 'vulnerable' and overlooks structure and agency. Policy also turns agency into choice and decision making where individuals are seen as maximising use and calculating costs and benefits. Not only, as numerous studies cited here have shown, does this not reflect choice, action and outcomes, it enables policy makers to recast agency as responding 'appropriately' to opportunities 'offered' by policy. In turn, there is a danger that policy makers and practitioners inadvertently infantalise 'non-traditional' or 'disaffected' young people and adults by creating more and more forms of emotional and practical 'support'.

In different ways, all three meanings of transition reinforce concerns about risk and suggest that everyone needs to have the emotional difficulty of transitions eased and soothed. Whether navigating norms created by institutions, creating a viable identity narrative, or understanding the effects of transitions on identity and agency, the idea that people cannot deal with transitions without formalised help sits uneasily with the possibilities of creative risk, opportunity and change that transitions can create. It also erases the positive effects of difficulty, challenge and overcoming problems and risks attributing 'problems' to particular groups so that people become a problem to be supported and managed more effectively: the combination of 'supporting and managing' only serves to mask the management.

Although there is a danger that policy discourses reduce transitions to the successful navigation by individuals through institutional arrangements and the expectations that accompany them, other perspectives offer different normative images. It might be argued, for example, that those who reject the growing compulsion, forced choice and instrumental outcomes of participation in formal education after 16 promote other normative benefits of lifelong learning, such as mental and physical health, social capital and cohesion, citizenship and inclusion. There is a danger that this leads to a different set of moral imperatives about participation, achievement and the need to be 'reflexive' about identity, whether about identity or agency.

Preoccupation with identity shifts, threats to identity, the need to create identity narratives, or narratives about agency as part of 'reflexive modernisation' not only presents transitions as risky, difficult and threatening to one's very sense of self. It also encourages the extension of 'support' through counselling and mentoring, the elicitation of biographical narratives, the smoothing of learning cultures and relationships and the insertion of requirements to develop 'learning to learn' skills or self-awareness.

In different ways, then, an emphasis on identity and agency, especially when considerations of structure are removed, creates the self and learning about the self as a 'subject' in both senses of the word: it constructs a new subjectivity but it also creates curriculum content and therapeutic forms of pedagogy and assessment around the self. This is perhaps illuminated by an invisible strand in research on transitions both at the CRLL conference and in the TLRP, namely that of transition or progression in ideas, thinking and learning in relation to specific subjects, skills or crafts. The depiction and management of transitions therefore raise new questions about how education helps people think and act for themselves, but, crucially, what they think and act about. This involves a struggle for the nature and realisation of subjectivity and for ways of shaping the conditions that shape us.

The concerns raised in this chapter also suggest that the research field around transitions is fragmented, full of small-scale studies and lacks conceptual clarity. There is a need to take stock of key work and its insights, and to build on that: the theorising and findings about transition, and debates they raise, could therefore be reviewed systematically for key implications before going further.

Finally, this chapter suggests the following questions:

1   To what extent is deep self-awareness (and a 'coherent' narrative) of agency and identity, with or without awareness of structural factors, necessary for successful life and institutional transitions? To what extent is such a narrative possible?
2   How far is awareness amongst policy makers and practitioners about identity, agency and structure necessary to make transitions more successful?
3   What *is* a successful transition?
4   How far do contemporary studies of identity and agency, with or without structure, add new knowledge to what we know already about the roles of identity, agency and structure for different individuals and 'types' of learners making different types of transition? How can we build on what we already know?
5   What should, and can, teachers, 'transition workers' and institutions do with our existing knowledge about transitions in order to evaluate structures and support systems, curriculum content, and teaching and assessment?
6   What new theoretical and empirical studies do we need on the topic of transitions?

But perhaps most crucially, we need to ask whether an overemphasis on identity and threats to identity encourage a curriculum and pedagogy of the self that, in turn, erodes educational goals and practices in favour of being supported and managed through transitions.

References

Ball, S.J., David, M. and Reay, D. (2005) *Degrees of Difference*, London: RoutledgeFalmer.

Ball, S.J., Maguire, M. and Macrae, S. (2000) *Choices, Pathways and Transitions Post-16: New youth, new economies in the global city*, London: RoutledgeFalmer.

Banks, M., Bates, I., Breakwell, G., Bynner, J., Emler, N., Jamieson, L. and Roberts, K. (1992) *Careers and Identities*, Buckingham: Open University Press.

Bates, I. (1994) 'Closely observed training: An exploration of links between social structures, training and identity', *International Studies in Sociology of Education* 1, 225–243.

Biesta, G. and Tedder, M. (2007) 'Agency and learning in the life-course: Towards an ecological perspective', *Studies in the Education of Adults* 39, 132–149.

Blair, S. (2007) 'The prevailing discourse of lifelong learning and the contrasting narrative from older people'. Paper given to CRLL International Conference, University of Stirling, 22–24 June.

Bloomer, M. and Hodkinson, P. (2000) 'Learning careers: Continuity and change in young people's dispositions to learning', *British Education Research Journal* 26, 583–598.

Brookes, J. (2005) 'Exploring the secondary transfer of gifted and talented pupils'. Paper from the TLRP Project on Home/School Knowledge Transfer.

Buckley, C. and Fielding, S. (2007) 'Building bridges for lifelong learning'. Paper given to CRLL International Conference, University of Stirling, 22–24 June.

Colley, H. (2003) *Mentoring for Social Inclusion: A critical approach to nuturing mentoring relationships*. London: Routledge.

Colley, H. (2006) 'Learning to labour with feeling: Class, gender and emotion in childcare education and training', *Contemporary Issues in Early Childhood* 7, 15–29.

Colley, H. (2009) 'Time in learning transitions through the life-course', in K. Ecclestone, G. Biesta and M. Hughes (eds), *Transitions and Learning through the Life-course*, London: Routledge.

Colley, H., James, D., Tedder, M. and Diment, K. (2003) 'Learning as becoming in vocational education and training: Class, gender and the role of vocational habitus', *Journal of Vocational Education and Training* 55, 471–496.

Collin, A. and Young, R.A. (eds) (2000) *The Future of Career*, Cambridge: Cambridge University Press.

Cullingford, C. (2006) *Mentoring: An international perspective*, Aldershot: Ashgate.

DfES (2004) *Every Child Matters*, London: Department for Education and Skills.

DfES (2006) *Success for All*, London: Department for Education and Skills.

Dixon, M. and Alcock, H. (2007) 'Managing the transition of pupils at the primary-secondary interface: Lessons for other major systemic transitions?' Paper given to CRLL International Conference, University of Stirling, 22–24 June.

Ecclestone, K. (2007a) 'Commitment, compliance and comfort zones: The effect of formative assessment on young people's learning careers in vocational education', *Assessment in Education* 14, 315–333.

Ecclestone, K. (2007b) 'Resisting images of the "diminished self": The implications of policy for emotional well-being in education', *Journal of Education Policy* 22, 455–470.

Ecclestone, K. and Hayes, D. (2008) *The Dangerous Rise of Therapeutic Education*, London: Routledge.

Ecclestone, K., Beista, G. and Hughes, M. (eds) (2009) *Lost and Found in Transition: Change and becoming through education*, London: Routledge.

Elder, G.H., Kirkpartrick, J.M. and Crosnoe, R. (2003) 'The emergence and development of life-course theory', in J. T. Mortimer and M.J. Shanahan (eds), *Handbook of the Life Course*, New York: Kluwer Academic/Plenum.

Evans, K. (2002) 'Taking control of their lives? Agency in young adult transitions in England and the New Germany', *Journal of Youth Studies* 5, 245–269.

Fabian, H. (2006) 'Secondary school transitions'. Paper given to ESRC Seminar Series 'Transitions through the life-course', University of Exeter, 19–20 January.

Fabian, H. and Dunlop, A.W. (2002) *Transitions in the Early Years: Debating continuity and progression for children in early education*, London: Routledge.

Frankel, H. (2007) 'Surviving the leap year', *The Times Educational Supplement Magazine*, 15 June, 14–20.

Fuller, A. (2006) 'Identity and occupational change'. Paper given to ESRC Seminar Series 'Transitions through the life-course', University of Nottingham, 12–13 October.

Gallacher, J. and Cleary, P. (2007) 'Learning careers: Exploring transitions between community-based further education to main college campuses'. Paper given to CRLL International Conference, University of Stirling, 22–24 June.

Gallacher, J., Crossan, B., Mayes, T., Cleary, P., Smith, L. and Watson, D. (2007) 'Expanding our understanding of learning cultures in community-based further education', *Educational Review* 59, 501–517.

Giddens, A. (1991) *Modernity and Self-identity: Self and society in late modern age*, Cambridge: Polity.

Hamilton, M. (2009) 'Transitions, identity and the individual learning plan in "Skills for Life" programmes', in K. Ecclestone, G. Biesta and M. Hughes (eds), *Transitions and Learning through the Life-course*, London: Routledge.

Hayward, G., Hodgson, A., Johnson, J., Oancea, A., Pring, R., Spours, K., Wilde, S. and Wright, S. (2005a) *The Nuffield Review of 14–19 Education and Training: Annual Report 2004–2005*, Oxford: University of Oxford.

Hayward, G., Hodgson, A., Johnson, J., Oancea, A., Pring, R., Spours, K., Wilde, S. and Wright, S. (2005b) *The Nuffield Review of 14–19 Education and Training: Annual Report 2005–2006*, Oxford: University of Oxford.

HEFCE (2005) *Young Participation in Higher Education*, Bristol, HEFCE.

Hodkinson, P., Hawthorne, R., Ford, G. and Hodkinson, H. (2007) 'Learning careers, learning lives and informal learning'. Paper given to CRLL International Conference, University of Stirling, 22–24 June.

Hodkinson, P., Sparkes, A.C. and Hodkinson, H. (1996) *Triumphs and Tears: Young people, markets, and the transition from school to work*, London: David Fulton.

Hughes, C. (2002) *Feminist Theory and Research*, London: Sage Publications.

Hughes, M. (2006) 'Knowledge and identity in home/school contexts'. Paper given to ESRC seminar series 'Transitions through the life-course', University of Nottingham, 12–13 October.

Hunt, C. and West, L. (2006) 'Learning in a border country: Using psychodynamic ideas in teaching and research', *Studies in the Education of Adults* 38, 160–176.

James, D. and Biesta, G. (2007) *Improving Learning Cultures in Further Education*, London: Routledge.

Lam, M. and Pollard, A. (2006) 'A conceptual framework for understanding children as agents in the transition from home to kindergarten', *Early Years* 26, 123–141.

Organisation for Economic Cooperation and Development (2004) *Careers Guidance and Public Policy: Bridging the gap*, Paris: OECD.

Osborn, M., McNess, M. and Pollard, A. (2006) 'Identity and transfer: A new focus for home-school knowledge exchange', *Educational Review* 58, 415–433.

Pallas, A. (1993) 'Schooling in the course of human lives: The social context of education and the transition to adulthood in industrial society', *Review of Educational Research* 63, 409–447.

Pollard, A. and Filer, A. (1999) *The Social World of Pupil Career: Strategic biographies through primary school*, London: Cassell.

Quinn, J. (2009) 'Re-thinking "failed transitions" to higher education', in K. Ecclestone, G. Biesta and M. Hughes (eds), *Transitions and Learning through the Life-course*, London: Routledge.

Quinn, J., Thomas, L., Slack, K., Casey, L., Thexton, W. and Noble, J. (2005) *From Life Crisis to Lifelong Learning: Rethinking working class 'drop out' from higher education*, York: Joseph Rowntree Foundation.

Reay, D., David, M.E. and Ball, S. (2005) *Degrees of Choice: Social class, race and gender in higher education*, Stoke-on-Trent: Trentham.

SEU (1999) *Bridging the Gap*, London: Social Exclusion Unit.

Torrance, H., Colley, H., Garratt, D., Jarvis, J., Piper, H., Ecclestone, K. and James, D. (2005) *The Impact of Different Modes of Assessment on Achievement and Progress in the Learning and Skills Sector*, Learning and Skills Development Agency. Online, available at: www.lsda.org.uk/cims/order. aspx?code=052284&src=XOWEB (accessed 17 December 2008).

Walker, M. (2006) 'Functional capabilities in managing transitions in higher education'. Paper given to ESRC Seminar Series 'Transitions through the life-course', London, 4 May.

Watts, A.G. and Sultana, R. (2004) 'Careers guidance policies in 37 countries: Contrasts and common themes', *International Journal for Education and Vocational Guidance* 4, 106–122.

Watts, A.G., Law, B., Killeen, J., Kidd, J.M. and Hawthorn, R. (1996) *Rethinking Careers Education and Guidance: Theory, policy and practice*, Routledge: London.

Wetherall, M. (2005) 'Identity and the ESRC Identities Programme'. Paper given to the Teaching and Learning Research Programme Annual Conference, University of Warwick, November.

Wetherall, M. (2006) 'Identities and transitions'. Paper given to ESRC Seminar Series 'Transitions through the life-course', University of Nottingham, 12–13 October.

Chapter 3

A view of Canadian lifelong-learning policy culture through a critical lens

André P. Grace

In the new millennium, lifelong learning has continued to emerge in many quarters as a pervasive policy phenomenon profoundly influenced by the economic logic of neoliberalism. In the face of this logic, contemporary lifelong learning has been more economistic than socially oriented in its intentions. As a result, its practice has been predominantly and variously reactive, instrumentalized, specialized, technicized, mandated and fragmented in response to such global change forces as an emerging knowledge economy. This state of affairs has prompted educators concerned with social and cultural education and the lot of ordinary citizens to demand that lifelong learning be something more (Edwards 2000; Field 2006; Grace 2006; Walters 2006). From critical and other perspectives, these educators envision broader conceptions and practices of lifelong learning. My analysis in this chapter aligns with this expanded vision.

Since its emergence in the 1970s, neoliberalism has become an economic convention and a practical influence on public policy including lifelong-learning policy; this ideology has turned into an invasive force in which its political project is to increase the power and wealth of economic elites (Harvey 2005). As Harvey explains, neoliberals, promoting unfettered global capitalism and deregulation, have astutely coded the liberation of the economic as the liberation of the individual and a valuing of the political ideals of human dignity and individual freedom. Seduced by this deceptive guise, many governments, educational institutions and international organizations like the Organization for Economic Cooperation and Development (OECD) have ardently persisted in linking individualism, which innervates learning for life and work, to economistic concerns and the global demands of privatization, competition and progress. However, the turn to neoliberalism has created a new classism in which the plight of those lacking relevant education and quality work is exacerbated by state abrogation of its social responsibility (Grace 2004, 2005). In the wake of this assault on the social, it is apparent that education for inclusive citizenship is, at best, a secondary focus in a neoliberal learning formation (Collins 1998; Welton 2005).

In the current messy neoliberal milieu, lifelong learning itself has become increasingly privatized so that its costs are now considered the responsibility of the individuals, communities and corporate interests viewed as its direct beneficiaries (Field 2006). With privatization of learning ascendant, and many

interest groups, including many learners, wanting pragmatic learning outcomes, the OECD, for example, has placed greater emphasis on the provision
of vocational and technical learning to meet the needs of contemporary
national and global economies; economic productivity is linked to learner
prowess and proficiency and individual or private responsibility (Grace 2004,
2005). Indeed, in a January 1996 meeting entitled *Lifelong Learning for All*,
the OECD justified such instrumental lifelong learning as an economistic
response to globalization and new developments in science and technology
(Field 2006). However, there were glimmers of hope for those concerned with
more holistic education. The organization also took the promising steps of
promoting informal learning and raising the need to attend to social cohesion
in the face of unstable occupations and the precarious nature of work (ibid.).
As well, the UNESCO-sponsored Delors Report was also released in 1996.
Entitled *The Treasure Within*, the report identified four pillars enabling individual development: 'Learning to do, Learning to be, Learning to understand
and Learning to live together' (Longworth 2002: 12). Longworth describes the
Delors Report as a broad-based response 'to the complexities of change,
culture, and civilization in the modern world' (ibid.: 14). Yet, despite a detect-
able critical accentuation of more encompassing individual development and
social cohesion in lifelong-learning rhetoric, a key reality remains: economistic
ambitions have generally engineered lifelong-learning policy development
(Grace 2006). For example, since the 1990s the OECD has spearheaded various
economistic lifelong-learning policy initiatives that expected the involvement
of all sectors of formal education (Grace 2005). However, these initiatives, predominantly driven by a neoliberal mindset that sees social progress as deriva-
tive of economic progress, are not confined to institutionalized forms of
education. They have infiltrated other learning spheres as well, criss-crossing
the domains of formal, informal and nonformal learning (Grace 2004, 2006).
While lifelong-learning policy development appears omnipresent across
domains of education and learning, policy execution nevertheless has generally
lagged behind policy generation. Reflecting on the British lifelong-learning
policy context, Field (2006) notes that policy development has not sufficiently
translated into innovative or dependable policy implementation. Moreover, he
adds that policy interventions, predominantly neoliberal in nature, have
usually centred on the production of a skilled and flexible workforce.

It is from these perspectives that I use a critical lens to examine trends in
Canadian lifelong-learning policy culture, which, for nearly four decades, has
been shaped by the emergence of a neoliberal change culture of crisis and
challenge. In doing so, I explore the involvement of a federal agency (Human
Resources and Social Development Canada), a federal corporation (the Canadian Council on Learning) and a federal centre (the Adult Learning Knowledge Centre). I critique how each entity approaches learning in a neoliberal
milieu in which the Canadian Government advocates cyclical lifelong learning in a national quest to produce highly skilled and productive workers
who are globally competitive. Throughout, I make suggestions regarding
what the Canadian Government and these various entities might consider

and do to engage learners in more holistic lifelong learning that addresses instrumental, social and cultural concerns.

The lifelong-learning policy culture in Canada

Human Resources and Social Development Canada (HRSDC) is the primary national agency that implements federal policy intended to build an educated, skilled and flexible workforce so Canada can prosper nationally and globally. In its current iteration, HRSDC, which has frequently liaised with the OECD on lifelong-learning policy development, has subsumed two former agencies: Human Resources and Skills Development Canada and Social Development Canada. In keeping with the public to private shift in responsibility for lifelong learning, HRSDC's goal is to create citizens who are more self-reliant, self-sufficient and adaptable workers who take responsibility for their own learning. This emphasis on individualism, coupled with a primary emphasis on economic productivity, abets more education for the already educated and affluent. This is having a major influence on postsecondary education, which has increasingly focused on learners 'being equipped with the skills and knowledge needed to succeed in a globally competitive economy' (Canadian Council on Learning 2007: 2). However, the uneducated, the undereducated, the underemployed, the unemployed, the poor and others underserved within a neoliberal approach to lifelong learning, are left to experience nihilism; that is, a sense of helplessness and hopelessness. For them, the quest to find a more secure and decent life seems ethereal as they struggle to attain educational access and accommodation, and a way to prosperity. In the contemporary Canadian learning milieu, lifelong learning is cast as both a necessity for economic advancement and a preventative measure so workers can keep up with learning-and-work cycles (Grace 2007). To keep workers updated in knowledge and skills, learning and work are conjoined, seeking dynamic equilibrium in a world where much of lifelong learning is about controlling workers (ibid.).

The Canadian Council on Learning

Over the past few years, HRSDC has given significant responsibility for lifelong learning to the Canadian Council on Learning (CCL). The CCL had its genesis when it entered into a five-year funding agreement with HRSDC in March 2004. One month later, it was operational. During its first year (2004–2005), the CCL (2005: 5) 'founded on a model of collaboration, inclusion, and partnership', focused on building and communicating a strategic pan-Canadian perspective on lifelong learning. The CCL has framed its core efforts in synchronicity with HRSDC's message emphasizing a melding of the social and the economic.

> Canadians are becoming increasingly aware of the social and economic benefits of lifelong learning for individual citizens, and for the competit-

iveness of our country. We are also coming to appreciate the contributions that ongoing learning makes to our health and wellbeing, and to the quality of life within our communities.

(2007: 1)

In his message in the CCL's (2005) first annual report, Robert Giroux, Chair of the Board of Directors, related that the CCL would zero in on Canada's need for a highly educated and skilled workforce to help the nation succeed in the global knowledge economy. Indeed business and labour felt that the CCL could be the nucleus for assembling national perspectives and solutions that would use learning to abet workplace innovation and productivity. In another message, Paul Cappon, President and CEO, suggested that the CCL's learning model would be something more, focusing on continuous learning that enables learners, sustains relationships among interest groups, including governments, learning organizations and researchers, and 'achieve[s] the nation-building character of an enterprise that expresses values shared by all Canadians' (CCL 2005: 5). In terms of nation building, attention would be paid to issues including learner participation, individual development and the perennial federal add-ons: community involvement and social cohesion. In general though, learning for social and cultural purposes that might address literacy problems, citizenship issues, multiculturalism and the learning needs of groups, including Aboriginals and new immigrants, continues, in large part, to be treated peripherally in federal initiatives in the rush to economistic learning (Grace 2006, 2007).

Still, the CCL is well aware of Canada's social and cultural problems and might be better able to solve them with a stronger and extended mandate that could come from increased government support of this federal corporation. In its first major report on the state of learning in Canada, the Council positioned itself as 'an independent, not-for-profit corporation whose mandate is to promote and support evidence-based decisions about learning throughout all stages of life, from early childhood through to the senior years' (2007: 2). In this regard, the CCL views lifelong learning as an ongoing foundational process that starts 'in early childhood [and continues] at school, through adulthood, [and] in the workplace' (ibid.: 1). Noting that significant numbers of Canadians, starting with the very young, still lack in individual, social, educational and economic terms, the CCL insists that lifelong learning begin with Canada's 'youngest citizens' (ibid.: 1) because research indicates that children's experiences during the first five years of life have a deep impact on future success in schooling, later learning, work and life. Since 25 per cent of Canadian children enter Grade 1 with learning or behavioural problems, the CCL asserts that they ought to be a primary focus of lifelong learning 'from their prenatal environment to school age' (ibid.: 1). Drawing on research indicating that many kindergarten-aged children from low-income families show delayed development in building literacy skills (21 per cent) and numeracy skills (26 per cent), the CCL also asserts that lifelong learning needs to address class differences. This raises two key questions. What will the CCL do to begin to address these social and cultural issues during its limited temporal mandate? What can it do to have an impact now? For a sizeable number of children and youth, public (kindergarten to Grade 12) schooling is marred by problems: many are variously bullied, hungry, unhealthy, truant, socially disengaged and dropping out of school (Grace and Wells 2007; Schissel 2006). Focusing on individual success that prepares them to be tomorrow's citizens won't cut it if education fails to network with other institutions to address the social and cultural ills that impair many young lives. Children and youth need to be helped, and they need to learn to help others as they mature as a principle of lifelong learning as critical action for citizenship. Sadly though, as the CCL notes, public schooling in Canada has been marked by a failure in citizenship education since at least the 1960s. Canadian youth have declining political knowledge and diminished civic engagement. Obviously, there needs to be a return to education for citizenship in order to engender success in advancing the social and re-engaging the public in Canada. Since public schooling is a provincial/territorial jurisdiction in Canada, the CCL might partner with the Council of Ministers of Education Canada so both work together to address the need for education for citizenship.

The CCL might also emphasize education for citizenship in adult learning for life and work. Such learning should be significantly motivated by intrinsic values associated with the desire to improve self and community; it can include (but should be more than) learning extrinsically triggered by the desire to enhance functional employability, earn more or get promotions. This will be a challenge, of course, since the Canadian Government prioritizes the latter kind of learning: adult learning is expected to focus on building the knowledge and skills necessary to bolster an adaptable and globally competitive workforce. By default, such economic engagement is supposed to promote greater social development and more social cohesion. However, this consequential advancement of the social is not particularly obvious in Canada (Grace 2005, 2007). In this regard, the CCL could lobby the federal government to promote more holistic lifelong learning by providing increased funding not only to the more instrumentally focused HRSDC, but also to the more socially and culturally focused Canadian Heritage so this federal department can fund more community education focused on political and cultural participation, active citizenship, social cohesion and the needs of civil society.

The Adult Learning Knowledge Centre

The Adult Learning Knowledge Centre (ALKC), which the CCL established in September 2005, has as its primary mandate to make a stronger and more visible adult-learning culture in Canada:

> [The ALKC's mandate is] to serve as a national centre of expertise and action in the arena of adult learning, facilitating an exchange of ideas, best practices, and common challenges.... [It assists] the Canadian

Council on Learning (CCL) in developing a pan-Canadian roadmap of educational models and practices designed to result in improved learning outcomes for all Canadians.

(CCL 2006: 2)

During its tenure, the ALKC aims to make the implementation of important advances in adult learning its primary commitment: 'The mission is to foster a vital, informed, and coherent pan-Canadian culture of adult learning, accessible and relevant to all Canadians, as individuals, as communities, as a nation' (Flanagan 2006: 2). This lofty goal has been translated into four action priorities (PRCI 2007). The first two focus on the social context: to advance a right-to-learn strategy focused on the needs of Canadians in relation to literacy, high-school completion and prior learning recognition; and to assist adult-learning practitioners to develop facility in conducting action research in the communities they serve. The third priority is political in nature: to increase the profile of adult learning as a useful endeavour. The fourth priority is instrumental: to develop criteria for monitoring progress in adult-learning activities.

In carrying out its action priorities, the ALKC emphasizes knowledge mobilization and research; knowledge exchange and distribution, including monitoring, reporting and establishing performance benchmarks; communication; and community connections and networking. At its first annual national symposium in 2006, the ALKC focused participant energies on building a three-step process to assess the pan-Canadian state of adult learning (What?), reflect on this status report and its implications (So what?), and move adult learning forward through adult-learning initiatives that are 'accessible, relevant, and action-oriented' (Now what?) (CCL 2006: 4). Particularly targeted were groups categorized as non-participants in adult learning: the undereducated, those with poor self-images as learners, immigrants and refugees, older adults (over 50 years old), and adults with sensory, mobility and learning disabilities. It was clear that the social context was a concern of the ALKC in the development and delivery of forms of adult learning.

The notion of learning community was also deliberated at the 2006 symposium as a concept needing greater theoretical and practical definition. Learning communities were discussed in relation to community development, social capital, advocacy, social change, inclusion and research needs. The symposium recommended that future emphases be placed on 'communities of practice, diversity of adult learning, community-based research, and university–community research alliances' (CCL 2006: 16). As a post-symposium example of doing this work, the ALKC, in conjunction with Literacy Nova Scotia, provided a workshop in Halifax to help community-based practitioners learn basic action-research skills to share with peers and colleagues in an effort to build research capacities to enhance their work. As well, the ALKC, in conjunction with the Canadian Policy Research Networks (CPRN), co-sponsored a series of roundtable events across the country with the intention of influencing adult-learning policy change through dialogue with targeted governmental and educational agencies. Networking to build communities of practice has been a key goal in this work:

this work: 'Communities of practice need to be inclusive, encompassing govern-ment, educational institutions, [and] researchers as well as practitioners.... [They] also need to be interconnected with each other, with cross-disciplinary alliances' (ibid.: 5). Through networking, communities of practice focus on common social, cultural and community-based purposes, shared practices, defined learning needs and community-enhancing knowledge building.

The ALKC provides key stakeholders in businesses, labour, communities, education and government with a vehicle for networking to determine and meet adult learners' needs at the grassroots level. In this regard, there is value in stakeholders supporting the ALKC to continue fulfilling this role. Indeed the centre could have an enhanced role in assisting these stakeholders to build communities of practice where lifelong learning is nurtured as a key element in achieving instrumental, social and cultural goals. Here the CCL might encourage the federal government to assist the ALKC to develop new pan-Canadian models for adult learning that attend to diverse learner popu-lations, their learning needs, their ways of learning and issues of inclusive pedagogy. This could be part of the CCL's communicative role to emphasize the importance of holistic lifelong and life-wide learning in helping citizens to achieve a range of goals in relation to personal and social development, basic and cultural literacies, workplace learning, community development, homeplace homeostasis, citizenship education, volunteerism and so forth. Here the CCL has to work to convince government that attending to the whole life needs of citizens through broad-based lifelong learning is not a mere resistance stance to an emphasis on economistic forms of learning. Instead it is encompassing outreach to citizens so they can function well in the workplace, live quality lives and contribute to community sustainability. Indeed all stakeholders should recognize that, in the sum of this learning, matters of democratic participation (access and accommodation), equity, ethical treatment, individual freedom and social justice are at stake.

Making it work: a joint responsibility

Of course, the work expected here is challenging for the CCL and the ALKC as entities with time-limited mandates that require particular political will to extend. Key questions need to be addressed within the dialogic process and networking called for above. How do government, business, labour, educational institutions, researchers and community groups variously under-stand what constitutes lifelong learning, and what models ought to be developed in a Canadian context? What does each group see as the purposes of lifelong learning? How do we make policy making timely and more influ-enced by the interest groups that it affects? How do we create a more dynamic equilibrium between policy making and policy implementation? How do we educate governments to learn from advocacy initiatives so they are not threatened by them to the point that they further downplay the 'public'? How do we translate the lifelong-learning research that academics do into something that community-based groups would find meaningful, useful and valuable? How do we manage time and resources so that all of this work takes place in ways in which interest groups feel appropriately informed and involved?

Answering these questions as part of building communities of practice is a complex process in the face of the contemporary neoliberal mantra melding the social and the economic. This mantra has been chanted for some time in Canada. Indeed the last several Canadian prime ministers and their governments, whether Liberal or Conservative in ideological positioning, have chanted it in unison. Of course, these governments have downplayed the high level of illiteracy among Canadian adults. According to the International Adult Literacy and Skills Survey, nine million workers or 42 per cent of Canada's potential workforce (adults aged 16–65) have low literacy skills below the minimum considered requisite to function effectively in a knowledge economy (CCL 2008). These adults are often unemployed or engaged in more menial types of service labour (CCL 2007). With adults aged 66 and over driving the percentage up to 48 per cent, the situation is made even worse (CCL 2008). While this percentage might seem implausible to many Canadians, the reality requires action on the part of different interest groups because literacy levels affect possibilities and opportunities that individuals have to improve their quality of work, life, health, social and economic well-being, and participatory citizenship. In stressing the importance of literacy to the social and economic stability of citizens and their abilities to engage effectively in lifelong learning, the CCL (2008) accentuates the importance of governments, employers, unions, community groups and individuals all playing roles to advance the nation's literacy level. The Canadian Government ought to provide adequate funding and establish policy and programmes focused on communicating the importance of literacy training and ensuring access and accommodation to it. Employers should visibly support literacy training by helping employees assess their learning needs and by providing follow-up literacy training. Unions should provide learning advocates who point out the importance of literacy to fulfilling roles at home, in the workplace, in the union, in the community and, more broadly, to achieving community development and social equity. In the ways they can, individuals should be self-directed, conducting inventories to identify personal and family learning needs in relation to improving the quality of their lives.

All this work is pressing since the upshot of the neoliberal approach to governance in Canada has been an erosion of the social and a weakening of the public. Competitive individualism, privatization and the economistic emphasis have coalesced as the driving forces in this approach. In recent years, federal cuts to literacy programmes across Canada, which comprised an assault on community-based literacy groups, have been a profound expression of this erosion. Sadly, at the same time, the CCL (2007) recognizes a major discrepancy in Canada's claim to having one of the most highly educated populations in the world: more than 40 per cent of Canadian adults lack the levels of literacy and more than 50 per cent lack the levels of numeracy needed to mediate more demanding kinds of work. As a key consequence, these Canadians are functionally unemployable in certain sectors of the labour market. Since they are restricted in terms of what is possible in their work lives, they will never be able to participate fully in the contemporary knowledge and skills-driven economy. Moreover, the CCL adds that Canadians with low levels of literacy who find employment are perpetually disadvantaged in the workplace: relative to comparable 'developed' nations, Canada provides inadequate levels of workplace training – only 25 per cent of workers received any employer-sponsored training in 2002 – and those workers with low functional capacity are the least likely to have access to such training. Obviously, workplaces are ignoring what government sees as their private responsibility to address workers' learning needs. Regarding health literacy, the CCL relates that 55 per cent of Canadians lack the acceptable levels needed to make knowledgeable choices that promote health and well-being in the workplace and beyond. This is further evidence of the erosion of the social in Canada.

As a member of the ALKC's national advisory group, it seems to me that the CCL is ill-prepared to address these issues effectively. There are two key reasons for this: the temporal limitations placed on its mandate and the voluntary, ad hoc nature of stakeholder involvement in CCL initiatives. Yet the CCL is not without good intentions and a plan. In its mandate, the CCL has placed a primary focus on literacy, emphasizing the need for cross-jurisdictional, collaborative problem solving whereby governments, education, labour, individuals, the private and non-profit sectors, and other entities work together to overcome social, economic, work-related and developmental and health-related challenges. As I see it, the CCL's stance obliges the Canadian Government, if it is truly concerned about ordinary citizens, to listen to the CCL and take public responsibility by providing more fiscal support for its initiatives. Beyond this, various interest groups have to address the needs of learners and workers more broadly. In addition to roles suggested above, employers have to focus on in-house learning and provide enhanced workplace training; unions have to intensify advocacy for workers and rejuvenate labour education; and communities have to engage in informal and nonformal citizenship education aimed at enhancing political and civic engagement. If all this work were carried out, then it would invigorate the social. In this milieu, the economy would still benefit, perhaps even more so.

In the name of social cohesion, ethical and inclusive policy making and implementation, and participatory and democratic citizenship, lifelong learning has to be holistic, embracing the social, the cultural and the economic. For this to happen in Canada, the federal government should enable the CCL to be more than an expert think tank and a clearing house for resources. As a national, independent and non-profit corporation, the CCL's primary commitment ought to be to build and communicate a strategic pan-Canadian perspective on lifelong learning that has integral instrumental, social and cultural components. In this regard, the Canadian Government should see the CCL as a national pulse on lifelong learning and as a conduit between itself and the grassroots learning communities it has to serve. The federal government should systematically utilize CCL expertise before it changes policy or alters spending affecting lifelong learning in communities across the nation. Moreover, it has to make a long-term commitment to provide funds to the CCL, and it has to enable the CCL to be a real change agent with clout in its advisory and functional capacities. The CCL could then play a substantial role in building and sustaining Canadian communities of practice as interactive, dynamic places where educators and learners critically frame lifelong learning to emphasize citizenship, social responsibility and inclusion, as well as economic development. Such an approach to lifelong learning cannot be construed as oppositional by the Canadian Government and other stakeholders if they believe in nation building as well as building the economy.

Concluding perspective

Acknowledging the need for broad visions of education and learning, the CCL accentuates that 'we can no longer afford to view the purpose of education and learning primarily as the preparation of young people for the labour market.... Learning trajectories across the life course are as complex, unpredictable, and nonlinear as individuals' lives' (2008: 4). This perspective challenges the ways that learning has been commodified and selective in the era of neoliberalism. Moreover, as the CCL points out, it demands that learning focuses not only on economic productivity, but also on noneconomic outcomes such as improved health and longevity, and enhanced community and civic engagement. In sum, the CCL asserts that the nature and purpose of learning need greater immersion in the social context as part of a process of understanding how shifting workplace demographics, rapid technological change and increased globalization impact the potential, the needs and the positionalities of learners, which, in turn, impact cumulative learning and the quality of life across the lifespan. Possibilities for a better world increase in the hands of informed and involved citizens who transgress a location as compliant learners to become productive learners who complement their need for instrumental learning (as workers) with their need for social learning (as advocates, social activists and cultural workers). It would seem that Canada still has a long way to go to enable such learners. As the CCL points out, 'Canada does not have a lifelong learning system in place, nor a plan to transform the rhetoric of lifelong learning into a coherent vision and a plan of action' (ibid.: 5). Moreover, 'adult learning in this country remains underdeveloped, largely because we do not have a concerted, comprehensive strategy to address the needs and aspirations of the adult learner' (ibid.: 9). Thus the economic and social marginalization of our citizens remains a possibility. This is shameful in the face of low literacy skills and other markers of the need for lifelong learning in Canada.

Whether it's the Canadian Government or governments elsewhere looking at lifelong learning through a neoliberal lens, learning that is myopically focused on the instrumental is exclusionary learning. Such blinkered learning generally lacks any real concern with ensuring individual freedom and security, social justice and the ethical treatment of citizens (Grace 2006). Indeed, in the rush to economistic learning, lifelong learning as a neoliberal formation has grown more isolated from a critical vision that would juxtapose instrumental learning with social and cultural learning so the whole life needs of citizens can be met. Contemporary neoliberal lifelong-learning initiatives have couched the nature and meaning of lifelong learning in surviving-and-thriving terms that are not particularly attentive to historical, social and cultural contexts. This narrow focus is astounding given the extent of such assaults on humanity as global poverty, AIDS/HIV, terrorism, American imperialism, religious fundamentalism and racial and ethnocultural profiling. These tragedies are among the many social and cultural ills that assault the integrity of so many global citizens. Currently, this assault is being intensified by global economic upheaval in which a turn to global market regulation contests the economic logic of neoliberalism. In the face of new worries and fears, economistic lifelong learning will not be enough for ordinary citizens. Thus it is time for educators to take a stand and revitalize lifelong learning as the kind of holistic social, cultural and instrumental learning needed to transgress and transform what could be emerging as a post-neoliberal change culture of crisis and challenge.

References

Canadian Council on Learning (2005) *Annual Report 2004–2005*, Ottawa, ON: Canadian Council on Learning.
—— (2006) *Report on the 2006 National Symposium: Adult learning in Canada – What? So what? Now what?* Fredericton, NB: Canadian Council on Learning.
—— (2007) *State of Learning in Canada: No time for complacency*. Online, available at: www.ccl-cca.ca/CCL/Reports/StateofLearning/StateofLearning2007.htm (accessed 27 February 2007).
—— (2008) *State of Learning in Canada: Toward a learning future*, Ottawa, ON: Canadian Council on Learning.
Collins, M. (1998) *Critical Crosscurrents in Education*, Malabar, FL: Krieger.
Edwards, R. (2000) 'Lifelong learning, lifelong learning, lifelong learning: A recurrent education?' in J. Field and M. Leicester (eds), *Lifelong Learning: Education across the lifespan*, London: RoutledgeFalmer.
Field, J. (2006) *Lifelong Learning and the New Educational Order* (2nd edn), Stoke-on-Trent, UK: Trentham Books.
Flanagan, K. (2006) *First Year Report of the Adult Learning Knowledge Centre: September 2005–March 2006*, Fredericton, NB: Adult Learning Knowledge Centre, Canadian Council on Learning.
Grace, A.P. (2004) 'Lifelong learning as a chameleonic concept and versatile practice: Y2K perspectives and trends', *International Journal of Lifelong Education* 23(4), 385–405.
—— (2005) 'Lifelong learning chic in the modern practice of adult education: Historical and contemporary perspectives', *Journal of Adult and Continuing Education* 11(1), 62–79.
—— (2006) 'Reflecting critically on lifelong learning in an era of neoliberal pragmatism: Instrumental, social, and cultural perspectives', keynote address in D. Orr, F. Nouwens, C. Macpherson, R.E. Harreveld and P.A. Danaher (eds), *Proceedings of the 4th International Lifelong Learning Conference, Central Queensland University, Yeppoon, Central Queensland, Australia*, pp. 1–16. Also online, avail-

able at http://lifelonglearning.cqu.edu.au/2006/papers-ft/keynote-grace.pdf (accessed 11 November 2008).

—— (2007) 'Envisioning a critical social pedagogy of learning and work in a contemporary culture of cyclical lifelong learning', *Studies in Continuing Education* 29(1), 85–103.

Grace, A.P. and Wells, K. (2007) 'Using Freirean pedagogy of just ire to inform critical social learning in arts-informed community education for sexual minorities', *Adult Education Quarterly* 57(2), 95–114.

Harvey, D. (2005) *A Brief History of Neoliberalism*, New York: Oxford University Press.

Longworth, N. (2002) 'Learning cities for a learning century', in K. Appleton, C. Macpherson and D. Orr (eds), *Proceedings of the 2nd International Lifelong Learning Conference, Yeppoon, Central Queensland, Australia*, pp. 10–35. Rockhampton, Australia: Central Queensland University.

Praxis Research and Consulting Inc. (PRCI) (2007) *Mapping the Field: A framework for measuring, monitoring, and reporting on adult learning in Canada*, Moncton, NB: Adult Learning Knowledge Centre.

Schissel, B. (2006) *Still Blaming Children: Youth conduct and the politics of child hating*, Halifax, NS: Fernwood Publishing.

Walters, S. (2006) 'Realizing a lifelong learning higher education institution', in P. Sutherland and J. Crowther (eds), *Lifelong Learning: Concepts and contexts*, London: Routledge, pp. 71–81.

Welton, M.R. (2005) *Designing the Just Learning Society: A critical inquiry*, Leicester, UK: NIACE.

Chapter 4

Time, individual learning careers, and lifelong learning

Barbara Allan and Dina Lewis

Introduction

In this chapter we explore the complex relationship between an individual's perspectives on time, their learning careers, professional development and lifelong learning journeys. The study developed from our observation that we each had a particular and distinct relationship to time both in terms of managing our working lives on a daily basis and also through our approaches to developing our professional and learning careers. Through working closely together over more than a decade we observed that our individual temporal perspective had a significant impact on our learning and professional careers as academics and authors, and it also appeared to influence our individual lifelong learning journeys. We also noted that the research literature on lifelong learning often focused on 'life history' yet rarely adopted a temporal perspective: this is in contrast to the emerging literature in the fields of management and organisational studies, and also e-learning.

Another driver for this research was changes in employment legislation, e.g. European Working Time directive and the new Work and Families Act 2006, and changes in employment practices, e.g. the rise in work/life balance and lifelong learning policies and practices. At the same time, we noted that despite these changes in legislation, policies and practices and also current debates about diversity, the concept of individual temporal differences was absent. We believe that it is important to understand individual approaches to time and to take them into account in developing policies and practices related to supporting learning careers, lifelong learning and career development.

At the same time, we are conscious that society's approaches to time, work and leisure are changing, e.g. the rise of the 24/7 society, the development of 'anywhere/anytime learning' offered in some e-learning programmes and the blurring of boundaries between work, learning and leisure. The rise in the discourse of learning careers and lifelong learning appears to have shifted responsibility for managing learning from the employer to the learner (Raggett *et al.* 1995). Consequently, it has become even more important that individuals manage their own time and create time for learning and learning activities. In this study we wanted to explore how individuals manage this process with reference to their own temporal perspectives.

We therefore decided to focus our research on the following questions:

a   Do concepts of fast and slow time relate to the women's experiences?
b   How do time vision theories relate to the women's working lives?
c   Is there a relationship between the women's time horizons and their approaches to career development and career planning?
d   Is there a relationship between time depth and individual approaches to career planning and lifelong learning?
e   Do individual differences in approaches to time management affect individual approaches to work and learning?

Time

Time is a complex construct and it may be explored from a number of different perspectives, for example philosophy, sociology, education and management. Theorists (Adam 1998; Eriksen 2001; Friedland and Boden 1994; Virilio 2000) argue that society today is characterised by the acceleration and compression of time and space. Eriksen (2001) characterises this in terms of 'fast time' and 'slow time'. 'Fast time' is much more than being busy and it is linked to the rise in information communications technology resulting in increased access to information at ever-increasing speeds. One consequence of 'fast time' is that it may lead individuals to race about from one activity to another, receiving and reading e-mails or messages in virtual learning environments without spending 'slow time' integrating new ideas and concepts (Eriksen 2001). Another effect of this 'fast time' is that it replaces 'slow time', which is required for certain kinds of emotional and intellectual experiences including reflection (Land 2006). This is relevant to this study, as it suggests that individuals need 'slow time' for different types of learning activities and, in particular, for reflection. In this study we are interested in how individuals build in or provide spaces in their lives for 'slow time' for learning activities.

Saunders *et al.* (2004) explore time in the context of virtual teams and they present a framework of time that suggests different cultures develop their own conception of time based on a number of different dimensions. They identify four time visions: clock, event, timeless and harmonic. Clock and calendar time is the dominant time vision in American, Anglo-Saxon, Germanic and Scandinavian countries (Adam 1995) and this approach perceives time as discontinuous, unidimensional and takes a short-term perspective. The current study is located within this time vision. Hughes (2002) describes this approach to time as being gendered and quotes the work of Knights and Odih who describe female time as relational, processual, cyclical and continuous. According to Saunders *et al.* (2004), very different approaches to time are found in Eastern cultures and these are called 'event', 'timeless' and 'harmonic' time visions. These temporal approaches are described as continuous, multidimensional or recurrent, and long term.

Other approaches to exploring time include the concepts of temporal depth and timescapes. Bluedorn and Standifer (2006) introduced the concept of temporal depth, which refers to the distances into the past and future that individuals think about plans and events. This links to the work of Jacques (1994) who talks about time horizon – i.e. the boundary of an individual's perspective on time as illustrated by a goal. These dimensions of time and ways of describing the temporal landscape are very relevant to this study, which explores individual approaches to time with respect to their learning careers and lifelong learning journeys. The concept of a timescape was suggested by Adam (1998) and this idea is concerned with individuals' relationships with time and their practical approaches to time. For example, individuals may consistently arrive on time, early or late for a meeting depending on their own timescape. Brown (2005) explores the temporal landscape within higher education and identifies different approaches to time including public and private, home and work, past, present and future time, as well as cyclical time. Again, this concept appears relevant to the current study and offers a language and framework for exploring individual approaches to time.

Hassard (1990) explores the ways in which time is constructed at the level of society and suggests that from birth onwards individuals adapt to the temporal constraints of their society and the organisations in which they work. He calls this temporal structuring, and suggests that it takes place through child-rearing practices, schooling and other socially sanctioned practices. This is relevant to this study as the individuals investigated are employed by an organisation that has its own temporal practices and seasonal patterns including semester and vacations, timetables, deadlines and assessment periods. In addition, we explore the concept of lifelong learning and relate this to the temporal structuring of an individual's life.

Adam considers education and time, and suggests that clock and calendar time provide the dominant time experience in Western education and suggests that these norms of time that underpin Western education are rarely questioned and they relate to specific theories of time:

> Time as measure and as quantity ... express an understanding of the uni-directionality of processes, of cause and effect, and of the cumulative nature of knowledge. They imply an understanding of time that acknowledges that 'you cannot step into the same river twice,' that the past and future are inseparably tied to the present, and that there is a 'right' time for everything.
>
> (1995: 66)

This is illustrated by the existence of an academic calendar, course timetables that determine the structure of the educational experience, and also academic debates over the curriculum and how much time is 'given' for a particular subject. Adam (1995), building on the work of Weber, suggests that this particular approach to time, namely punctuated and sectioned time, was first developed in monasteries and, in particular, by the Benedictine monks. In addition, educational experiences are normally arranged in certain sequences, which presuppose a beginning, middle and end. In higher education, this is illustrated by the identification of levels of academic learning and also the notion of prerequisites. The rise in the concept of 'lifelong learning' has extended the traditional educational lifespan from a traditional one that involved Western children entering school at the age of four to eight years (depending on their country of origin) and then remaining within the educational system until their teenage years or twenties, to one that means that individuals may be engaged in educational processes throughout their lives.

Lifelong learning

The concept of lifelong learning has been widely used to underpin educational policies and political priorities. Rose (1999) outlined the rise of the concept during the 1970s when it was associated with the drive to encourage individuals to keep up with technological change and developments in order to remain in employment. This link between lifelong learning and employment resulted in a wide range of training initiatives aimed at enabling the unemployed to become active in the labour market. The second period of interest and development in lifelong learning came in the 1990s and this was associated with the rise in global competition, flexible lifelong learning was vaunted as the European panacea to the threat of the Pacific Rim economies and adult learning was heralded as the remedy to socio-economic disadvantage. Aspin and Chapman (2001), Delors (1996) and international bodies such as UNESCO, EU and OECD have identified support for lifelong learning as a response to economic, political, social and technological changes (Kreber 2005).

McIntosh (2005) considers the complexity of the concept of lifelong learning and identifies six distinct models. The functionalist model focuses on 'human capital' and teaching essential vocational skills; the critical literacy model is associated with the work of Freire (1970) and encouraging learners to develop a questioning attitude towards assumptions and concepts; the social justice model focuses on marginalised and minority groups; the reflective learning model may be characterised by the phrase 'learning how to think'; the compensatory model is concerned with educational institutions providing opportunities for learners to remedy deficiencies in their knowledge and skills; and the humanistic model, which is concerned with broadening learners' horizons and developing their minds. We are interested in the literature of lifelong learning as, although it may refer to time, e.g. with reference to age or stages in a career, we have been unable to find research that explores the temporal experiences of individuals.

Individual learning careers

The concept of a 'learning career' is used by Gallacher *et al.* (2002) to explore the process by which individuals make the transition to participating in education and becoming increasingly engaged in formal learning. In the context of this study, the concept is used to explore the process whereby individuals undertake further study and gain additional qualifications. The use of the word 'career' derives from symbolic interactionalist theory and the suggestion that this concept may be used with reference to continuous and discontinuous trajectories in an individual's life (ibid.). This study is concerned with the subjective dimensions of a learning career and considers individual experiences, the meanings that they attribute to these experiences and their sense of their own identity.

Gorard *et al.* (2001) illustrate the social determinants of lifelong learning careers and explore the determinants of participation and suggest that individual choices are made within a social context and this affects what individuals perceive as appropriate for themselves and their group. The purpose of this chapter is not to explore structural determinants but to explore individual agency of choice located within academic careers. We suggest that the process of engaging in an educational programme with its intrinsic learning community may change someone's 'horizons of action' leading to new career trajectories.

Methodology

This study is based on life history and autobiographical research methodologies. This approach offers an alternative to empirical methods for identifying and documenting patterns of individual lives. It allows us to explore individuals' experiences within a time framework. It is useful in helping individuals to understand current attitudes and behaviours and how they could have been influenced by initial decisions made at another time and in another place. It encourages individuals to note events from their lives and note the importance or comment on the meaning of those events. Life history research provides an opportunity for exploring social phenomena from the perspective of individuals and it 'enables us to know people intimately, to see the world through their eyes, and to enter into their experiences vicariously' (Shaw writing in 1931 and cited in Taylor and Bogdan 1984: 81).

We explore the working and learning lives of four academic women (identified as Claire, Jazz, Kath and Theresa) who are employed at the University of Hull and each has worked in higher education for more than ten years. The data was collected by interviews that were structured around the concepts of fast and slow time, time depth and time landscapes. The interviews were recorded and transcribed. The four women were then given the opportunity to read and comment on the findings. Minor amendments were made as the result of this process. We used narrative analysis (Barthes 1966) to identify general themes, and we then analysed these with reference to our theoretical frameworks. We view this study as an exploratory one and we intend to follow it up with a larger-scale study.

Results

Do concepts of fast and slow time relate to the women's experiences?

All four academic women regularly experienced 'fast time' and gave examples of their daily experiences, which typically involved moving from one meeting to another or lecture to lecture. In between times they caught up with e-mails, phone messages and other demands on their time. They commented on the volume of e-mails and information that they were required to manage at any one time and they used expressions such as 'pressures of time', 'no breathing time', 'no gaps' and 'racing from one thing to another'. This fitted into Land's description of *dromos* or fast time. All four women identified the need for slow time and adopted different approaches to including it in their working lives. Jazz kept the hour between 5 p.m. and 6 p.m. for slow-time activities and, in contrast, Claire never scheduled slow time into her diary but would regularly (about once a fortnight) work from home for one or two days as a means of giving herself this type of quality time. For Claire 'slow time' involved activities such as tidying up and dog walking, and this gave her 'space to think'. Kath created 'slow time' by working in her office with her light off and scheduling time to work at home. Theresa, whose subject specialism is computerised information systems, uses the internet to gain 'slow time' and this involves general surfing or engaging with people via discussion forum. She described this as giving herself time 'to be in touch with my inner teenager'. For each of these women, 'slow time' appeared to offer time to slow down and reflect on their current work and to identify areas for change and development. Without access to this quality of time there was a suggestion that there was reduced scope for personal development or learning.

How do time vision theories relate to the women's working lives?

All four women worked within the UK higher education system and stated that they were bound by clock time. They mentioned the annual academic cycle and the rise and fall of their workloads in time with annual events such as the start and end of semesters, module and programme boards, and conferences. One woman commented that the academic calendar was in fact structured around traditional natural cycles of the seasons and welcomed the differences she experienced between the winter months when she experienced her heaviest workload and the summer months when her workload was lighter. In contrast to this calendar-based perspective, all the women viewed their careers as being continuous, multidimensional or recurrent, and long term. In addition and with some laughter they all acknowledged their need to multitask (called polychronicity within the time vision framework). One of the women commented:

> I am bogged down by the demands of the semester and the annual university calendar. This doesn't match my own learning goals or career

development plans. It means that I have two calendars in my head: the university one and my personal one. They are often in conflict with each other and the demands of the RAE have made this much harder than normal. I'm being idealistic but if these two calendars could be integrated into a more holistic one then I'd probably be more productive and less stressed.

This quotation clearly demonstrates the temporal demands on this individual and the ways in which personal and organisational are in conflict with each other.

Do the women's time horizons impact on their approaches to career development and career planning?

Taking a broader perspective on their careers the women described different career trajectories. Jazz described her working life in terms of ten-year blocks: ten years at home with her family; ten years' part-time work; ten years' full-time work. Claire described her working life as full time although this included periods of part-time work. However, when she worked part time she normally had a series of part-time contracts that built up to full-time work. She described her working life as continuous. Kath described her career in terms of full-time work with 'breaks' while she engaged in further study. Theresa described her career as starting late and then being full time. She talked in terms of needing sabbaticals or gap years (or months) as a means of maintaining her equilibrium and keeping up-to-date with her subject.

Is there a relationship between time depth and individual approaches to career planning and lifelong learning?

Each woman demonstrated her own time depth and this clearly related to their approaches to their working lives and lifelong learning history. Jazz's time depth ranged from a year ago to about three years ahead. Associated with this she tended to set herself three-year plans or career goals that were specific in terms of income and progress within the higher education institution. Jazz linked this with her desire 'to catch up' with women who had not had the big family career influences. She felt that she had 'not much time' and so set targets so that she did not 'waste a minute'.

In contrast, Claire's time depth was very narrow from about one week ago to up to six months ahead. She rarely had long-term goals but tended to 'keep doing what she was doing until she became bored. It was then she would look for something different.' Claire linked her approach to not having any specific career plans but following her interests and enthusiasms. Kath's time depth was similar to that of Claire; she tended not to look back (except at specific incidents) and to look ahead for four to six months.

Theresa's time depth was quite different from the others. She defined a professional time depth that involved living in the moment and then looking forward for up to six months or a year. She linked this with the academic annual calendars. She identified that her domestic time depth was quite different and involved looking back intermittently over a long period of time and also looking forward to and, in general, making plans for the next five, ten and 20 years. She talked about this looking ahead in terms of 'lifestyles I want to taste'.

Do individual differences in approaches to time management affect approaches to career development and learning careers?

Individual differences to time were clearly identified in the women's discussions about their personal relationship with time. Jazz was normally on time or a few minutes late for meetings and was concerned about wasting time if she arrived at an event early and then had to wait for others. In contrast, Claire was always early and preferred to be prepared and wait for others to arrive rather than arrive just in time or several minutes late. Kath managed her time by lists and identified that it was important to her to include easy items on the list. She was sometimes late for or rearranged meetings. In contrast, Theresa described herself as obsessive about time: she arrived on time for meetings, and she always had her next semester's teaching materials fully prepared before the start of the semester. Theresa stated that she was very poor at managing her time and experienced lots of panics before she was able to start on a task.

Different women took different approaches to their learning lives. Jazz took a strategic approach and focused on undertaking qualifications and programmes that would help her achieve her specific career goals such as a Master's degree when she knew it was essential for progression and leadership and management training to enable her manage staff more effectively. In contrast Claire signed up for and completed academic programmes such as Master's degrees that enabled her to follow her subject interests. She was driven by her subject interest rather than her career, as demonstrated by her achievement of three Master's degrees. She also pointed out that these educational experiences had enhanced her career although that wasn't her motivation. Kath had completed two Master's degrees and she used these as a means of changing career direction and taking control of her work situation during times of institutional change rather than in response to an inner temporal career pattern. Finally, Theresa said that she felt that she didn't have enough time to pay attention to the dimension of formal educational programmes and she recognised their value and suggested that 'you can only go so far with self reflection and after a time you need to add formality'.

Discussions and conclusion

These initial findings suggest that these academic women all take quite individual approaches to time and their careers. All the women identified with the concepts of fast and slow time, and described the strategies they used for creating slow time in their working lives.

The concepts of time vision, time horizon and depth, and timescapes provided a useful framework for talking about and exploring individual approaches to time. Although their approaches to time were structured on a day-to-day basis by the academic annual cycle (clock or calendar time), each woman also appeared to work within her own temporal framework and this gave a structure to their working careers. These differences in individual approaches to time are interesting as they do not appear to be acknowledged within current policies and practices with respect to careers and lifelong learning. Although it is common to talk about flexible learning opportunities, these are often concerned with 'when and how' an individual engages with learning, rather than how a learning opportunity fits into an individual's inner temporal perspective. Individuals with a relatively short time depth (such as Theresa) may not take up learning opportunities that cannot be completed within her time depth, to the detriment of her opportunity to engage with lifelong learning. Finally, individual temporal frameworks appeared to have more in common with Eastern time visions than clock time vision, and this is an area for further research.

Their individual motivations for engaging in formal learning opportunities appeared to link with their career identities and they used these opportunities as a means of either directing their careers in a particular direction or to follow up a personal interest. The findings from the study illuminated the concept of lifelong learning and McIntosh's (2005) models of lifelong learning (the functionalist model, the critical literacy model, the social justice model, the reflective learning model, the compensatory model and the humanistic model). Different women appeared to use formal learning opportunities for different reasons and these appeared to map into the functionalist model as they used these learning opportunities for different reasons. These included the development of their 'human capital' as a means of updating or remedying their perceived deficiencies in their knowledge and skills, and broadening their horizons. Consequently individual women could locate their learning careers in the context of the functionalist model, the compensatory model and the humanistic model. In addition, they acknowledged that their educational experience enhanced their ability to reflect and learn from experience. However, these different models of lifelong learning appear to offer an oversimplification of the reality of individuals' lifelong learning experiences, which may involve elements of different models at the same or different times of their learning careers. This finding suggests that current models of lifelong learning need to be developed to provide a more holistic model that integrates elements from other models and also takes into account temporal perspectives. This will be an area for research in the future.

Finally, this is an introductory exploratory study. The findings indicate that the use of these different time concepts do offer a framework for exploring the experiences of academic women. Exploring and understanding individuals' temporal experiences is important as it provides a lens to explore the impact of different educational policies and management practices. In addition, an understanding of one's own temporal experiences and perspectives provides the basis for managing increasing complex work/life balances. We intend to follow up this initial study with an in-depth study that explores gendered aspects of academic women, time, individual learning careers and lifelong learning.

References

Adam, B. (1995) *Timewatch: The social analysis of time*, Cambridge: Polity.

Adam, B. (1998) *Timescapes of Modernity: The environment and invisible hazards*, London: Routledge.

Aspin, D. and Chapman, J. (2001) 'Lifelong learning: Concepts, theories and values'. Paper presented at SCUTREA, 31st Annual Conference, University of East London.

Barthes, R. (1966) 'Introduction to the structural analysis of narratives', in S. Sontag (ed.), *A Barthes Reader*, London: Vintage, pp. 251–195 (1993).

Bluedorn, A.C. and Standifer, R.L. (2006) 'Time and temporal imagination', *Academy of Management Learning and Education* 5(2), 196–206.

Brown, R.B. (2005) 'Mapping the temporal landscape: The case of university business school academics', *Management Learning* 36(4), 451–470.

Delors, J. (1996) *Learning: The Treasure Within*, Paris: UNESCO.

Eriksen, T.H. (2001) *Tyranny of the Moment: Fast and slow time in the information age*, London: Pluto.

Freire, P. (1970) *Pedagogy of the Oppressed*, New York: Herder and Herder.

Friedland, R. and Boden, D. (1994) *NowHere Space, Time and Modernity*, Berkeley, CA: University of California Press.

Gallacher, J., Crossan, B., Field, J. and Merrill, B. (2002) 'Learning careers and social space: Exploring the fragile identities of adult returners in the new further education', *International Journal of Lifelong Learning* 21(6), 493–509.

Gorard, S., Rees, G., Fevre, R. and Welland, T. (2001) 'Lifelong learning trajectories: Some voices of those in transit', *International Journal of Lifelong Learning* 20(3), 169–187.

Hassard, J. (ed.) (1990) *The Sociology of Time*, London: Macmillan.

Hughes, C. (2002) *Key Concepts in Feminist Theory and Research*, London: Sage.

Jaques, E. (1994) *Human Capability*, Falls Church, VA: Cason Hall.

Kreber, C. (2005) 'Charting a critical course on the scholarship of university teaching movement', *Studies in Higher Education* 30(4), 389–405.

Land, R. (2006) 'Networked learning and the politics of speed: A dromological perspective', Networked Learning 2006, University of Lancaster, Lancaster. Online, available at: www.networkedlearningconference.org.uk/ (accessed 21 June 2006).

McIntosh, C. (2005) 'Introduction', in C. McIntosh (ed.), *Perspectives on Distance Education, Lifelong Learning and Distance Higher Education*, Paris: UNESCO, pp. 1–10.

Raggett, P., Edwards, R. and Small, N. (1995) *The Learning Society: Challenges and trends*, London: Routledge.

Rose, N. (1999) *Powers of Freedom*, Cambridge: Cambridge University Press.

Saunders, C., Van Slyke, C. and Vogel, D. (2004) 'My time or yours? Managing time visions in global virtual teams', *Academy of Management Executive* 18(1), 19–31.

Taylor, S. and Bogdan, R. (1984) *Introduction to Qualitative Research Methods: The search for meanings* (2nd edn), New York: John Wiley and Sons.

Virilio, P. (2000) *Politics of the Very Worst*, New York: Semiotexte.

Chapter 5

Who is the 'responsible learner'?
Viewing learning careers through social narratives and recursive methodology

Sue Webb and Simon Warren

Introduction

When Edgar Faure argued in his UNESCO report 'Learning to Be' that life-long education should be 'the master concept for educational policies in the years to come for both developed and developing countries' (UNESCO 1972: 82), could he have envisaged the way this concept would be appropriated and adapted in all types of societies over the last three decades, irrespective of their different stages of development or ideological bases? There has been a strong Eurocentric dimension to this policy migration, assimilation and accommodation. Many of the influential policy documents have been produced by the European Union (EU) and the Organization for Economic Co-operation and Development (OECD). These have framed much of the conceptualisation of lifelong learning policy globally (Field 2006; Preece 2006; Warren and Webb 2007: 6). Given this, arguably, it is useful to examine the policy effects of these texts in one of the countries close to the European policy hub, in other words, to focus on England.

Specifically, this chapter explores the meanings of a policy construct, 'responsible learners', who are exhorted by current lifelong learning policy discourse to use learning in order to work upon themselves and become more amenable to the demands of a globalised world. The focus is on understanding what 'responsible learners' look like empirically. It asks the question what practices and understandings do social actors engage in when undertaking lifelong learning. A sub-question to this is: can these practices and learners' identities be understood in terms of reflexive agency or are there structural constraints on their practices that lead to a reproduction of the social order? We explore these questions in the context of a small empirical study of adults choosing to return to formal education in England, and more specifically we focus upon the decision-making process and learning career of one adult learner. The chapter is informed by the growing literature on learning career (Bloomer and Hodkinson 2000; Crossan *et al.* 2003).

We present a case study of the experiences and learning career of one adult learner, 'Jenny', developed through iteration between two interviews conducted at different stages of her engagement with formal learning. Our analysis of these interviews is informed by our theoretical concerns, an analysis of policy discourse and policy effects, and interviews with her course tutor, her course director and a practitioner from a regional Further/Higher Education partnership – a research model that elsewhere we have termed recursive methodology (Warren and Webb 2009). Beginning with Jenny's story, we identify specific turning points and key moments in her narrative and move to map these to theoretical understandings of changes in the gender division of labour, especially the gendered construction of the care economy, before returning to an enriched narrative of Jenny's situated practices. We continue enrichment of the analysis by continually oscillating between Jenny's original representation of herself, further representations she makes and the policy construction of the field of post-compulsory education and training; the institutional habitus of the further education college Jenny attends; and the strategies employed by the college in response to the policy regime (Webb and Warren 2007). Through this learner's story of transition we reveal the material conditions for the constitution of her identity and by stressing the contingent and historical location of this formation we glimpse the possibility of alternative futures in her learning career.

Where are the 'responsible learners'?

A range of policy texts argues that global processes of economic and technological restructuring have reconfigured the relationship between national economies and global markets, refashioning the kinds of skills and knowledge perceived as necessary for economic growth and competitiveness, and transforming the labour process, with consequent impacts upon education, traditional notions of career and working lives (see Brown and Lauder 1992; Coffield 1999; Department for Education and Employment 2001; Department for Education and Skills 2005, 2006; Department for Trade and Industry 1998; Department for Innovation, Universities and Skills (DIUS) 2008).

In particular, globalisation is seen as introducing new risks and uncertainties, disrupting traditional patterns of transition into and through employment and creating new purposes for post-compulsory education (Department for Education and Skills 2006; Field 2001, 2006; Leitch 2006; Strain and Field 1997). Leitch argues, for example,

> The global economy is changing rapidly, with emerging economies such as India and China growing dramatically, altering UK competitiveness.... There is a direct correlation between skills, productivity and employment.... As a result of low skills, the UK risks increasing inequality, deprivation and child poverty and risks a generation cut off permanently from labour market opportunity. The best form of welfare is to ensure that people can adapt to change. Skills were once a key lever to prosperity and fairness. Skills are now the key lever.
>
> (2006: 3)

In response to this politically constructed policy problem, policy solutions invoke the 'responsible learner' as a central character in educational policy narratives. These policy discourses are informed by areas of social theory, particularly 'reflexive modernity' and 'risk society' (Beck and Beck-Gernsheim 1996; Beck *et al*. 1994; Beck 1992), where the 'responsible learner' is imagined as a reflexive agent in a post-traditional society. James Avis (2000: 196) writing about England has noted this process in the field of post-16 education and training as one where 'We are to become responsible for our own actions as individuals, investing in our own development thus increasing our capacity as human capital.' Similarly, Andreas Fejes has noted this process of responsibilisation of adult learners in Sweden (2005). And the foreword to the policy text, 'Higher Education at Work, High Skills: High Value' illustrates this well in the claims it makes for the relationship between acquiring skills and individuals:

> High level skills – the skills associated with higher education – are good for the individuals who acquire them and good for the economy. They help individuals unlock their talent and aspire to change their life for the better. They help businesses and public services innovate and prosper. They help towns and cities thrive by creating jobs, helping businesses become more competitive and driving economic regeneration. High level skills add value for all of us.
>
> (DIUS 2008: 3)

So where are these 'responsible learners' in practice; are they acquiring high-level skills, and if so, what does this learning mean for them, or are they simply figments of the policy discourse? It is a matter for empirical investigation to discern to what extent they exist in practice. In particular, for individuals who appear to be engaging in reflexive practices – adults who 'choose' to engage with formal learning, what is it that they do and what is it about their practices that makes them a 'responsible learner'? Do the discursive constructions of people as reflexive agents adequately capture the real practices people engage in when responding to the policy exhortations that they need to adapt to change and acquire high-level skills? Is the 'responsible learner' simply an ideological deceit that disguises the reproduction of the social order? These are the questions that inform the wider research on which this chapter is based.

Researching the responsible learner

The research drawn upon here is derived from a larger study that has focused on the following research question and two sub-questions. How are adults engaging with formal lifelong learning over their lifetime? How are 'decisions' made to engage with formal learning? What meaning does this learning have in their lives and identities? These interrelated questions were examined through qualitative methods including documentary discourse analysis and interviews focused on different levels in the field of post-compulsory education and training in order to elicit understandings of the context of learning within which adults are engaging and the meanings learning has in their lives. A critical case study approach was adopted. This involved selecting a region in England that exemplified the transformative changes brought about by globalisation. The area selected was Sheffield, which over the past three decades along with the rest of the South Yorkshire region, has shifted from an economy dominated by manufacturing, specifically steel production, to one where the service sector predominates (Sheffield City Council 2004; Sheffield First Partnership 2002).

In the South Yorkshire region of England transitions play a large part in people's lives and the educational and training practices of the region have foregrounded the role of lifelong learning in these. It provides a critical case to explore how learners are engaging with learning. In order to examine this question and what might be understood by the term the 'responsible learner' we used theoretical sampling to identify learners to exemplify different types of transitions in learners' lives and whose entry to formal learning provided an opportunity to examine moments where the policy discourse suggests there should be heightened reflexivity. We recognised three types of transitions where we hypothesised that there were different forms of engagement with learning. First, there were those who were in a skills transition, often undertaking work-based learning in order to adapt to changing workplace requirements in order to improve their employability or maintain their labour market position; second, there were those in a migratory transition, either as a consequence of economic or forced migration, for example, new migrants, refugees and asylum seekers and those learners who might be using learning to support their transition into and through employment in the host country; and finally there were those who were in a home-to-work transition, who were using a return to education to acquire new skills and knowledge to move into the labour market as an older worker after a break in employment. In this chapter we concentrate on the third category, the home-to-work transition experienced often by older unemployed learners, commonly women, who had returned to learn in spite of appearing to have slipped down the policy agenda because they were not the prime focus of social inclusion and widening participation nor of work-based learning initiatives. Our third type of learner was an older British female, Jenny, who had made a decision to return to education at the age of 39 and had chosen the health care area for study. It is Jenny's transition that is the focus of this chapter.

Data to examine the structural analysis context that Jenny experienced was collected through interviews with spokespersons from different levels of the field of post-compulsory education and training in further and higher education (F/HE). These included interviews with a practitioner (1) from a regional F/HE educational partnership promoting post-compulsory vocational learning routes and widening participation, course directors (2) and course tutors (3), each from a college and a university, and Labour Market statistics. Learners were interviewed twice and their accounts were located within a web of identifications using snowball sampling of key influencers such as other 'learners', friends, work colleagues, family members, partners and so on in order to capture something of their multiple identities at this point of transition.

Jenny realises her caring identity: the importance of her underlying 'identity' as carer

At first sight Jenny's story appears as an amazingly reflexive and rational account of a 'caring' identity being given the opportunity to be realised. 'Caring' appeared in her narrative as a central feature of her identity work. Jenny's narrative conveys linearity and the motif of 'caring' was used to link different points in the story. This linearity may have been partly imposed by the fact that she was being interviewed about her participation on a 'caring' course. However, as with the women in Beverley Skeggs' (1997) study of gender, social class and 'respectability', caring appeared to provide Jenny with certain symbolic resources with which to construct a particular gendered and moral identity. We can detect in the narrative five distinct 'caring' periods.

The first period covers her post-school transition into employment. Jenny informed us that when leaving school she had wanted to work with children. This appeared to be motivated by her general sense of being good at 'caring' and good with children, something that would later be confirmed by her participation in formal adult learning. She was encouraged by her parents to go into the family occupation of catering. Yet, Jenny claims, she held on to the idea of working with children. Marrying and becoming pregnant offered a way out of catering and into another period where 'caring' could become predominant. Jenny provided a clear rationale for being a stay-at-home mother. While this was partly pragmatic, looking after four young children was incompatible with the work patterns of catering, it was the centrality of providing good caring that overlaid this part of her story. For Jenny, to be a 'good' mother meant being a full-time mother. There was an ethical element and moral identity to this that would reappear later in her role as a care worker.

This sense of being good at caring was reinforced by her experience of looking after her dying aunt, the third period. Although caring was a shared family activity, Jenny recounted how her aunt commented that she had a natural aptitude for caring, that she cared for her aunt's dignity as much as her body and was prepared to do things others found repulsive. There appeared to be a direct connection between caring for her aunt and Jenny taking up caring jobs working with the elderly in community care settings. In retrospect this fourth period of 'caring' appears to have set down roots that would flourish later in her decision to participate in formal adult learning. Jenny's account of working for private sector care companies was anchored around the ethical struggles she found herself engaged in. Jenny had a very strong ethical approach to caring and so disagreed with the way many people were treated in the community care settings. She conveys a strong sense that people should be treated with dignity, as with her aunt. She was not happy with the level of training provided and spoke about the way she found herself in situations she knew intuitively were wrong but did not have the relevant skills or knowledge to question them. These experiences reinforced her sense that a more appropriate form of caring was required, simultaneously reinforcing her own sense of being a 'carer' and propelling her towards formal learning to gain some qualifications in order to be taken seriously in the world of paid-for caring. Although she was not able to realise this 'caring' role for a number of years, the narrative sets it up as the antecedent to the fifth period.

Jenny appears to have used her engagement with formal learning on the health and social care course in a further education college to provide a reflective space. The part-time nature of the course fitted around her child-care commitments and her perception that she did not have the capacity to engage with the academic content and workload of a full-time course. The breadth of the course provided space to reflect on which area of care she preferred. Jenny views the course as a 'life-changing' experience. She has confirmed her sense as a 'carer', and more specifically as somebody who can make a difference to children in care. Jenny's narrative also speaks of the raising of her self-confidence in her academic abilities and looking forward to continued study. Indeed, at this point in her narrative she has taken on a counselling course, which she sees as enhancing her 'caring' identity and providing important vocational skills.

Key moments and turning points in realising the caring identity

Jenny's narrative is marked by a number of key turning points or critical moments. Bourdieu has remarked on the difficulty of empirically investigating habitus (1984). Turning points, or moments where there might be a disjuncture between habitus and the social fields they are deployed within, provide moments where habitus can be viewed. These critical moments appear to function within the narrative as opportunities for Jenny to realise her 'caring' identity and display responsibility for developing her learning career.

One such moment concerns the death of her aunt. In the account provided by Jenny the caring for her dying aunt becomes the key moment where a caring identity is imagined in terms of employment in caring work.

> My aunty died 11 years ago with cancer and various family members helped to look after her in the last few months and it was her that actually said you ought to go into something like this and she said you're the only one in the family didn't make her feel uncomfortable. She thought I'd got a natural aptitude for it.
>
> (Jenny, first interview)

Caring is depicted as a 'natural aptitude', as something that Jenny is good at, and that should be realised through paid employment. Within the whole narrative this moment is pivotal. This moment is seen as laying the foundation for Jenny's eventual entry into caring work and re-engagement with formal learning.

As suggested above, there is a sense of linearity in Jenny's story. This sense is reinforced with regard to another critical moment. This occurred while employed as a care worker. Jenny talks about the inadequate on-the-job training provided by the private sector employers. Importantly, as a turning point, this is depicted as necessarily connected to her later engagement with formal education.

> I was sent on a handling and lifting course. Apart from that the only other training was working with somebody else for 6 weeks, you do this, this way, and if I'm totally honest I didn't agree with what they were doing anyway. They just didn't show people dignity and compassion. And every time I wanted to go on a course, because the companies run courses themselves, like in-house training, and 'oh sorry this one's full', and I just got so frustrated in the end I thought right that's it, I've had it.
>
> (Jenny, first interview)

There are two related elements here. One is the poverty of training opportunities in this highly gendered field (see, for example, Colley 2006; Crompton 2001; England *et al.* 2002; McKie *et al.* 2001, for accounts of the gendered nature of care work). The second is Jenny's antagonism to the ethical base of the practices she encounters. Both are presented as factors pushing Jenny to find her own route into formal learning and leading her to the present course on which she is enrolled. In contrast, the learning on the formal college course is described as providing a space to reflect on the kind of caring work she wants to do. For Jenny this is intimately related to the ethical base of caring practices that is articulated through the language of giving dignity and respect to those for whom you are caring.

The final critical moment relates to Jenny as a mother. Throughout Jenny's story there is the depiction of herself as committed to being a 'good mother', which included being a full-time carer. Once Jenny's children became older, this presented Jenny with another opportunity to realise her 'caring' identity through employment. It is this moment in her life course, connected to a strong sense of a 'caring' identity, articulated in terms of employment in caring work that makes this a pivotal moment. Later Jenny talks about understanding that she has had to make realistic choices about future career possibilities because of her age. There is a sense then that for Jenny it is either now or never, yet far from being desperate, Jenny's story is full of potential and hope and the realisation of her moral identity as a carer.

Future orientated rational planning and becoming a responsible learner

Jenny's story with its strong sense of linearity is also a story of progress. The linearity is provided by a narrative coherence that links the idea that 'caring' is Jenny's core identity with the realisation of this identity through lifelong learning. It is also a 'progress' narrative that seems to echo the progress narrative of the policy discourse in which lifelong learning is presented as the key to 'help individuals unlock their talent and aspire to change their life for the better' (DIUS 2008: 3) (see Goodson 2005, for a discussion of how life stories are linked to the context of public narratives). Taken together the strong sense of identity and the sense of progression suggest there is reflexivity in Jenny's story, a certain cognitive understanding that she applies to her life story giving us a greater sense of the life history. For half the story this is constructed through the linking together of the critical moments with her core identity. The events become critical moments because they provide opportunities to realise this identity, albeit within constraints. For example, her account of how she ended up on the caring course suggests an element of rational planning. At the same time she shows awareness of how her 'choices' were structured by the strictures of family commitments and limited career opportunities for unqualified women in low-level caring jobs. She had this to say about her paid work in the community and the decision to return to education.

> I was actually stuck in a rut, neither of them [her employers] would help me progress and I wanted to get more qualifications through it, but they just kept putting things off and then through family commitment I ended up having to leave anyway. Now the time's right for me to go back to work so this is why I've decided to get some training first.
>
> (Jenny, first interview)

However, it is later in the story, when she is discussing the college course and her post-course aspirations that a more calculating element is introduced.

For Jenny the course has become a space that allows her to take her bearings. The course provides her with an opportunity to clarify what caring work she wishes to engage in. She recounts how she had originally wanted to work with children, but that the experience of caring for her aunt had introduced the idea of elderly care. Nevertheless, Jenny articulated the caring identity through the actuality or possibility of caring employment. While being a 'good mother' is closely associated with her sense of caring as a core identity, the stress is always put on paid employment. Having worked in elderly care, the course has confirmed for Jenny her desire to move into a different area of care work, that of working with young people and imagining a future as follows: 'Eventually working with children. With children with difficulties, either learning or like I said, I would really like to work in a children's home with children that are in care for whatever reason' (Jenny, first interview).

One way of reading this statement of ambition is the potential this avenue offers of maximising Jenny's personal experiences. Jenny discusses this aspiration in terms of drawing on her own experiences for the benefit of those in children's homes. This links back to Jenny discussing the way she had become a confidante to both her own family and her children's friends. Again this infers a 'natural' aptitude, and reflexive cognition that by maximising her personal resources she has the abilities to deal with the challenges presented by working at management level in children's homes. Yet this recognition of her potential and aspiration is contrasted to the most likely employment available to her – working as a classroom assistant. She acknowledges that this is the destination identified by the course tutor as the normal employment route from the caring course rather than progression to higher learning.

Not surprisingly, at the time of first interviewing Jenny she had applied for a job in a children's home. She did not think she would be successful in her application. She fully understood that the care market mainly comprised low-skill opportunities, and that this progression route would not immediately provide the kinds of employment challenge she wanted. Jenny's story at this point suggested a rational calculation. She knew that she would now have to improve her skills and knowledge through continued study if she was to have a chance of realising her ambition, although she recognised that this study may have to take place through work-based learning rather than college or university.

The second interview took place a few months after Jenny had completed the caring course and at the point at which she had taken up a job as a support worker to children in a care home following six months of unemployment. There is still a strong thread of rational planning running through this second interview and awareness not only of her ambition and core identity, but also the contexts and structures through which she needs to negotiate her way to fulfil this ambition. In gaining a position in a care home working with young girls Jenny has realised part of her ambition and she is now intent on increasing her qualifications in order to become a children's home manager.

Jenny reveals that in pursuing employment and a work-based learning route she had undertaken cost–benefit analyses about her learning career.

> I did consider training to be a social worker but for me, I left it too late. I know a lot of people have said to me 'It's never too late' but I don't want to go to university for three years, get into debt and be 45, 46, 47 by the time I've finished and then start a career, so this is why I stepped back from that and have gone down this pathway I wanted to.
>
> (Jenny, second interview)

The financial implications of studying for a university-level qualification provide strict limits on Jenny's ambition. Instead she lowers her horizon. This decision also matches with one of the entry points into the labour market and enables her to construct a pathway to a managerial role as a children's home manager by working from the bottom up. Besides, it avoids the financial burdens involved in studying for a social work qualification, the type of qualification that would be needed for direct entry to managerial level and avoids the unknown, that is, what a learning career in education might look like and the potential for disappointment.

For Jenny, the transition from employment as an unqualified care worker of the elderly, to working with young people has not been straightforward. Having enjoyed the formal college course Jenny was keen to continue with full-time study. Yet she did not continue with her studies. Her narrative suggests this was the result of rational planning and a cost–benefit analysis. However, interviews with the course tutors and college managers revealed another aspect of the context that Jenny does not mention, that is, the structure of the college's learning progression routes. These are revealed as predicated on recruiting different types of learners and constructing different transitions into and out of the lower-level vocational and the higher-level academic and professional programmes. The higher-level learning programmes that would provide the preparation for university study or high-level skills at the college and essential for employment in the care sector at a managerial level were not normally open to adult learners such as Jenny.

This understanding of the context provides a different way of making sense of Jenny's decision to begin looking for work immediately her vocational course finished and her choice to rely on her own networks and personal knowledge of the caring field, not those of the college. She said she applied for 'God knows how many jobs' and at one point gave up the idea of care work and began to apply for secretarial work. She explained that this was because she failed to get two jobs, because she was less qualified than others. Instead she was offered two jobs in companies where she had worked previously as an unqualified care worker, but she did not want to go back to the places where she had been denied access to further training. Her narrative reveals an awareness of the circularity of the career path or 'jobs roundabout' she was trapped in. She could not break out of low-paid, low-skilled caring work without gaining further qualifications. Yet, in spite of becoming a 'responsible' learner, by enrolling on the caring course, it was not enough to lift her to the level where she could have access to the higher-level qualifications necessary for employment as a qualified care worker and ultimately a care manager. Becoming a 'responsible' learner had not been enough to ensure a smooth transition to her ideal employment and so Jenny drew on her own personal social capital and networks and secured a job in a private company that her friends had worked in, and where she thought she would have more opportunities for lifelong learning. She said:

> The company I'm with is the company I wanted to be with. [It] had the best staff support and training ... I have a friend ... and there is another girl that I know ... [I] ended up going to work for this one because of that fact.
>
> (Jenny, second interview)

The role of structure in responsibilisation

The institutional context is critical to understanding how it has been possible for Jenny to realise her caring identity in particular forms. How is it that this is the trajectory that is being constituted rather than the reproduction of a former caring self as mother and wife or a work role in catering in line with the family habitus? One of the factors to help us explore and answer this question is that of the institutional context of the college where she studied.

Jenny was enrolled on a course at a level equivalent to the qualifications taken by early school leavers, a Vocational GCSE course within a health and social care programme within a further education college. Jenny was not an 'active chooser', someone who had the kinds of cultural and social capital to enable her to make informed choices about course, college and qualification (Ball *et al.* 2000). Jenny relied on what has been called 'cold knowledge', the formal information provided by the college (Ball and Vincent 1998). This kind of orientation towards the choice process in education markets has been noted as characteristic of working-class participants who often cannot avail themselves of inherited knowledge of how the system works, nor have access to social networks where trusted information on institutions can be gained. Consequently, Jenny's 'choices' were immediately constrained. These constraints are structural in nature; they are partly a product of the location of the further education college within particular circuits of post-compulsory provision, and the active position-taking of the college management in the context of specific policy frameworks and local opportunity structures. Jenny's potential for realising her caring identity was tied to the way the caring course she was enrolled on was located within the post-compulsory education market.

Although there is a national funding framework for post-compulsory education, this is mediated regionally to meet local priorities, and colleges have some discretion to decide how to apply these funding steers. The particular college Jenny attended had chosen to position itself as a widening participation provider and the course that Jenny studied, the part-time VGCSE, was free to the learner as long as they did not have a previous qualification at that level and were in receipt of state welfare benefits. However, this situation is unlikely to continue. The course director anticipated a growth in work-based adult learning and a reduction in funding for academic college-based courses. It seems that Jenny was in the right place at the right time to develop her learning career to begin to realise her caring identity.

In view of these impending changes to the college provision, simply having a disposition to continue learning was not sufficient to enable Jenny to continue with this learning career at the college. At the first interview she imagined a future where she could progress from this part-time Level 2 course to a full-time Level 3 course,[1] and move from caring for the elderly to realising her early ambition for 'something in childcare'. Instead the location of the college within the local post-compulsory education market, and the structuring of this market through policy priorities and funding mechanisms, impacted upon Jenny's imagined progression into paid employment in relation to work with children in care and of becoming a care manager.

Performing well at Level 2 is unlikely to translate into progression on to Level 3 if the learner falls outside the college's designated targeting of learners. In the Course Director's opinion, many older students would be better advised following a work-based learning route to gain qualifications:

> People who want to get into health and social care [should] ... go and get a job. At the moment they are better [off] and they'll get qualified more quickly if they were in employment. Because they're wanting employment in care, and generally people can get jobs in care ... there would be the pressure on all [to have] minimal qualifications to level 2, so the employer is under pressure to get them qualified, and that's where the money's been directed to.
>
> (College Course Director)

For Jenny, 'choosing' the work-based learning route was her only option, in effect, and it has meant starting again, retaking a Level 2 qualification in Childcare before having the opportunity to take a Level 3. She said:

> I've got to do an NVQ in childcare ... but I can't start that until I've done 3 months' probationary period. Because of finances actually for the company that's why ... I don't like it after 3 months or they don't like me, but as soon as 3 months is up I start a childcare course and then there's induction that I have to do in the next few weeks, that's a 2-week course and that's basically first aid, food hygiene, all the basic things like that. I don't know exactly what the rest of the courses are, all I do know is the company is very good at providing the courses and helping you to get on them.
>
> (Jenny, second interview)

But this 'responsible learner' is not fazed by the additional steps she needs to take to fulfil her ambition, and has volunteered to take on an extra course because, as she put it, she intends to:

> Do all the courses that's available through the company, I'm actually starting on Friday a 9-week training course with home start. That's voluntary work. And once I've completed that course I can then be put with families which is more like a social work job without being qualified so if I get the experience in that, as well as the job I'm doing, then even after I've done the level 3 there is training courses where you can take qualifications to be a manager within the company, which is quite good.
>
> (Jenny, second interview)

Indeed, in spite of the apparent failure of the college course to provide a smooth transition in the progression of Jenny's career as an employed care worker, Jenny viewed the experience of this learning as something that set her on the learning career for further lifelong learning. She said:

> It was brilliant. I really enjoyed it, finished it and passed. Very proud of myself and I knew I could go on and do more courses which I will be doing through work and I've confidence in doing things like that. I won't be frightened any more so I want to do any course that's available to me.
>
> (Jenny, second interview)

Conclusion

The combination of the institutional habitus of the further education college, its location within circuits of post-compulsory education and life-long learning and the growth in private training and work-based learning in the privatised care sector (in part funded by the state) made it possible for Jenny to realise her caring identity in a particular form. Her disposition towards seeing this core identity realised in terms of paid employment in the health and social care market, and especially as a care manager, is mediated through her engagement with formal learning, initially, in the college, and now, in the workplace. There is what some regard as serendipity here. The initial engagement was made possible in large part because of the further education college's institutional ethos and commitment to widening participation. Institutionally the college was disposed to make it possible for learners such as Jenny to engage in formal education.

This combination of institutional habitus and structural location has created conditions that allowed Jenny to begin to realise her caring identity, or at least formulate a particular social trajectory. The experience of this learning instilled a confidence in Jenny to seek employment, not just in any part of the care sector, but with children. Her family habitus, which involves employment and self-employment mainly in the service areas of catering and retail, seemed to inform her engagement with the educational choice process, in particular her reliance on 'cold knowledge' about the college rather than inherited cultural and social capital. However, the recent policy shift in the focus of the college away from learners like Jenny seems to have resulted in her feeling a need to spurn the advice of college staff at the point of transition to further learning or employment. Instead she chose to fall back on her personal knowledge and networks in seeking to realise her caring identity and learning career in paid employment with children.

Class position, and therefore its relation to class and familial habitus can help create meanings around Jenny's particular orientation towards the choice process in lifelong learning and employment. Equally in order to understand in what ways Jenny is a 'responsible' learner we need to understand another level of structure, that is, the location of the college and the private care companies within particular circuits of post-compulsory education and training. We read this story of Jenny as being produced at the nexus of movements within the domains of the economy, culture and politics. Through Jenny's story these moments are articulated, revealing both her reflexivity and agentic practices, but within contexts that are heavily structured and constrain her opportunities. Whether or not Jenny, the responsible learner, will be able to realise fully her ambitions to become a care manager through work-based lifelong learning or whether the old order will simply be reproduced remains an open question.

Note

1 These levels refer to levels within the National Qualifications Framework for England, Wales and Northern Ireland; see online, available at: www.qca.org.uk/libraryAssets/media/qca-06–2298-nqf-web.pdf (accessed 8 February 2009).

References

Avis, J. (2000) 'Policy talk: Reflexive modernization and the construction of teaching and learning within post-compulsory education and lifelong learning in England', *Journal of Education Policy* 15, 185–199.

Ball, S.J. and Vincent, C. (1998) 'I heard it on the grapevine: Hot knowledge and school choice', *British Journal of Sociology of Education* 19, 377–400.

Ball, S.J., Maguire, M. and Macrae, S. (2000) *Choice, Pathways and Transitions Post-16: New youth, new economies in the global city*, London: RoutledgeFalmer.

Beck, U., with Ritter, M. (1992) *Risk Society: Towards a new modernity*, London: Sage.

Beck, U. and Beck-Gernsheim, E. (1996) *Detraditionalization*, Oxford: Blackwell.

Beck, U., Giddens, A. and Lash, S. (1994) *Reflexive Modernization: Politics, tradition and aesthetics in the modern social order*, Palo Alto, CA: Stanford University Press.

Bloomer, M. and Hodkinson, P. (2000) 'Learning careers: Continuity and change in young people's dispositions to learning', *British Educational Research Journal* 26, 583–597.

Bourdieu, P. (1984) *Distinction, A Social Critique of the Judgement of Taste*, London: Routledge and Kegan Paul.

Brown, P. and Lauder, H. (1992) 'Education, economy and society: An introduction to a new agenda', in P. Brown and H. Lauder (eds), *Education for Economic Survival: From Fordism to post-Fordism*, London: Routledge, pp. 1–44.

Coffield, F. (1999) 'Breaking the consensus: Lifelong learning as social control', *British Educational Research Journal* 25, 479–499.

Colley, H. (2006) 'Learning to labour with feeling: Class, gender and emotion in childcare education and training', *Contemporary Issues in Early Childhood* 17, 15–29.

Crompton, R. (2001) 'Gender restructuring, employment, and caring', *Social Politics* 8, 266–291.

Crossan, B., Field, J., Gallagher, J. and Merrill, B. (2003) 'Understanding participation in learning for non-traditional adult learners: Learning careers and the construction of learning identities', *British Journal of Sociology of Education* 24, 55–67.

Department for Education and Employment (2001) *Opportunities and Skills in the Knowledge Economy: A final statement on the work of the national skills task force*, Nottingham: DfEE.

Department for Education and Skills (2005) *Skills: Getting on in business, getting on at work*, London: The Stationery Office.

Department for Education and Skills (2006) *Further Education: Raising skills, improving life chances* (Cm 6768), London: The Stationery Office.

Department for Innovation, Universities and Skills (2008) *Higher Education at Work, High Skills: High Value*, London: The Stationery Office.

Department for Trade and Industry (1998) *Our Competitive Future: Building the knowledge driven economy*, London: DTI.

England, P., Budig, M. and Folbre, N. (2002) 'Wages of Virtue: The relative pay of care work', *Social Problems* 49, 455–473.

Fejes, A. (2005) 'New wine in old skins: Changing patterns in the governing of the adult learner in Sweden', *International Journal of Lifelong Education* 24, 71–86.

Field, J. (2001) 'Lifelong Education', *International Journal of Lifelong Education* 20, 3–15.

Field, J. (2006) *Lifelong Learning and the New Educational Order*, Stoke-on-Trent: Trentham Books.

Goodson, I.F. (2005) *Learning, Curriculum and Life Politics*, London: Routledge.

Leitch Review of Skills (2006) *Prosperity for All in the Global Economy: World class skills*, London: The Stationery Office.

McKie, L., Bowlby, S. and Gregory, S. (2001) 'Gender, caring and employment in Britain', *Journal of Social Policy* 30, 233–258.

Preece, J. (2006) 'Beyond the learning society: The learning world?' *International Journal of Lifelong Education* 2, 307–320.

Sheffield City Council (2004) *Creative Sheffield: Prospectus for a distinctive European city in a prosperous region*, Sheffield: Sheffield City Council.

Sheffield First Partnership (2002) *Sheffield City Strategy 2002–5*, Sheffield: Sheffield First Partnership.

Skeggs, B. (1997) *Formations of Class and Gender*, London: Sage.

Strain, M. and Field, J. (1997) 'On "the myth of the learning society"', *British Journal of Educational Studies* 45, 141–155.

UNESCO (1972) *Learning To Be, The World of Education Today and Tomorrow*, Paris: UNESCO.

Warren, S. and Webb, S. (2007) 'Challenging lifelong learning policy discourse: Where is structure in agency in narrative-based research?' *Studies in the Education of Adults* 39, 5–21.

Warren, S. and Webb, S. (2009) 'Accounting for structure *in* agency: Recursive methodology, social narratives and habitus', in B. Merrill (ed.), *Learning to Change: The role of identity and learning careers in adult education*, Frankfurt am Main: Peter Lang.

Chapter 6

Older men's lifelong learning
Common threads/sheds

Barry Golding

Introduction

This chapter is based on a suite of completed research in Australia into informal learning by older men (age over 45) in community contexts that forms the first part of an international comparative study of men's informal learning. A number of research projects since 2002 in rural and remote Australian communities sought to look beyond what are conventionally regarded as education providers and to examine closely whether and what learning takes place informally by men, particularly by older men, who participate in community-based organisations.

The research began with studies of learning in small and remote towns (Golding and Rogers 2002) including men's learning (Golding *et al.* 2004), which identified men as largely missing in many adult and community education providers but very involved in some surrogate learning organisations including sport, fire services and land care. It led to a dedicated study of the learning role and function of volunteer fire brigades and emergency service organisations in small and remote towns across Australia (Hayes *et al.* 2004). The research then shifted to informal learning through men's sheds in community contexts (Golding *et al.* 2007). These shed-based workshops, configured mainly for older men have recently evolved and proliferated across much of southern Australia, largely as a grassroots response to the difficulties men often face coping with changes in their lives beyond the workplace. What has emerged from all of the research is a picture of older men with a strong desire to socialise and learn, particularly with other men, in productive, social and informal contexts but a reluctance to be formally taught. The research on community men's sheds demonstrated the degree to which many older men's early and negative experiences of formal learning adversely affected them both lifelong and life-wide.

In 2009 the research was broadened to include the important learning that occurs through participation in the diverse range of organisations found in Australian urban, regional rural and remote communities in 12 new sites in four Australian states. One research project for the Western Australia Department of Education and Training (Golding *et al.* in progress 2009a) is examining men's learning in community settings. The other research for

National Seniors Australia (Golding *et al.* in progress 2009b) is focusing specifically on learning by men over age 50 years in three Australian states.

This chapter seeks to take what had been learnt from this suite of Australian studies to 2007, and pull together some of the common threads in order to locate the findings against what is known from some of the comparable international research literature about older men's learning in the community, particularly from the work of McGivney (1999a, 1999b, 2004). It includes an examination of common motivations for older men to learn, common barriers and preferred pedagogies as well as some common and valued outcomes. The ongoing research seeks to determine whether what has been found from this research in Australian community contexts is similar to or different from what has been found for older men in other countries and cultural settings. Part of the chapter includes consideration of issues associated with men's identities as they age as well as gender issues associated with learning. It also briefly examines the role and legitimacy of creating informal learning spaces and organisations specifically for men, for older men in particular.

The research emphasis on men was originally motivated by evidence from reviews of adult and community education (ACE) research (Golding *et al.* 2001) that showed that a relatively low proportion of men, particularly older men, participate in ACE settings in Australia. It was widely but mistakenly believed that older men (age over 45 years) were less involved essentially because they were not interested in learning. A number of research projects in Australia since 2002, particularly in rural and remote communities (Foskey and Avery 2003) found that most men certainly *are* interested in learning: the key is to create the right context for that learning. This suite of ongoing research therefore seeks to look at learning beyond what are conventionally regarded as 'formal' learning organisations where men tend not to participate, and closely examine whether and what learning takes place informally by men who do participate in community-based organisations and where learning is one of many positive outcomes. The first phase of the research to 2005 into the learning function of these surrogate learning organisations that many men tend to prefer, was summarised by Golding (2006). The second phase of the research involved studies of men's sheds in community contexts, a relatively new and apparently wholly Australian phenomenon until their recent spread to New Zealand[1] and the Irish Republic[2] in 2008. The third and ongoing stages of the research involve comparative studies of aspects of men's learning in Australia (Golding *et al.* in progress 2009a, in progress 2009b) with men's learning in other, culturally similar, Anglophone countries including sites and community organisations in which men participate, particularly in the UK and the Irish Republic. While this research programme is seen as an extension of the previous research programme based in Australia it has been informed particularly by some similar findings from the UK about men's learning by McGivney (1999a, 2004) and about the benefits of informal learning in the community (McGivney 1999b).

Method

The research reported in this chapter involved extensive surveys and audio-recorded focus group interviews between 2001 and 2007 with men who participate either in adult and community education or community-based organisations. All studies involved multiple research sites and two studies included several Australian states. The particular method used is identified when each study is introduced. In cases where surveys were employed, sufficient surveys were administered and high response rates (all greater than 50 per cent) were obtained, allowing for reasonably confident findings based on frequency tables and tests of significant difference of most variables by sub-group. The paper-based survey focused on men's perceptions, opportunities and recent experiences of learning within particular community organisations. Steps were taken within each organisation to sensitively encourage men with low formal literacies to complete the survey. Most studies, including those incorporating audiotaped focus group interviews involved two on-site visits, which led to better organisational understanding and active participation in the research process. All audiotapes were fully transcribed and data were extracted by word or thematic searches using a qualitative data analysis program.

Findings

Initial studies from ACE that crystallised the issue about men's learning

The initial findings about men's informal learning in community settings come from research into ACE in small and relatively remote towns by Golding and Rogers (2002). That interview-based research in adult education providers in 20 small towns across the Australian state of Victoria found very few men regularly or actively involved in ACE. It found that the attitudes and skills necessary for the 'new world' of work, enterprise and community were increasingly falling to women, as the main learning leaders, community networkers and enrolled learners in these small towns. Women were welcomed and included as learners in ACE by virtue of its rich and historic patronage, management and volunteerism by women. Men were of course welcome to participate but there was a previously unspoken gender blindness associated with what were typically and essentially women's learning centres. It is important to note in passing that in the seven years since, ACE in Victoria has acted positively on these findings and implemented policies and action research (Golding *et al.* 2006; Foley 2007) that has begun to change this situation. ACE in the state of Western Australia (Learning Centre Link 2004) has similarly recognised a need for 'Bringing in the blokes'.[3]

The first men's learning study by Golding *et al.* (2004) relied on surveys. It was also based in small rural towns (ten Victorian towns, each with populations less than 3,000) but this time anticipated that most men would be missing from ACE. The research was therefore deliberately inclusive of organisations in which men were known to be involved as participants or volunteers and that provided opportunities for men to learn informally. It included five small towns without adult education centres but that had other voluntary, community-based organisations, typically including a volunteer rural fire brigade, a football club,[4] a senior citizens' club and a land care organisation. The method set out to test whether the presence of an ACE organisation made a difference to men, which turned out not to be the case. The 2004 research led to a number of important new insights. There was new evidence of the ongoing and debilitating effects of negative experiences at school on involvement in lifelong learning and community activity for men of all ages. Being part of a community organisation was found to play a key role in men's learning. There were strong preferences for informal learning through existing local organisations that men were involved with, in practical group settings and wherever possible outside.

Almost counter-intuitively, the most effective learning organisations, as judged by the men surveyed, were those in which learning was not *the* major organisational role. Learning was found to be most effective for men through active community involvement in organisations with other men, other than in ACE, that provided social contexts and pedagogies that more closely matched men's desired learning preferences. Men said that they learnt best through regular practice with other men, by taking on responsibilities through community-based organisations as well as through one-on-one learning. Though not known to us when we completed our (Golding *et al.* 2004) study, men's sheds in community contexts, discussed in detail later in this chapter, were already beginning to take on many of the pedagogical and lifelong learning attributes deemed to be desirable by men surveyed in this earlier study, but remained essentially below the 'radar' of most academic research. In effect, the study anticipated what some men were already in the process of creating through their innovative, shed-based organisations. The 2004 study showed that adult learning in some form is critical for men of all ages. As remoteness from services increased and as town size decreased, the need to learn though informal community networks became more acute. Men's informal involvement in networks through voluntary community activity, particularly through volunteer fire and emergency service organisations and through football clubs, became a critical part of their learning as well as for social, family and economic well-being in small Australian towns. Men who participated in sporting and emergency services organisations were found to be less likely than other men to take advantage of opportunities, even where they existed in small towns, through a local ACE provider.

While most men were not 'at home' in ACE, local learning centres in small rural towns were found to play a critical role as a focus for ongoing lifelong learning, mainly for women. In many cases it provided the only public access to information and computer technologies (ICT) as well as to adult and sometimes vocational education programmes. However, the research showed that ACE in small rural towns was not orientated to the particular and different learning needs of most men, particularly for older rural men who had left school early with negative recollections of formal learning. While men were found to have a keen desire to learn, an ACE provider setting seldom met men's particular learning needs, preferences or styles. Men who did use ACE were found in Golding *et al.*'s (2004) study typically to be occasional users and marginally attached to adult and community learning organisations, not only as learners, but also as teachers, coordinators or on management committees. In summary, the physical space, the décor, the programmes, the staff and pedagogies were regarded as being for women, and run by women. Even in the smallest towns where the ACE provider was one of the only public facilities, many men did not relate positively to ACE or know enough about ACE to use it and many men did not feel comfortable going there.

Most men expressed a strong desire for learning provided in less formal, practical, group settings, locally and on site through organisations they knew and felt comfortable within, consistent with Lave and Wenger's (1991) theory of situated learning. Men indicated through surveys that they generally learnt best by doing and through practice, via organisations and people they knew and trusted rather than via abstracted learning 'about' something in contrived situations. Men, particularly older men with typically negative previous experiences of school and formal learning, generally preferred to learn through being involved in an activity in real and familiar situations, wherever possible outside. ACE located in community house-type settings therefore tended not to be welcoming to or comfortable for such men. As with lower utilisation of men's health services (Department of Health and Ageing (DHA) 2008, p. 10), while lower utilisation of ACE to address men's perceived learning needs 'is often attributed to the idea that "masculinity" – men's gender identity – precludes men from seeking help appropriately ... it may be that it is the nature of services that determines willingness to seek help'. The strongly expressed need for men to learn but their strong reluctance to learn in ACE has for this reason become an important rationale for our research programme. Rather than looking at where men are not learning and asking why, we are determined to look first at where and what they are learning. As with parallel research seeking to address men's health needs (DHA 2008), some of the answers we are seeking in relation to men's unmet learning needs are likely to be found in the current mismatch between preferred pedagogies and services. These needs include considerations of availability, access and suitability of services in line with men's values and practices, rather than being restricted to rural masculinities as argued by Kenway *et al.* (2006).

The surprising finding in Golding *et al.*'s (2004) study, repeated in subsequent studies and consistent with the hypothesis above about the inappropriateness of existing ACE services to men's needs and pedagogies, was that, counter to prevailing perceptions about Australian men not caring about their health or well-being, most men surveyed wanted to learn about how to stay fit and healthy. The particular difficulty for governments concerned about lifelong learning and men's health and well-being is that the men most likely to be 'put off' by ACE are older, more likely to have fewer networks and with the most need (and fewest opportunities) to learn elsewhere. However, even younger men with good ICT skills were found to have dismissive, uninformed and negative attitudes towards adult education and were less likely to learn through leadership and informal involvement in other organisations, raising important questions about future rural community sustainability.

Findings about learning through participation in voluntary fire organisations

A related national study followed up the learning role and function of rural fire brigades and emergency service organisations in small and remote towns across four states in Australia (Hayes *et al*. 2004) where men comprised 85 per cent of members. The study, which involved both survey and interview of participating volunteers, allowed the separation of findings by gender. In part, because of their critical importance in a dry and seasonally fire-prone Australian landscape, the study identified fire and emergency services organisations as the most widespread and active adult learning and training organisations in non-metropolitan Australia outside business and industry. The direct and indirect benefits to men in small and remote towns of regular (and often accredited) fire and emergency services training was found to be positive and extensive, in employment, business, family, personal and community life. The research found that men, who meet regularly in this way for a common community purpose, develop the high levels of bonding social capital within their organisational structure that are essential for providing quick and coherent responses to community emergencies. Again, the research identified a reluctance on the part of older men, with lower levels of school and post-school education and training, to submit to formal training and assessment that occupational, health and safety and legal liability regulations increasingly required. This finding is of such interest that it has been incorporated into our in-progress (2009) studies but extended to include coast rescue and surf lifesaving clubs along Australia's extensive coast, where the majority of the nation's population are differentially located.

Findings about learning through participation in men's sheds in community contexts

Research with others has recently focused on informal learning through men's sheds in community contexts (Golding *et al*. 2007) based on surveys and interviews in 24 community-based men's shed organisations across four Australian states. Unlike backyard and garden sheds popular with men in several Anglophone nations, community men's sheds are available regularly to groups of men for gathering, socialising and making things (Hayes and Williamson 2005). These workshops specifically for older men recently have sprung up and proliferated across much of southern Australia to a point that approximately 250 sheds were open in late 2008. While some are stand-alone most have auspicious arrangements with other community organisations including local government, health and adult education providers, churches and war veterans' organisations. Men's sheds in community contexts are of particular interest in terms of gender politics and pedagogy in that rather than being created by government equity policy that traditionally targets women, they have been set up primarily and deliberately to meet the informal social, health and learning needs of men. Shed organisations reach their highest density in southern Australia in areas where men in prime age or in retirement but not in paid work comprise a greater proportion of all men as mapped by Lattimore (2007), as well as in socially disadvantaged areas and localities as mapped by Vinson (2007).

In some ways men's sheds organisations mirror aspects of the gendered, workshop-based spaces that many working-class tradesmen, farmers, factory workers and labourers have experienced for most of their working lives. Like workplaces, they encourage practical, productive, regular and hands-on activity in teams with other men. Though the activity is work-like it is also voluntary, social and without compulsion. Unlike some paid work situations it is not like the difficult, stressful or dangerous workplaces that many men have either been injured in or rejected by, or else withdrawn or retired from. Men in the surveys and interviews (Golding *et al.* 2007) liked the fact that the men's sheds were voluntary, social, safe and inclusive. The emphasis was on the men and not on the product or on workshop efficiencies. The shed is, in effect, one place where older men not in work can simultaneously feel at home, experience important and positive aspects of masculinity outside home with other men, give back to the community and informally access a wide range of services in a relatively seamless way. Importantly, the shed allows older 'men of experience' to be active co-participants in a community activity rather than being patronised and problematised from a deficit model as clients, students, customers or 'users of services'.

Discussion and conclusion

Some common threads from shed-based research

What has emerged from the suite of research is a picture of older men with a strong desire to socialise and learn, particularly with other men, collaborating and mentoring each other in productive, informal contexts, wherever possible outside. Older men's experiences of learning as well as their lives generally have often been adversely affected over a lifetime by negative experiences of formal learning, starting with school. Men who are not in the workforce for whatever reason often lack access to former work-based professional and friendship networks. If with a female partner there are often good reasons for men to seek friendships beyond work with other men that have not always been kept or maintained whilst working. There is strong evidence from the men's sheds research of a mutual recognition amongst married couples of the benefits for both men and women regularly to 'get out from underfoot' at home and to establish independent post-work or post-retirement identities, that typically include socialisation with other men through active community involvement.

What many men's sheds do particularly well is informally create mentoring and friendship relationships between two groups of older men whose needs are somewhat different. They provide unique opportunities for married, former 'working-class' men experiencing 'underfoot syndrome' to meet regularly and work alongside single men or widowers who for a range of reasons have 'fallen on hard times'. Men living with partners are typically in relatively secure retirement or enforced early withdrawal from work, experiencing the 'underfoot syndrome' at home and keen to share their trade skills. Men without a partner are typically experiencing a combination of boredom, social isolation, loneliness or ill-health and are typically without other connections to community. The 'magic' of community men's sheds revolves around the informal learning that takes place based around the mutual mentoring relationships that this mix of men sets up. The learning that men experience with and through other men typically goes well beyond the woodwork, metalwork or gardening activity that form the basis of most (but not all) shed practice. It includes critically important but informal discussion about changes in their lives, particularly to do with men's health and well-being, masculinities, relationships, families and retirement.

The research raises the important, unanswered questions about whether and which similar places, spaces and community organisations positively embrace men, particularly men not in paid work, in other national and cultural contexts. It is anticipated that while community shed-based models beyond Australia might be positive and therapeutic for some older men from other countries with Anglo-Irish cultural traditions (such as the UK, Irish Republic, Canada and New Zealand), there will be other community-based places that men frequent and benefit from participating in for other reasons in other nations and cultures. It is important to ask the related question as to whether these places, spaces and organisations, be they sporting, religious, community-service orientated, social or learning related, serve to reinforce gender stereotypes and/or perpetuate negative or hegemonic masculinities. Some of these questions form the focus of our international research planned beyond 2009 alluded to in the introduction.

Being grassroots and developed some way ahead of government policy and research, community-based men's sheds provide a unique glimpse of what some future masculine environments, shaped to meet older men's particular and arguably different social, learning and health needs, might look like. The research snapshot of men's informal learning through community-based men's sheds in Golding *et al.* (2007) provides a view of a rapidly growing community shed-based movement for men that has some tantalising analogies to the birth and growth of community houses for women in Australia (Golding *et al.* 2008). In both cases the emphasis has been on the perceived gender friendly and social nature of the shed/house, and the learning has been 'the icing on the cake'.

Some thicker threads about service delivery for older men

While the research projects reported in this chapter adopted learning as their underlying foci, the research method anticipated that informal learning was only one of several important outcomes from regular, voluntary, hands-on community participation by men. Indeed, the survey and interview data confirmed many other motivations, benefits and outcomes for men participating in football clubs, voluntary fire services and community-based men's sheds. The data prompt the conclusion that community shed-based organisations reach, involve and excite precisely those older men that are least easily reached in Australia by conventional gendered services organisations and their delivery models, *particularly* in areas of highest social disadvantage and men's labour market withdrawal. These services include health, aged care and welfare as well as adult and community education. It is essential to recognise that some apparently equitable services, organisations and professions for older people such as adult and community education, health, aged care and welfare are already highly gendered and sometimes also gender blind – particularly to men's different service delivery preferences and needs. It seems timely to recognise the importance and effectiveness of creating some separate spaces (houses or sheds) for both women *and* men that allow them to socialise informally and separately and share their diverse feminine and masculine identities.

The benefits to women from active involvement with other women in informal, house-based service and programme provision are well known and widely accepted in adult and community education. It should not be surprising that similar benefits accrue to some (but not all) men from shed-based activity in community settings. What is new from this research is that these new spaces for men show very few signs of the stereotypical negative and hegemonic masculinities – that even this researcher expected might be found there. What is new is that partners and families of men who participate in community-based men's sheds as well as their communities also benefit from men having a place to go and be productive, typically for community and recreational purposes.

In case governments and others misread the policy implications of this research, the intention should not be about using sheds (or houses) for more of the same service delivery. One undesirable outcome would be for governments to take these research findings and find new ways for 'labour market trainers' to ambush 'disadvantaged' people with 'low literacy' who are 'unemployed' in 'disadvantaged areas' with accredited vocational education and training based on deficit models and perceived 'skill shortages'. Nor should sheds (or houses) be set up in ways that patronise individual 'clients' and ignore their identity and humanity and regard them primarily as 'ripe for retraining' and amenable to easy reinsertion into the workforce. All parties in service delivery need to recognise that the overwhelming majority of people not in the paid workforce, or in education and training, have left, are avoiding or cannot return to either for very good reasons, that are not often directly training related. All older people are experienced, wise and knowledgeable in several ways and can be empowered to be active agents with other people in community contexts in shaping their own lives, learning, work, leisure and ageing.

The overarching common thread from all of this research, gender and learning aside, is that the provision of services (such as adult education and training, health and welfare) appears to more attractive and effective for adults if the service itself is social, informal, community based, integrated and preferably not contained in the title of the organisation. This general finding is particularly true for older adults who have led highly gendered working and home lives with negative previous experiences of formal service provision that is sometimes gender blind.

Notes

1 Approximately eight community men's sheds were either open or being set up in New Zealand in late 2008.
2 A men's shed based on the Australian model was being developed in New Ross, County Wexford, Ireland (John Evoy, personal communication).
3 The noun 'bloke' and adjective 'blokish' in Australia appears to have a somewhat similar meaning to 'lad' and 'laddish', respectively, in the UK as used by McGivney (1999a).
4 In Australia the term 'football' refers specifically to Australian Rules football.

References

Department of Health and Ageing (2008) *Development of a National Men's Health Policy: An information paper*, Canberra: Department of Health and Ageing.

Foley, A. (2007) 'Encouraging men's learning', Research Circle 2, Final Report to Adult, Community and Further Education Board, Victoria, Melbourne: ACFEB.

Foskey, R. and Avery, A. (2003) 'Older rural men: Learning for change'. Paper given to Adult Learning Australia Conference, Communities of Learning: Communities of Change, Sydney, 27–30 November.

Golding, B. (2006) 'Men's learning in mall and remote towns in Australia', in J. Chapman, P. Cartwright and E. McGilp (eds), *Lifelong Learning, Participation and Equity*, Dordrecht: Springer, pp. 175–203.

Golding, B. and Rogers, M. (2002) 'Adult and community learning in small and remote towns in Victoria' (June and November). Reports to ACFE Board, Bendigo: Bendigo Regional Institute of TAFE and Centre for Sustainable Regional Communities, La Trobe University Bendigo, Victoria.

Golding, B., Brown, M. and Foley, A. (in progress 2009a) 'Beyond the workplace: Men's learning and wellbeing in Western Australia'. Research Report for Western Australia Department of Education and Training, Perth.

Golding, B., Brown, M., Foley, A., Harvey, J. and Gleeson, L. (2007) *Men's Sheds in Australia: Learning through community contexts*, Adelaide: NCVER.

Golding, B., Brown, M. and Naufal, R. (2006) 'Encouraging men's learning, Research Circle'. Final Report to Adult, Community and Further Education Board, Victoria, Melbourne: ACFEB.

Golding, B., Davies, M. and Volkoff, V. (2001) *A Consolidation of ACE Research 1990–2000: Review of research, online*. Online, available at: www.ncver.edu.au/publications/638.html (accessed 12 December 2008).

Golding, B., Foley, A. and Brown, M. (in progress 2009b) 'Senior men's informal learning and wellbeing through community participation'. Research Report for National Seniors Australia, Canberra.

Golding, B., Harvey, J. and Echter, A. (2004) 'Men's learning through ACE and community involvement in small, rural towns'. Report to Adult, Community and Further Education Board, Melbourne: ACFEB.

Golding, B., Kimberley, H., Foley, A. and Brown, M. (2008) 'Houses and sheds: An exploration of the genesis and growth of neighbourhood houses and men's sheds in community settings', *Australian Journal of Adult Learning* 48(2), 237–262.

Hayes, R. and Williamson, M. (2005) *Preliminary Evidence-based, Best Practice Guidelines for Victorian Men's Sheds*, Bundoora, Victoria: School of Public Health, La Trobe University.

Hayes, C., Golding, B. and Harvey, J. (2004) *Adult Learning through Fire and Emergency Services Organisations in Small and Remote Australian Towns*, Adelaide: NCVER.

Kenway, J., Kraak, A. and Hickey-Moody, A. (2006) *Masculinity Beyond the Metropolis*, Basingstoke: Palgrave Macmillan.

Lattimore, R. (2007) *Men Not at Work: An analysis of men outside the labour force, staff working paper*, Canberra: Australian Government Productivity Commission.

Lave, J. and Wenger, E. (1991) *Situated Learning: Legitimate peripheral participation*, New York: Cambridge University Press.

Learning Centre Link (2004) *Bringing in the Blokes: A guide to attracting and involving men in community neighbourhood and learning centres* (2nd edn), Perth: LCL.

McGivney, V. (1999a) *Excluded Men: Men who are missing from education and training*, Leicester: NIACE.

McGivney, V. (1999b) *Informal Learning in the Community: A trigger for change and development*, Leicester: NIACE.

McGivney, V. (2004) *Men Earn, Women Learn: Bridging the gender divide in education and training*, Leicester: NIACE.

Vinson, T. (2007) *Dropping off the Edge: The distribution of social disadvantage in Australia*, Sydney: Report for Jesuit Social Services and Catholic Social Services Australia.

Chapter 7

Biography, transition and learning in the lifecourse

The role of narrative

Michael Tedder and Gert Biesta

Introduction

Historically, adult education has been connected with learning for personal development and empowerment and for social inclusiveness and democratic understanding and activity (see Aspin and Chapman 2001). In the last 20 years in the UK, however, there has been a shift in the policy discourse away from adult education in favour of lifelong learning and towards a notion of lifelong learning that emphasises learning for economic progress and development (Biesta 2006a). Associated with this shift has been an increasing use of a 'new language of learning' (Biesta 2004, 2006b) that promotes conceptualisation of education as an economic transaction in which education becomes a commodity, a 'thing' for consumption. This inevitably has implications for the quality of the relationships that can develop between those who learn and those who teach.

It is evident that there is a struggle over the definition of learning: a struggle over *what* counts as (worthwhile) learning and a struggle over *who* is allowed to define what (worthwhile) learning is. In this context one important task for adult education researchers is to highlight the significance of the broad range of learning processes and practices that occur in the lives of adults so as to show that there is more to learning than what is acknowledged in the economic definitions of lifelong learning. Doing this has been one of the main ambitions of the Learning Lives project.[1] The project gave the participants opportunities to tell stories about their earlier lives and it also enabled the researchers to hear stories about changes in the participants' lives during the course of the project and to discuss such changes with them. All the interviews were transcribed for analysis and interpretation and copies of the transcripts were provided to the participants.

Unsurprisingly, we found that some people were more adept at engaging in processes of telling stories about their lives than others and this suggested that the potential for their learning from such processes also varies. Drawing on literature on narrative in the human and social sciences (Polkinghorne 1988; Bruner 1990; Czarniawska 2004; Elliott 2005) and with the emerging body of work on narrative learning in adult education (Rossiter 1999; Rossiter and Clark 2007), we analysed the life-stories of the participants.

Our analysis revealed that in a significant number of cases, they had come to some kind of understanding about their lives and themselves and we found that this learning had had an impact on the ways in which they led their lives. We became particularly interested in the role of life-stories and life-storying in such learning processes and in the relationship between the 'narrative quality' of such stories and their learning potential.

Our findings suggest that the rise of the 'learning economy' (Biesta 2006a, 2006b) has not completely displaced learning processes that are significant for people's agency and in our conclusions we reflect upon the importance of the conditions under which narrative learning might contribute to those dimensions of lifelong learning that have come under pressure as a result of the rise of the learning economy. We also address practical issues concerning whether and how narrative learning might relate to established provision in adult education, and what the implications might be for the training of teachers in this role.

Theoretical background: biographical learning and narrative theory

The idea that life itself can be or become an 'object' of learning is, as such, not new. The idea of biography as 'itself a field of learning' (Alheit 1995: 59) has particularly been developed by Alheit and Dausien through the notion of 'biographical learning', which they define as:

> a self-willed, 'autopoietic' accomplishment on the part of active subjects, in which they reflexively 'organise' their experience in such a way that they also generate personal coherence, identity, a meaning to their life history and a communicable, socially viable lifeworld perspective for guiding their actions.
>
> (Alheit 2005: 209)

Alheit and Dausien (2002) highlight three aspects of biographical learning: the implicit dimension, the social dimension and the 'self-willed' dimension (see Alheit and Dausien 2002: 15–16). They note how learning that is implicit and tacit 'forms a person's *biographical stock of knowledge*' (ibid.: 15; emphasis in original) and that we can retrieve such learning 'when we find ourselves stumbling or at crossroads' (ibid.). They emphasise that such reflexive learning processes do not exclusively take place 'inside' the individual 'but depend on communication and interaction with others' (ibid.: 16). And they argue that while learning within and through one's life history is interactive and socially structured, it also follows its own 'individual logic' generated by the specific, biographically layered structure of experience (see ibid.).

Although the stories people tell about their lives can be taken simply as accounts or descriptions of these lives, we start from the assumption that such stories may already reflect aspects of what people have learned from their lives, either in a more self-aware or in a more tacit and implicit manner. Moreover, rather than only looking at life-stories as the *outcome* of biographical learning, it seems reasonable to assume that the construction, and narration, of such stories itself forms an important part of such learning processes. To think of the life-story as a 'site' for biographical learning and to think of life-story*ing* as central to this activity, is captured in the notion of 'narrative learning' (see Biesta *et al.* 2008). The reason why we refer to this as narrative learning rather than 'storied' learning or learning through story-ing has to do with an important conceptual distinction within narrative theory between story and narrative.[2] Narratives, to put it briefly, are those stories that are characterised by a *plot*, that is, 'a type of conceptual scheme by which a contextual meaning of individual events can be displayed' (Polk-inghorne 1995: 7; see also Polkinghorne 1988). Although 'emplotment' (Ricoeur 1992) is often understood as a temporal and sequential organisation of events, this is not necessarily the case. Plots can also organise stories in a thematic, non-temporal manner. As Polkinghorne (1995: 5) explains: 'Nar-rative is the type of discourse composition that draws together diverse events, happenings, and actions of human lives into thematically unified goal-directed purposes.' A plot thus provides structure to a story and enables the selection of events for their relevance in the story – thus making the story into a narrative.

For the analysis of life-stories, this raises the possibility that the pres-ence of a particular plot – or particular plots – may be an expression of what narrators have learned from their lives. Empirically the question is not only whether it is possible to discern one or more plots within a life-story, but also how such plots function. One important distinction here is between those situations in which the narrator seems to be aware of the plot and actively uses it to construct a particular 'version' of his or her life, and those cases where the plot can be reconstructed from a research per-spective but does not seem to be part of the narrative 'strategy' of the nar-rator. With regard to the question of the function of plots, Bruner has suggested that we construct narrative – both at an individual and societal level – in order to justify the *departure* from established norms and patterns of belief (see Bruner 1990: 47). Autobiographical accounts are therefore not simply descriptions of one's life but should be understood as accounts 'of what one thinks one did in what settings in what ways for what felt reasons' (ibid.: 119). Narratives thus reveal why it was necessary (*not* caus-ally, but morally, socially, psychologically) why the life had gone in a par-ticular way (ibid.: 121).

This means that narration is not only about the construction of a particu-lar 'version' of one's life; it is at the same time a construction of a particular 'version' of the self. Narrating one's life-story can therefore be understood as the act of constructing 'a longitudinal version of the Self' (Bruner 1990: 120). The self is not only the object or product of the narrative but at the very same time the subject of narration. Although stories about one's life are about the past, Bruner argues that 'an enormous amount of work is going on here and now as the story is being put together' (ibid.: 122). This is not so much because the narrator needs to work hard to bring events back from memory, but more importantly because in telling about the past the narrator must decide 'what to make of the past narratively at the moment of telling' (ibid.). This is another reason why the narration is not simply to be seen as the outcome of a learning process, but can be seen as (narrative) learning-in-action.

A narrative perspective on biographical learning

In our reading and analysis of life-stories of participants in the Learning Lives project we made use of the foregoing ideas in order to characterise and explore processes and outcomes of narrative learning. One of the reasons for this was our interest in the question whether a focus on the narrative quality of life-stories could reveal something about the 'learning potential' of different narrative forms. Another reason for this was that we were also interested in the 'action potential' of life-stories, i.e. the way in which and the extent to which particular narrative forms or characteristics correlate with agency, which we understood roughly as the ability to exert control over and give direction to one's life (for more on our conception of agency see Biesta and Tedder 2006, 2007). In this way our analysis focused on the key terms of the Learning Lives project, namely, learning, identity, agency and life-course.

Perhaps the most significant finding emerging from our analysis is that the differences between the stories people tell about their lives do indeed correlate with ways in which people learn from their lives and with ways in which such learning bears significance for how they conduct their lives. This not only suggests that life-stories and life-storying are important 'vehicles' or 'sites' for learning from life. It also suggests that the differences between stories matter for such learning.

One relevant dimension in this regard is the *narrative intensity* of life-stories (Biesta *et al.* 2008). Narrative intensity refers to the length of the initial life-story, but also to the amount of detail and 'depth' of the account offered. The extent to which life-stories are more or less elaborate not only has to do with length and detail but also with the question whether the life-story is predominantly *descriptive* or whether it is more *analytical or evaluative*. (Note that stories can be analytical without passing any judgements.) In our analysis we found stories that were at the more descriptive end of the spectrum as well as stories that presented themselves more explicitly as attempts to 'make sense' of the life.

To make sense of one's life – or, to be more precise, to construct a story that presents the life as 'making sense' – is related to the ideas of 'plot' and 'emplotment' and also to questions about justification. If we see the plot of a (life)-story as an organising principle by which the contextual meaning of individual elements can be displayed, then we can see that the presence of a plot is a strong indication that the narrator has learned something from his or her life. In most of the stories we analysed we were able to identify a plot and this coincided with the narrative being more evaluative and analytical than descriptive. However, not in all cases in which there was a discernible plot did this function in the self-understanding of the narrator. Some participants appeared to be aware of the plot in their life narrative from the outset, whereas for others the plot only emerged throughout the interviews. In some cases a plot was only discernible from the point of view of the researcher but there was little evidence that the narrator was aware of this plot. Not all stories carried a single plot and in cases with multiple plots we could also see that they functioned differently in the narrator's self-understanding. The absence of a plot does not automatically coincide with the absence of learning. We found examples of life-stories that lacked any emplotment but where there was still evidence that the person had learned from life. This not only suggests that narration is only one of the possible ways of learning from one's life. It also highlights the fact that the life-story is itself a particular genre (with a particular history) and that some people may be simply unfamiliar with this genre.

The question of the awareness of a plot can be connected to the question of the *efficacy* of the life-story, the question to what extent particular stories allow people to *do* something – in the broadest sense of the word. This partly has to do with the question of the 'learning potential' of life narratives, i.e. the extent to which particular narratives make learning from one's life possible, and partly with the 'action potential', i.e. the extent to which such learning 'translates' into action. We found examples of very extensive and elaborate narration with clear episodes of analysis and evaluation that still appeared to have a different efficacy. It seems as if in some cases people are 'caught' in their story more than that their story and storying helps them to 'move on'. People can be 'stuck' in their life-story, so we might say, which means that having a 'strong' version of one's life can actually sometimes prevent further learning. There is clear evidence of this in our data.

The question of *script* is important in this regard as well, but not in the way in which this notion is often used in the literature, i.e. to highlight the extent to which individual stories and narratives make use of templates, plots and narrative structures that are available in particular cultures or segments of culture. It is evident that the stories we tell and construct about our lives always make use of 'public material' and in this respect are never completely subjective – although, as Alheit and Dausien (2002: 16) have argued, they are at the same time unique in that they are linked to the unique biographies of individuals. What is more important from the perspective of the learning potential of life-stories is the question of *flexibility*. We call a life-story scripted when there is little flexibility in the storying, when the life is lived and understood in relation to one particular 'version'. There is, as such, nothing wrong with this and the research provides evidence that for a category of people it is very important to have a 'strong' story about themselves and their lives as this gives them direction, orientation and a sense of self. Where this may become a problem is in those situations where the 'fit' between the story and the conditions under which the life (and perhaps we could also say: the story) is lived begins to shift. We did find cases where individuals did not use the potential of narrative learning to respond to important changes and transitions in their life, whereas we also found cases where the narration did function as such a resource. We are neither saying that people should act in this way, nor that narrative learning is the only way in which people can respond to change and transition. Our research only provides evidence that it can be an important resource, provided that there is a degree of flexibility in the story or, to put it differently, that there is a 'capacity' for narrative learning from life. It is important to add that this capacity is not fixed. Some of the participants in the project clearly developed their ability to use narration as a way to reflect upon their lives. In this regard a certain familiarity with the 'genre' and perhaps even a certain amount of practising of storying one's life may be an element that can help develop the ability to learn narratively from one's life.

The question of the 'action potential' of life-stories is not necessarily connected to an ability to change one's story in relation to changing circumstances. Within the project we also found evidence of situations where holding on to a particular story or version of the life – often based on strong normative ideas about what a good life should look like – was effective for individuals to achieve a degree of agency in particular situations. As we have argued elsewhere in more detail (see Biesta and Tedder 2006, 2007), the ability to achieve a degree of agency in particular 'ecological' situations partly depends on opportunities for 'imaginative distancing', that is, for considering different ways of acting and being. In this regard flexibility of life-storying is relevant since it allows for the construction of different possible versions of one's self and one's life. The achievement of agency is also related to opportunities for 'communicative evaluation', i.e. the evaluation of different 'scenarios' of life and self in communicative context and settings, in conversation and communication with others. For many of the participants in the Learning Lives project the project itself has provided them with such opportunities. This raises two important issues.

One has to do with the artificiality of the stories we collected in the project. Although we do not wish to doubt the authenticity of the stories nor wish to question the integrity of the participants, we have evidence that stories were told in function of the project setting and also in function of the more specific dynamics of the relationships between interviewers and interviewees. In some cases the participants were very clear that they had only given us a particular part of their life-story. Although this does not alter our conclusion about the role of narrative in learning from life, it does help us to retain a perspective on the 'nature' of our data.

The second issue this raises has to do with the question of to what extent there are opportunities for narrative learning and communicative evaluation in everyday life. The important point here is that we do not wish to psychologise narrative learning and see it simply as an individual capacity that some people have and other people lack. Although there is an element of 'internal conversation' in narrative learning and although some people seem to be able to do quite a lot of 'narrative work' at this plane, we wish to see narrative learning first and foremost as a social and communicative endeavour – which goes back to the fact that stories are first and foremost 'things' we *tell*. If narrative learning is considered to be important – and our research suggests that it is or can be – then the question is not simply how we might increase the capacity of individuals to engage with such learning processes; the question is also and first of all about the opportunities that might be created for such learning. While our chosen methodology clearly has an individualistic bias, this does not mean that the implications that follow from our research should be entirely individualistic too.

We turn now to present stories from two of the participants in the Learning Lives project to illustrate some of the foregoing themes. They were chosen on the basis that they were both particularly willing and loquacious story tellers and both were undergoing significant transitions in their lives during the time that they were participants in the project. Further cases can be found in other publications related to the project (see, for example, Tedder and Biesta 2007; Biesta *et al.* 2008).

Anne Wakelin

Anne Wakelin was interviewed six times between November 2004 and May 2007. With her husband and three children, Anne had uprooted in 2002 from one part of the country to go and live in another. Our project gave Anne the opportunity to tell stories about some of the ramifications of that life-changing transition.

When we first met, Anne was aged 38, had been married for 16 years and was the mother of a teenage daughter and two infant sons. The family came originally from Staffordshire where Anne had lived all her life until she and her husband decided to move to a village in the south west. She came from a close-knit family where she was accustomed to visiting parents, grandparents and sisters regularly and, despite close family ties and an established pattern of life – and in the face of considerable scepticism from friends and family that they would go ahead with their move – Anne and her husband took the risks involved in making a major change. They had no previous connection with the village they moved to and yet were willing to leave behind their familiar lives for the sake of living somewhere new that was close to the sea.

When she left school, Anne had trained and worked for several years as a hairdresser. She described herself as being a 'people person' who found her *métier* in that profession. Through her son's primary school, Anne came into contact with a government initiative, Sure Start, and became a volunteer mentor for the scheme. Subsequently she was invited to become 'parent rep' for the village at Sure Start organisational meetings and became active in a number of community groups. In time, she was employed by Sure Start as a community development officer with responsibility for leading several projects for parents and children. Alongside her learning in the workplace were elements of formal education. Anne had started an NVQ 3 in Early Years and Education though found it difficult to put aside time to do the necessary paperwork. With the end of Sure Start, Ann continued to be employed by her local authority as a community development officer.

Narrative quality

Anne is an enthusiast for life and the interview transcripts frequently quote her saying that things are 'fab', 'fantastic', 'lovely', 'brilliant'. Ann's narratives were primarily *descriptive* of events and the most distinctive characteristic of her stories was an intense *dialogic quality*: as an enthusiastic narrator of events in her life, she would frequently reconstruct conversations between key players in the events she described. There was usually little analysis or reflection in Anne's stories; however, the final interview achieved an unprecedented depth in terms of its *analytical* and *evaluative* quality when Anne was asked to comment on her experiences of taking part in the Learning Lives project.

Plot

The plot that emerges from Anne's narrative is of the wife and mother who resumes a career. A researcher's perspective on the plot would be sensitive to the way she presents as a vigorous, active, enthusiastic and sociable person engaged in an exuberant quest to engage in life's opportunities. At various times in the interviews she emerged as the epitome of the uninhibited multitasking mother: attending to her toddler, taking care of a pet, dealing with phone calls from work and phone calls about house improvements while also responding to interview prompts. She is excited by life and the possibilities it offers and this exuberance characterises her narratives about her own life, even when talking about family problems and conflicts. Most striking during the time span of the research was Anne's resumption of her identity as a woman with a career that resulted in stories about changes to routines, knowledge and skills and that was also manifest in an embodied, physical change.

The clue to Anne's perspective on the existence of a plot in her narrative is contained in the frequently used comment that she sees herself as a 'people person'. Her post-school training was as a hairdresser and she ran her own business for several years. In her new location she has become a community development worker, which enables Anne to pursue her interest in people in new ways – going into estates of houses and caravans to locate small children and ensuring their carers are aware of their rights and responsibilities. Anne relishes 'being on a mission' and meeting the challenge of coordinating people and resources in projects. She loves doing this in a work environment where she can cooperate with others she finds congenial. However, she has a daily challenge of reconciling her aspirations and preferences with her concerns about her domestic life.

Learning potential

In early interviews we heard many stories of Anne's learning as she commented on learning from moving to a new home. Some adjustments were material such as how to cope with everyday matters like transport and shopping in a rural area after moving from the Midlands to the rural south west. Other adjustments were more essential and involved the way she related to her husband and children as she started to develop a new sense of identity in her new home in a new community. We heard of the skills and knowledge she gained from her voluntary and employed work for Sure Start.

During the final interview Anne was asked to reflect on the experience of taking part in the project and this shifted the quality of her responses, away from a descriptive account to a more reflective discourse. She commented on what a rare opportunity it had been:

> I've really enjoyed doing it. I've enjoyed doing it because it's, it's not very often that somebody sits there and lets you tell them about what you are and what you do and how you do your [pause] how your life has been, has been really.
>
> (Interview 6, June 2007)

It was suggested that perhaps the experience was like talking with friends or with relatives. While she agreed that friends may well get together and reminisce, it was never to the extent that someone talks about themselves at length. She added that family members have so many interests and commitments that they would not listen for long either.

Action potential

There was a physical manifestation of the changes that Anne had experienced by our fifth interview. Anne had started attending a slimming club and lost weight. She resembled far more the glamorous young hairdresser who features in photographs in the family home. She spoke of having regained interest in buying new clothes and caring once more about her appearance.

A change in Anne's approach to telling stories was in the way she reported chronology: in our early interviews, Anne's sense of time was mainly 'family-centric' – she recalled chronology in terms of when things had happened to family members. By the final interviews she was 'organisation-centric' and using standard chronology.

She said she enjoyed taking part in the interviews and reading the transcripts and they offered an important insight into herself. She was able to characterise the changes she had experienced in terms of her new identity:

> I'm doing more for a starter. I'm completely different in what I do. I'm working now. More confident in myself as I was three years ago, and more knowledgeable in what I do as well. The different outlook on

things, you know, in my work, because I'd only ever been, as I say I'd only ever been a hairdresser.

(Interview 6, June 2007)

However, in the final interview Anne communicated some of her underlying anxieties about getting older and the personal costs that were involved in pursuing her job. She said it was a 'horrible feeling that I've no baby in the house anymore'. She was moving beyond her motherhood identity to being someone who enjoys being at work and sees it as necessary to fulfil herself as a 'people person':

> I would have been a right miserable bugger or, you know, I don't know how I'd have been. So life takes you in such funny ways you never know what's there. You never know how it's going to turn out, so just go with it … I mean [my son] does say to me, he says 'I hate your job, I hate your work,' and I say, 'Why' ''Cos you're not here for me.'

(Interview 6, June 2007)

There is some indication in Anne's case that we can see someone construct-ing a narrative to justify a *departure* from her established norms and patterns of belief (Bruner 1990). There are several respects in which Anne's life could be circumscribed and scripted: she has working class origins in the West Midlands, she is female and a mother, she has values, beliefs and goals in life that reflect her social and cultural origins. There is a striking agentic quality, nonetheless, revealed in the narrative in that Anne and her husband shared a dream of moving to another part of the country and achieved that change. More recently, Anne effected an opportunistic change in her occupational identity as hairdresser by becoming a community development officer. She is driven on by her energy and enthusiasm to engage with the opportunities life presents and she learns from such opportunities; at the same time she is cognizant of the personal cost that she is no longer available for her children and husband in the way she once was.

Bob Davidson

Bob Davidson was interviewed three times between April 2006 and April 2007 when he was in the process of leaving the Royal Navy. He was 39 when first interviewed and engaged in what the Navy terms a 'resettlement process', a transition to civilian life. Our project gave Bob the opportunity to tell stories about his reflections on making the transition from a successful armed forces career back into civilian life and he emerged as a thoughtful interviewee, capable of being self-analytical and self-critical.

Bob Davidson has a wife and three young children. He had served in the Royal Navy for 24 years, ever since he left school at the age of 16 years. He had joined as a rating, worked and studied to become a marine engineer and by 1997 was a chief petty officer. In 2000 he transferred to the Royal

Marines and was serving as an engineer with them at the time of the Iraq War. His experiences in that conflict contributed to a personal transformation: Bob told how he had become disillusioned with his job, with the politicians whose decisions led to the war and with some of the officers who were responsible for managing the war. In relation to engineering, Bob said that he had become deeply bored with the field. He no longer felt comfortable with naval structures that he perceived as incompatible with his desire for personal growth and learning. He described as an epiphany the realisation that 'it was no longer [pause] suitable or apt for me, with the feelings that I had, to stay in the armed forces'. Instead, his family had assumed much greater significance:

> I'm talking about the emotional side of things there, intellectual side of things that the things you always *think* about telling your children, you never do. The things about you always think about telling your wife and you never do.
>
> (Interview 1, April 2006)

Having made the decision to leave, an extended period of transition started during which Bob was supported by the Royal Navy in his exploration of various possibilities, which included periods of placement with civil engineering companies in New Zealand and in the UK. Bob spoke of one particular moment that encapsulated his situation:

> I was in ... a sewage treatment works, in a six ... six metre excavation and the rain was pouring down and um – the rain was pouring down and the effluent was also pouring down on my, my wellies and I just thought to myself, 'there *must* be something better than this!' [laugh] And I kind of sacked myself.
>
> (Interview 2, August 2006)

The alternative that started to emerge was based on Bob's passion for houses and building. By the time of our third interview in 2007, he had left the Navy and was managing his own building company that was successful in attracting a substantial number of projects and employed five workers in addition to Bob and his partner. The economic circumstances in Britain and the associated building boom at the time ensured that Bob's skills and expertise quickly found an outlet.

Narrative quality

Bob is a lover of language who takes pleasure in using words that few others have within their active vocabulary. He has a strong disposition for story telling and is able to tell stories about himself at length: he was *descriptive* of his family background, formal education and naval career. There was a detailed, though inevitably superficial, account of his involvement in the

Iraq War. He rarely uses dialogue in his stories but uses direct speech to articulate questions. Bob claims that he constantly self-analyses and this tendency is evidenced in the transcripts that also reveal how he refines his answers, sometimes modifying comments in mid-sentence. His story-telling can be characterised therefore as *analytical and evaluative*.

Plot

The plot that emerges from Bob's narrative is of a man of action negotiating a mid-life transition. A researcher's perspective on plot in Bob's narrative would note the objective circumstances at the time. No other Learning Lives respondent in the south west was in such a clear situation of self-reconstruction, a process that seemed to encourage him to tell stories, to be reflective about their meaning, to consider the implications of achieving insight into his character and abilities. The narrative outlined the complexity of factors involved in the decision to leave the Navy, including retrospective and projective elements. The retrospective elements included Bob's disillusion with serving in the armed forces – with politicians who made the decision to invade Iraq and with officers whose motives and competence Bob suspected. It was likely also that Bob had advanced as far as was likely within the naval hierarchy – he had become too old to build a further career as an officer. The projective elements of Bob's decision relate to his self-concept as someone with abilities and talents whose life-course challenge is to find out how best he might use his abilities – and this was the primary plot in Bob's stories. He commented that:

> There are three types of people, those who look back in life, those who live in the present, and those who live into the future. I was looking for the next thing and I think I'm quite – it's quite clear that I, I, I like to look in the future ... I'm impatient and I want to know what I'm going to be *now*, rather than undertake something and find out it's the wrong thing. I want to know that I'm going to be good at something.
>
> (Interview 1, April 2006)

Bob's own view of the plot in his narrative could be observed in his stories of himself as an 'action man' responding with commitment to challenge and would emphasise the importance of his family. The period of transition was one in which Bob sought to use various strategies to reframe his ideas of himself, what he could do and who he could be. On several occasions he referred to the importance of responding to challenge and Bob appeared to think that his commitment to action in his life should be transferred from the pursuit of a career to the pursuit of family life and self-fulfilling ideals.

Learning potential

Bob values traditional education and people he sees as 'educated' and several times was dismissive of the functional nature of his own engineering qualifications. What he valued more for learning were experiences and circumstances that enabled him to recognise his own strengths and abilities. He spoke about learning that could become a substantive part of his understanding of everyday life. The Royal Navy makes generous provision for people with Bob's length of service to explore options and possibilities in civilian working life and he had availed himself of the placement opportunities that the resettlement scheme provides. Our interviews gave him opportunities to be reflective and self-analytical about what he was learning about himself through such experiences.

Bob also spoke frankly of fears that he might be 'boring' or 'average' or 'just another statistic'; however:

> the more the interviews have gone on, the more I've talked, the more I've realised that, you know, that I am a part of this rich fabric of life ... you realise how many people have helped you in the past, I think, because the more you help people, the more you think, oh somebody did that to me once.
>
> (Interview 3, April 2007)

Action potential

Much of the importance of learning for Bob related to his ability to control and effect change in his life. Bob stated that he had a commitment to change but feared he lacked the right skills to achieve it; one of his concerns during our interviews was to identify what such skills might be and what he could do to acquire them. He was able to express aspirations, such as his interest in learning for personal development; and he had practical strategies for his resettlement that included placing himself in contexts where he could gauge experientially whether he was sufficiently interested in the work and able to function with colleagues. Eventually Bob opted to run his own building firm so that he could be autonomous at work and take part more actively in his family life.

Thus Bob spoke of learning that would show him how to change, about learning that would show to him and others what he could become and there were continuing visions of future possibilites:

> I've always hoped to have a little farm or a little smallholding [pause] and the more and more you hear about becoming environmentally friendly, the more and more I want to become environmentally friendly and the more I want – more I want to live in a sustainable house, or community.
>
> (Interview 2, August 2006)

Conclusions

We started by stating that an important task for adult education researchers is to highlight the significance of the broad range of learning processes and practices that occur in the lives of adults in order to show that there is more to learning than what is acknowledged in the economic definitions of life-long learning. In this chapter we have presented stories from two participants in the Learning Lives project to show some of the complexity of formal and informal learning processes sustaining two individuals through periods of transition in their lives.

We found in the project that some people (though not all) are effective 'narrative learners'. By narrative learning we mean that learning can take place as a result of articulating stories from one's life, through the process of talking about and reflecting on life experiences, in other words from the very *narration* of one's biography; and can take place as a result of presenting stories from one's life, by having stories with content and structure, by *having a narrative* that says something about what and how you have learned. Narrative and narration are not simply a vehicle for such learning processes but can be understood as a 'site' for learning.

Anne Wakelin and Bob Davidson reveal different ways in which narratives can have different learning potential and they show something of the conditions under which narrative learning might operate. There remain many questions about practical issues, concerning whether and how narrative learning might relate to established provision in adult education. Both participants said that their experience of telling stories for our project was quite unlike telling stories to family or relatives. The support and promotion of narrative learning therefore first of all raises questions about the provision of social settings in which such stories can be told to others and constructed with others, so that communicative evaluation and imaginative distancing can become possible. But it also raises questions about the 'quality' of such settings and interactions. Many authors have commented on the 'individualisation' of adult learning and, more importantly, on the de-politicising effects of this individualisation (see Martin 2003; Biesta 2006b), i.e. the loss of opportunities to translate 'private troubles' into 'public issues' (Wright Mills 1959). Supporting narrative learning is therefore neither only about improving people's 'capacity' for narration, nor only about providing opportunities for doing this together with others. What matters is also the extent to which such learning processes can be understood in a political way and can be lifted from the level of private troubles to the plane of public and political issues so that the learning economy might eventually transform into a 'learning democracy' (Biesta 2005).

Notes

1   *Learning Lives: Learning, Identity and Agency* was a three-year longitudinal study of the learning biographies of 150 adults of 25 and older during which participants were interviewed up to eight times between 2004 and 2007. The research also used quantitative data collection from panel surveys. The project was funded by the Economic and Social Research Council, Award Reference RES139250111, and was part of the ESRC's Teaching and Learning Research Programme. Learning Lives was a collaborative project involving the University of Exeter (Gert Biesta, Flora Macleod, Michael Tedder, Paul Lambe), the University of Brighton (Ivor Goodson, Norma Adair), the University of Leeds (Phil Hodkinson, Heather Hodkinson, Geoff Ford, Ruth Hawthorne) and the University of Stirling (John Field, Heather Lynch). For further information see www.learninglives.org.

2 Surprisingly, this distinction does not play a role in Rossiter and Clark's (2007) book on narrative and adult education.

References

Alheit, P. (1995) 'Biographical learning: Theoretical outline, challenges and contradictions of a new approach in adult education', in P. Alheit, A. Bron-Wojciechowska, E. Brugger and P. Dominicé (eds), *The Biographical Approach in European Adult Education*, Vienna: Verband Wiener Volksbildung, pp. 57–71.

Alheit, P. (2005) 'Stories and structures: An essay on historical times, narratives and their hidden impact on adult learning', *Studies in the Education of Adults* 37, 201–212.

Alheit, P. and Dausien, B. (2002) 'The double face of lifelong learning: Two analytical perspectives on a "silent revolution"', *Studies in the Education of Adults* 34, 3–22.

Aspin, D.N. and Chapman, J.D. (2001) 'Lifelong learning: Concepts, theories and values'. Proceedings of the 31st Annual Conference of SCUTREA, University of East London: SCUTREA.

Biesta, G.J.J. (2004) 'Against learning: Reclaiming a language for education in an age of learning', *Nordisk Pedagogik* 24, 70–82.

Biesta, G.J.J. (2005) 'The learning democracy? Adult learning and the condition of democratic citizenship', *British Journal of Sociology of Education* 26, 693–709.

Biesta, G.J.J. (2006a) *Beyond Learning: Democratic education for a human future*, Boulder, CO: Paradigm Publishers.

Biesta, G.J.J. (2006b) 'What's the point of lifelong learning if lifelong learning has no point? On the democratic deficit of policies for lifelong learning', *European Educational Research Journal* 5, 169–180.

Biesta, G.J.J. and Tedder, M. (2006) 'How is agency possible? Towards an ecological understanding of agency-as-achievement'. Working Paper 5, Exeter: The Learning Lives Project.

Biesta, G.J.J. and Tedder, M. (2007) 'Agency and learning in the lifecourse: Towards an ecological perspective', *Studies in the Education of Adults* 39, 132–149.

Biesta, G.J.J., Goodson, I., Tedder, M. and Adair, N. (2008) 'Learning from life: The role of narrative'. A summative working paper for the Learning Lives project, Exeter: The Learning Lives Project.

Bruner, J. (1990) *Acts of Meaning*, Cambridge, MA and London: Harvard University Press.

Czarniawska, B. (2004) *Narratives in Social Science Research*, London: Sage.

Elliott, J. (2005) *Using Narrative in Social Research, Qualitative and Quantitative Approaches*, London: Sage.

Martin, I. (2003) 'Adult education, lifelong learning and citizenship: Some ifs and buts', *International Journal of Lifelong Education* 22, 566–579.

Polkinghorne, D. (1988) *Narrative Knowing and the Human Sciences*, Albany, NY: SUNY Press.

Polkinghorne, D. (1995) 'Narrative configuration in qualitative analysis', in J.A. Hatch and R. Wisniewski (eds), *Life History and Narrative*, London: Falmer, pp. 5–23.

Ricoeur, P. (1992) *Oneself as Another*, Chicago, IL: University of Chicago Press.

Rossiter, M. (1999) 'A narrative approach to development: Implications for adult education', *Adult Education Quarterly* 50, 56–71.

Rossiter, M. and Clark, M.C. (2007) *Narrative and the Practice of Adult Education*, Malabar, FL: Krieger.

Tedder, M. and Biesta, G. (2007) 'Learning *from* life and learning *for* life: Exploring the opportunities for biographical learning in the lives of adults'. Paper presented at the ESREA Conference on Life History and Biography, Roskilde University, Denmark, 1–4 March.

Wright Mills, C. (1959) *The Sociological Imagination*, London: Oxford University Press.

Part II

Changing places of learning

Chapter 8

Approaches to lifelong learning

American community colleges and age inclusiveness

W. Norton Grubb

Introduction

In contrast to countries (like Austria) with specialized institutions for adult learning, the US provides most lifelong learning within its mainstream educational institutions, particularly community college. As comprehensive institutions, community colleges provide a variety of programmes for students often described as non-traditional, including lifelong learning for adults seeking upgrade training to improve their skills, retraining to change their occupations, remediation to develop basic academic skills or avocational education of many sorts. Lifelong learning in community colleges takes place in several ways, often difficult to disentangle: in "regular" credential programmes; in evening classes geared to adult students; in non-credit programmes with particularly easy access; in customized training funded by specific employers. In addition, colleges have developed several practices to support adult students, and several ways of enhancing transitions both into and out of colleges. In contrast, lifelong learning in separate adult education and job training programmes suffers from more difficult transitions, a lack of transparency and often low-quality teaching. The chapter ends with some criteria by which the effectiveness of different approaches to lifelong learning might be judged.

A conventional narrative about the role of education has developed in many countries, both developed and transitional, as well as in many international agencies including the European Union and OECD. I call it the Education Gospel because it expresses a faith that education, focused on preparation for occupations, can resolve many individual and social problems including access to well-paid jobs, equity, transition to the Knowledge Economy, growth and competitiveness in a globalizing world (Grubb and Lazerson, 2004). One strand of the Education Gospel emphasizes that individuals are more likely to find their skills becoming obsolete as technology and knowledge progress, and that they are more likely to change jobs, so that the need for lifelong learning is increasing. Often the need for lifelong learning is taken as an article of faith rather than demonstrated, like other strands of the Education Gospel.[1]

After the rhetoric for lifelong learning has quieted, a crucial question is how to enhance access to education for adults. This may happen in educational institutions created specifically for adults; for example, Austria has created a number of adult institutions sponsored by employer associations, trades unions, Chambers of Commerce, *Volkschule* and other local groups, while their mainstream postsecondary institutions (universities and *Fachhochschulen*) are rarely attended by adults.[2] In a different pattern, the US provides most lifelong learning in its mainstream education institutions, especially community colleges and to a lesser extent universities, in programmes that include individuals of all ages. It's difficult to say which of these two polar models, as well as intermediate approaches that combine specialized practices in age-inclusive institutions, is more effective. However, examination of the US practices in this chapter suggests that certain dimensions of lifelong learning (including certain types of transitions) are enhanced by age-inclusiveness, while others may become more difficult. After describing the variety of ways that community colleges facilitate lifelong learning in the first part of the chapter, and then briefly describing the problems with specialized adult programmes in the US, I end by turning to the question of effectiveness.

Including adults in American community colleges

Over time, community colleges in the US have adopted a great variety of purposes, in part the result of responsiveness to community demands. Among the purposes relevant to lifelong learning are retraining for workers switching jobs, upgrade training for employed individuals who need additional skills, "remedial" training for individuals whose basic academic skills are insufficient to enter the labour market and avocational education in a variety of hobbies and subjects linked to intellectual and civic goals. In general, Americans generally prefer comprehensive rather than specialized institutions. Comprehensive institutions seem more equitable, because they are less likely to segregate some individuals (especially working class or minority) in separate institutions. They also facilitate student choice and transition among programmes; for example, individuals who start in academic (or general) education programmes designed for transfer to university can shift into occupational programmes, or vice versa. Finally, occupational programmes have greater access to related academic coursework, like biology and chemistry for nursing programmes, in comprehensive institutions.

The comprehensive community college has therefore included adults with a variety of purposes, and it has done so in a variety of ways.

Inclusion in credit programmes

Community colleges pride themselves on being open-access institutions, meaning that there are no prerequisites for entry; therefore older individuals past their initial education can enroll in the "regular" credit courses of community colleges. In the most recent national data from the federal fall enrolment survey, for example, 60.1 per cent of community college students were over 24, compared to 32.2 per cent of public university students and 38.6

per cent of private university students. Indeed, community college administrators often proclaim that "our average age is 29", implying that most students are older. However, this is misleading in several ways. A few much older individuals, in their fifties and sixties, can skew the average, and the *median* age of students is closer to 26. In addition, conventional-age students (18–24) are much more likely to attend full time and to take three to four courses, while older individuals are much more likely to take just one or two courses at a time, often for specific purposes (as in upgrade training) rather than aspiring to a degree. As a result, the median *course* is taken by someone who is between 22 and 23; the majority of courses, therefore, and the majority of funding are generated by conventional-age students.

Indeed, some community colleges look like two institutions under one roof: a daytime college for conventional-age students taking a full load, usually taught by full-time instructors who prefer teaching during the day; and an evening college with older students taking one or two courses at most, taught almost exclusively by part-time instructors. Many colleges offer a different roster of courses during the evening, at times that are convenient for older students, and sometimes devise open-entry/open-exit courses that students can enter at any time during the semester, rather than only at the beginning of each semester. Distance education courses have also become more common, although their costs and uncertain effectiveness have prevented them from expanding as some enthusiasts would wish. Many colleges have therefore made some accommodations for the particular needs of lifelong learners, a combination of age-inclusiveness with some degree of specialization. The drawback of these practices is that an ancillary benefit of age-inclusiveness – the function of older students as role models for younger students without much life experience – is weakened, even though older students may be better served.

Learning communities and older students

A different form of accommodation has been to develop learning communities for older students. Learning communities are created when two or more instructors coordinate their courses, and students take all these courses at the same time; they provide ways of providing more integrated curricula, support groups of similar students and different disciplinary perspectives. In the case of the Program for Adult College Education (PACE) in a number of colleges, older students – often women returning to college and the workforce after their child-rearing years are over – take a series of classes together, with schedules and distance learning devised to meet their schedules. The older students with similar goals and problems can also form a community of mutual support. Similarly, some colleges have developed learning communities for older welfare mothers (and a few fathers), trying to improve their skills so they can increase their earnings and move off welfare; in these cases the learning communities focus on those occupations that a group of welfare recipients would like to enter.

Bridge programmes

While many adults enrol in regular credit programmes on their own, some – particularly those without a history of success in conventional schooling including many working-class individuals, black and Latino students, and immigrants new to the country – may be distrustful of large, impersonal educational institutions, or unable to navigate the bureaucratic demands of enrolling, or too unsure of their purposes to know how to start retraining or remedial education. A number of colleges have therefore devised "bridge" programmes to provide additional support to such students. One at Laney College in California has been extensively described by its founder (Wilson, 2007); it uses a variety of especially student-centred teaching approaches to bring these students back to academic work, especially in reading and writing. Similarly, the Puente (Spanish for "bridge") programme was developed in a number of California colleges to provide special approaches for Latino students, including a variety of Latino and Mexican literature, different approaches to teaching writing, special roles for counsellors and mentors from the Latino community. These various bridge programmes may, like all credit programmes, enrol students of different ages, but by focusing on the special needs of certain kinds of students they also provide greater support for older students.

Non-credit programmes and the transition to credit programmes

In addition to credit programmes leading to credentials – certificates, Associate degrees and then the baccalaureate through transfer – most colleges provide a variety of non-credit courses, some of which are avocational, some of which are remedial courses in basic reading, writing, maths and English as a Second Language (ESL), some of which are employer-sponsored courses mentioned below and other forms of specific upgrade training. These usually cannot count towards credentials, particularly not the baccalaureate degree; they are often funded in different ways, and at lower rates, than credit courses. Colleges develop non-credit programmes for different purposes, then, though one purpose in some colleges is facilitating access of students (and especially adult students) into the college.

One illustrative example of the use of non-credit programmes is San Francisco City College.[3] The college, with a long history of providing adult education, has nine major centres and about 150 sites throughout the city, many of them specialized for the populations in different neighbourhoods – with a focus on the Chinese population in Chinatown, for example, or the Latino population in the Mission. These centres are smaller and more personable than a central campus would be; teachers and administrators often create distinctive cultures in these smaller centres. Non-credit courses have certain advantages: they are free to students, eliminating the tuition barrier; they are open to all immigrants, reportedly eliminating the fear of illegal immigrants that enrolment will involve them in bureaucratic procedures that might lead to the dreaded Immigration and Naturalization Service. The college has worked to facilitate movement from credit to non-credit programmes by integrating credit and non-credit divisions, by creating multiple pathways from non-credit to credit programmes, by instituting several counselling and information mechanisms to support students through the bureaucratic process of transition. The college has discovered that roughly 50 per cent of its students earnings degrees have taken some non-credit courses, and it claims that non-credit enrolment enhances the likelihood of completing a degree, so it views non-credit education as a central part of its mission rather than a peripheral and low-status service. A large proportion (70 per cent) of non-credit students are older than 24, so that by providing non-credit education in special forms this college and a few others have in effect devised special ways of serving adults.

Customized training

As part of their roles in economic development, or supporting employment in local communities, community colleges often provide short courses customized to the needs of specific employers. These might be, for example, training in statistical process control, or in specific computer systems or production processes, or remedial reading or maths for low-skilled workers (see Dougherty and Marianne, 1998, for a review). Often employers pay for such upgrade training, though in some states colleges receive conventional subsidies for such training, and most states have special programmes to subsidize some customized training. By definition, all individuals in such programmes are adults beyond their initial preparation for the labour force and engaged in some form of upgrade training. Reportedly the provision of customized training within comprehensive colleges enables these workers to see the extent of college offerings and facilitates the transition of workers into other credit and non-credit courses, though I have never been able to find statistics on rates of such transition. Indeed, colleges usually organize customized training in a different division from credit and non-credit courses, with more entrepreneurial and employer-oriented (rather than student-centred) attitudes, so in practice such transition is likely to be individual and idiosyncratic – unlike, for example, the systematic efforts to bridge non-credit and credit programmes in San Francisco City College.

Transition possibilities and problems

Community colleges face at least four well-known kinds of transition problems. One is the transition into the college, either from secondary schools for younger students or from employment (or unemployment) for older students. A second, for those who aspire to baccalaureate degrees, is the transition from community colleges to four-year colleges or universities, commonly referred to as the transfer function. A third, described above, is the transition from non-credit education to mainstream credit-bearing programmes that can lead to credentials. A fourth is the transition into employment, a crucial transition because students who fail to find employment related to their fields of study earn much lower economic returns.

Colleges have devised many ways to smooth these transitions. So-called 2+2 programmes linking the last two years of secondary school with two years of community college, and dual enrolment where secondary students enrol in community college courses, are intended to smooth the transition from secondary school. Bridge programmes and non-credit efforts try to improve the transition from employment. Most colleges have transfer centres as well as counselling to provide information about transfer, though the complexity and opacity of the transfer process – particularly with the enormous variety of admissions procedures at universities – is a favourite target of critics. The example of San Francisco Community College and several other colleges with similar approaches illustrates that there are ways of improving the transition from non-credit to credit education. And many colleges have employment centres, though some of these are small and weak and others concentrate on "stay-in-school" jobs to help students pay for colleges, rather than providing information on the "adult" jobs that students want to get when they leave the college. More generally, I have argued that community colleges can serve as bridging institutions among the various postsecondary options, especially for adults (Grubb and Lazerson, 2004, Ch. 3; Grubb, 1996, Ch. 4), facilitating the movement among secondary schools, universities, short-term job training programmes, adult education and employer-based programmes.

However, the problem is that, while a variety of transition mechanisms exist, they tend to be sporadic, fragmented and idiosyncratic. For each of them, a few colleges have developed exemplary efforts, while many more colleges have very little in place; these transition programmes have never been institutionalized very well. One problem is that the bridging role is really a "system" responsibility, and should be funded and supported by a variety of institutions in the education and training *system* and not just colleges; providing strong transition mechanisms does not generate additional funding the way that providing additional courses and increasing enrolments do. A second problem is that the elements that make up most transition programmes – information to students including guidance and counselling, particular approaches to pedagogy, the provision of basic skills instruction and ESL, the creation of small communities of students in institutions that are often large, impersonal and designed for commuter rather than residential students – are among the most difficult for most community colleges to carry out. And a third problem is that colleges have many roles or missions to perform. The bridging role may be emphasized by some colleges,[4] but others may focus on transfer, or occupational education, or customized training for high-profile companies; the non-credit divisions of most colleges seem to emphasize upgrade training, rather than the emphasis on remediation and transition in San Francisco Community College and a few other similar institutions. So in practice the transition programmes to facilitate the movement of students vary enormously among colleges.

A final problem associated with the provision of lifelong learning in so many different ways is that it is impossible to estimate how important each of these forms of provision is. Consistent national information is unavailable on non-credit enrolment, for example, and colleges usually do not keep figures even on their own customized training programmes.[5] In addition, the intensity of enrolment varies among the five options I have reviewed: customized training efforts tend to be short, taking as little as 10–20 hours of contact, whereas full-time credit programmes usually involve 12–15 contact hours per week over a semester of 10–15 weeks, or at least 150 contact hours; a count of students may badly misrepresent the intensity of efforts. So, while it is reasonably clear that the majority of lifelong learning in the US takes place in community colleges, particularly in credit programmes open to all students, the data necessary to confirm this statement or to examine variation in its accuracy are simply unavailable.

Lifelong learning in other American programmes: transition problems

While community colleges provide a substantial amount of publicly supported lifelong learning in the US, there are two other sources of public support that deserve mention: adult education and short-term job training (Grubb and Lazerson, 2004, Ch. 4). Each of them is a form of second-chance education, with funding largely from the federal government, and each illustrates the problem of placing lifelong learning in relatively narrow programmes disconnected from broader educational concerns.

In its broadest sense encompassing the many forms of education for adults, adult education in the US has a glorious history. During the nineteenth century and well into the twentieth, self-initiated learning took place in a wide variety of forms, under the sponsorship of many different churches, working-men's clubs and unions, self-improvement associations, summer encampments and retreats. These usually took place outside the education system, reflecting the distrust of bureaucratic education and government intervention (Kett, 1994). Since 1900, however, much of organized adult education has been redirected towards vocational purposes, away from the great variety of efforts aimed at cultural improvement and moral uplift. In addition, a great deal of adult education shifted from informal and community settings into educational institutions, and increasing support from the federal and state governments made a good deal of this public in the sense of its funding. Currently adult education is usually sponsored by elementary-secondary school districts, along with community colleges in a few states; it provides a great deal of ESL and basic skills instruction, along with a smattering of avocational and occupational education. But the rich and varied forms of adult education evident in the nineteenth century have generally decreased.

The effectiveness of current adult education programmes, even given their narrow educational goals, is highly suspect. As one evaluation concluded:

Adult literacy programs have failed to produce the life-changing improvements in reading ability that are often suggested by published evaluations … the average participant gains only one or two reading levels, and is still functionally illiterate by almost any standard when he or she leaves.

(Dieckhoff, 1989, 629)

One problem is that programmes are usually short, and fail to lead to any credential other than the GED (for General Equivalency Diploma, supposedly the equivalent of a high school diploma but in practice the equivalent of perhaps Grade 8 or 9). This is precisely the situation where transition into a community college, with its variety of both basic skills courses and occupational courses, might benefit participants. But in a decade of examining community colleges and their connections with other programmes, I uncovered almost no examples of adult schools cooperating with colleges to improve the transition between the two; on the contrary, the opinion of one welfare programme director – who bemoaned the problems of referring welfare recipients to the "black hole of adult education" from which they never emerged – is more typical. In practice, then, adult education remains an isolated corner of the education system, providing short programmes to the individuals whose basic skills are the weakest – far from the conventional view of lifelong learning as a response to the Knowledge Revolution.

Similarly, short-term job training in the US has developed, independently of the education system, to provide remedial training to the long-term unemployed, welfare recipients, dislocated workers displaced from employment by shifts in regional or industry employment patterns and others on the margin of the labour force. They then provided short programmes – often about 15 weeks – of relatively job-specific training, again to individuals who are among the least skilled and experienced in the labour market. It's not surprising, then, that most job training programmes have been found ineffective, and that any short-term gains dissipate after four or five years. Like adult education, job training has sometimes provided a second-chance route into the labour force, but it certainly does not provide the kind of lifelong learning that the majority of individuals want to access.

In prior years, job training was reasonably well coordinated with both secondary education and community colleges, partly because the legislation set aside funds specifically for cooperation between the two. In addition, forward-looking states began creating their own coherent *systems* of vocational education and training (VET), combining resources from a variety of federal and state sources to create more rationalized approaches in place of multiple fragmented programmes (Grubb and Associates, 1999). However, when Congress revised federal legislation for job training in 1998, funding for coordination vanished, and the ability of community colleges to cooperate with job training was seriously limited by rigid accountability measures. In practice job training has given way to a system of providing information to individuals about local education and training opportunities, and so this particular (albeit largely ineffective) form of training for adults and of transitions into community colleges largely vanished.

The weak cases of adult education and job training illustrate that transitions among lifelong learning providers can be very difficult. Indeed, there is a substantial literature bemoaning the lack of cooperation, not only in education and training but also in a variety of social services. Where there are funds set aside for coordination, then it is much more likely to occur than when coordination is mandated or encouraged without resources. And the efforts of programmes to maintain their separate identities, and to insist (as job training and adult education programmes often do) that their specific approaches are superior makes transitions in lifelong learning much more difficult.

Evaluating approaches to lifelong learning

The differences between countries like Austria, with an array of specific lifelong learning programmes for adults, and the US, which embeds a great deal of lifelong learning in its mainstream education institutions like community colleges, pose the question of whether one approach is more effective than another. In its general form this question is impossible to answer, since there are generally too many differences among practices in different countries that affect the quality of lifelong learning. In addition, the either/or form of the question – asking whether one form of lifelong learning is more effective than another – is not the best way to pose the issue of effectiveness, as John Dewey argued.[6]

However, while the overall question of effectiveness is impossible to answer, there are still criteria by which to evaluate lifelong learning that can be used to examine different approaches.

Visibility and transparency

In the US, community colleges have become increasingly visible institutions; they are ubiquitous, and so are physically close to most of the population (except in rural areas). Most adults therefore know of their existence and how to gain further information, whereas adult schools and job training efforts are much harder to learn about. Even though community college students complain about the lack of transparency in constructing programmes, and guidance and counselling are often weak (Grubb, 2007), there are informative catalogues in all colleges, a great deal of information on the Web and some forms of guidance and counselling. Location in large and well-known education institutions therefore enhances the transparency of lifelong learning. In other cases – again, Austria provides a good example – adult-specific programmes are associated with other institutions that individuals have contact with – employers and unions, for example – and so appear to be quite visible. But if lifelong learning is provided in small, local programmes without much visibility, then visibility and access may become problems.

Access and suitability for adults

Adults operate on different schedules from conventional-age students,[7] and so incorporating them into education institutions created for younger individuals may require them to distort their schedules to accommodate lifelong learning. On this criteria, programmes created specifically for adults, with their schedules in mind, may be superior. However, in the US the general solution to this problem has been to create the "dual" community college, with evening and weekend classes scheduled specifically to meet the needs of adults. Similarly, an educational institution dominated by younger students without family or employment possibilities may create a culture that is unwelcoming to lifelong learners, and here too specific adult programmes may be more effective. But again many community colleges have developed what is effectively a hybrid approach, in which learning communities like the PACE programme, evening programmes dominated by older part-time students and organizations for older students, provide a different atmosphere or culture for adult learners.

The problem of access to lifelong learning is often an issue of money: potential students lack financial support, or cannot get the grants or loans that younger students get. The excellence of the Austrian approach is partly a result of the willingness of employers, unions and chambers of commerce to provide a great deal of funding. On this issue, community colleges have the advantages of relatively low tuition levels, ubiquity (so that travel costs are low) and flexible schedules (so that opportunity costs are low). However, low-income adult students are less likely to get access to grants and loans for which they would otherwise qualify (Grubb and Tuma, 1991). A more difficult problem is what I call the work–family–schooling dilemma: many older students have families and employment obligations, and when their carefully scheduled lives suffer a disruption – a sick child, a broken-down car, a change in work schedules – they may be forced to suspend their schooling. Many colleges offer some childcare and counselling on time management, but the US welfare state is too stingy to provide the income support that such older students need.

Effective teaching

In the US there is a substantial literature arguing (though rarely demonstrating) that effective teaching methods for adults differ from those for younger students – that adult programmes should be more student-centred, should draw on the experiences of older students and should use materials (textbooks and problems) reflecting adult rather than childish concerns. Some of this discussion is pointless because many precepts for adult learning are equally true for learning by younger students,[8] but the point that the pedagogy of lifelong learning should be carefully considered is surely true. Here the incorporation of lifelong learning into educational institutions may be beneficial, because it puts programmes for adults into a context where pedagogical discussions are more likely to occur.[9] In contrast, in the adult education, job training, and welfare-to-work programmes in the US disconnected from mainstream education, the teaching is usually the most arid form of lecture and drill, and indeed the very question of appropriate pedagogies rarely comes up (Grubb and Kalman, 1994). One question to pose consistently, therefore, is how the organization of lifelong learning – in mainstream education institutions versus specialized adult institutions disconnected from pedagogical discussions – affects approaches to teaching.

Transitions into mainstream education

One of the advantages of locating lifelong learning within community colleges is that adult learners are already part of a mainstream institution with connections to the baccalaureate degree and above. Indeed, a recent version of the archetypical rags-to-riches story is that of a welfare mother who enters a short training programme in a community college to become a health technician, moves into a credit-based nursing programme, transfers to a university and then goes on to medical school! The point of such stories is not that such paths are common, but that the education system as a whole provides such paths. In contrast, locating lifelong learning in programmes disconnected from mainstream education requires additional transitions, and at least in the US this transition has been difficult.[10]

Effectiveness in attaining adult goals

Perhaps the most difficult question to pose is whether various forms of lifelong learning are effective in helping adults reach their goals, whatever they may be. Quite rightly, community college educators point out that earning credentials or transferring to a university is not the goal of many students: some want shorter vocational certificates and licences, for upgrade training or retraining; some are "experimenters" trying to figure out whether postsecondary education is suitable for them, or students exploring different occupational areas; some want to correct deficiencies in basic skills, especially literacy; some are avocational students; and some want to continue their education as part of their own sense of self, like this community college student (Grubb, 1996, Ch. 2), "I couldn't stand not being in school, it's like wallowing in your own shit ... I learned how to wait tables and bar tend, and I thought my brain was becoming mush ... I love school!" Similarly, proponents of lifelong education have stressed the variety of goals adults have, even though lifelong learning often emerges in the context of vocational preparation and the Education Gospel. One problem is that of identifying these disparate goals, since prospective students may not always be articulate about them. The second problem is developing programmes to meet these different needs. Here is whether the comprehensive community college is particularly appropriate, since it provides a variety of occupational education, academic or general education, remedial education, avocational opportunities and a broad enough array of options so that experimenters and explorers can find a variety of experiences. In contrast, a system of more specialized programmes cannot provide such a broad array; for example, many of the Austria programmes are designed specifically for upgrade training, and cannot serve the other goals of adult students.

So there is no simple way of judging the effectiveness of different institutional approaches to lifelong learning, even though there are some criteria we can apply. However, what is perhaps most noteworthy about the best community college programmes in the US is that they develop a hybrid or both–and approach: that is, they locate lifelong learning within a mainstream education institution, *and* they provide different schedules and specialized support to meet the particular needs of adults – for example, in learning communities like PACE and Puente, in evening programmes and other non-traditional schedules, in efforts to integrate non-credit and credit programmes, in organizations intended to provide adult learners with their own community. Under these conditions, the strengths of each of these different approaches can develop.

Of course, this does not always happen. Learning communities, while widely known, are not all that prevalent; institutional approaches to improving instruction (including adult learning), while familiar to most instructors, are often neglected in favour of individual approaches to improving teaching; the transitions between non-credit and credit programmes are weak in most colleges; the problems of the family–work–schooling dilemma have not been resolved, even though some services exist. Like all institutions, then, community colleges are often imperfect versions of what they could be. But they provide a basic structure of age-inclusiveness and some practices supporting adults that have been conducive to lifelong learning, and these provide potential lessons both for other institutions and for other countries.

Notes

1 A terrific example is Pusser *et al.* (2007), with the histrionic subtitle: "Adults' success in college is key to America's future."
2 See OECD (2004), for which I was rapporteur, as well as the final report on adult education (OECD, 2005).
3 My thanks to Leslie Smith and Gregory Keech for providing me information about non-credit programmes at San Francisco City College.
4 A few urban community colleges intend to be "the only game in town", an institution relied on for every conceivable education service and they are likely to cooperate with all other education and training programmes. Rural colleges are often forced into this role because there are few other institutions around.
5 On the problems of data, see Pusser *et al.* (2007) and other reports from the Emerging Pathways project.
6 In his introduction to *Experience and Education* Dewey wrote: "Mankind likes to think in terms of extreme opposites. It is given to formulating its beliefs in terms of Either-Ors, between which it recognizes no intermediate possibilities" (1938, 17). In discussing traditional and progressive pedagogies, for example, he lamented that "the problems are not even recognized, to say nothing of being solved, when it is assumed that it suffices to reject the ideas and practices of the old education and then go to the opposite extreme" (ibid., 22).
7 This is decreasingly true in the US since such a large proportion of postsecondary students, in both community and four-year colleges, work.

8 See, for example, the distinction between "pedagogy" for children and "andragogy" for adults in Knowles (1984). Many practices labelled "pedagogy" are conventional behaviourist approaches like lecture and drill that are also ineffective, or at least incomplete, for children as well as adults.

9 I stress that educational institutions are more likely than others to engage in pedagogical discussion and improvement, but this does not always take place; see Grubb and Associates (1999) on the relatively weak efforts to improve the quality of teaching in many community colleges. This problem is even more serious in four-year universities.

10 There is a similar rags-to-riches story associated with adult education: an individual with low skills earns a GED in an adult school, then attends a university and goes on to graduate school! However, in general the GED does not enhance access to postsecondary education; see Quinn and Haberman (1986).

References

Dewey, J. (1938) *Experience and Education*, New York: Macmillan Publishing.

Dieckhoff, G.M. (1988) "An appraisal of adult literacy programs: Reading between the lines", *Journal of Reading* 31(April), 624–630.

Dougherty, K.J. and Marianne, F.B. (1998) *The New Economic Development Role of the Community College*, New York: Community College Research Center.

Grubb, W.N. (1996) *Working in the Middle: Strengthening education and training for the mid-skilled labor force*, San Francisco: Jossey-Bass.

Grubb, W.N. (2007) "'Like, what do I do now?' The dilemmas of guidance and counseling", in T. Bailey and V. Morest (eds), *Defending the Community College Equity Agenda*, Baltimore: Johns Hopkins University Press, pp. 195–222.

Grubb, W.N. and Kalman, J. (1994, November) "Relearning to earn: The role of remediation in vocational education and job training", *American Journal of Education* 103(1), 54–93.

Grubb, W.N. and Lazerson, M. (2004) *The Education Gospel: The economic power of schooling*, Cambridge, MA: Harvard University Press.

Grubb, W.N. and Tuma, J. (1991, Spring) "Who gets student aid? Variations in access to aid", *Review of Higher Education* 14(3), 359–381.

Grubb, W.N. with Byrd, B., Webb, E. and Worthen, H. (1999) *Honored but Invisible: An inside look at teaching in community colleges*, New York and London: Routledge.

Grubb, W.N., Badway, N., Bell, D., Chi, B., King, C., Herr, J., Prince, H., Kazis, R., Hicks, L. and Taylor, J. (1999, January) *Toward Order from Chaos: State efforts to reform workforce development systems* (MDS-1249). Berkeley, CA: National Center for Research in Vocational Education.

Kett, J. (1994) *The Pursuit of Knowledge under Difficulties: From self-improvement to adult education in America, 1750–1990*, Stanford, CA: Stanford University Press.

Knowles, M. (ed.) (1984) *Andragogy in Action: Applying modern principles of adult learning*, San Francisco, CA: Jossey-Bass.

OECD (2004) *Thematic Review on Adult Learning: Austria country note*, Paris: OECD.

OECD (2005) *Promoting Adult Learning*, Paris: OECD.

Pusser, B., Breneman, D.W., Gansneder, B.M., Kohl, K.J., Levin, J.S., Milam, J.H. and Turner, S.E. (2007) *Returning to Learning: Adults' success in college is key to America's future*, Indianapolis: Lumina Foundation.

Quinn, L. and Haberman, M. (1986, Fall) "Are GED certificate holders ready for postsecondary education?" *Metropolitan Education* 1(2), 72–82.

Wilson, S. (2007) *"What About Rose?" Using teacher research to reverse school failure*, New York: Teachers College Press.

Chapter 9

Two conceptual models for facilitating learners' transitions to new post-school learning contexts

Jill Lawrence

Introduction

This chapter introduces two conceptual models for facilitating transitions to new post-school learning contexts. The theoretical perspectives generated by critical discourse theory (CDT) underpin the first model, the 'New Learning Framework' whereas the perspectives stemming from constructivism and cross-cultural communication theory inform the second model, the 'Model for Transition Practices'. Both models are process orientated and therefore applicable to a range of new learning contexts. Those related to the higher education (HE), workplace and inter-cultural contexts are advanced here. The models are supported by data derived from two research studies, one on a regional Australian university and the second an analysis of conference papers presented to a multicultural conference held at the Australian National University (ANU), Canberra, Australia.

Theoretical insights

CDT contributes three main insights to clarify issues in relation to new post-school learning contexts and lifelong learning. First, by visualizing pedagogical practices and outcomes as discourse (Fairclough 1995; Van Dijk 1995), CDT highlights the role played by discourses in learning contexts. Luke (1999: 67) argues that if the primacy of discourse is acknowledged, then mastery of discourse can be seen to constitute a principal educational process and outcome. Edwards (2005) sees that discourses of lifelong learning could frame a practice-based understanding of polycontextuality and relationality, but also that such a notion of learning can be better understood through being situated within such discourses. The processes of facilitating effective transitions into new learning contexts, with these insights, can be visualized as the processes of becoming familiar with a context's discourses. This focus not only makes more explicit mainstream discourses, it also prioritizes the processes by which students learn to engage and master them.

Second, the application of CDT reveals the role of cultural diversity and the presence of literacies, or multiliteracies in the new learning context (Cope and Kalantzis 2000; New London Group 1996). If the learning context is perceived as a culture, then student engagement can be viewed as becoming literate in this culture. This insight makes more transparent the crucial nature of the interrelationships between students' cultural capital (Bourdieu 1999) and institutional or mainstream literacies, as well as the consequences for transition. Edwards (2005, citing Eraut 2004) notes that these are complex processes that include the transfer of knowledge encompassing:

> The extraction of potential relevant knowledge from the context(s) of its acquisition and its previous use; understanding the new situation – a process that depends on informal social learning; recognising what knowledge and skills are relevant; transforming them to fit the new situation; and integrating them with other knowledge and skills in order to think/act/communicate in the new situation.

Third, CDT focuses attention on the discursive practices that can operate as power relationships in constructing and maintaining dominance and inequality in the university context (Fairclough 1995). This understanding is critical in settings where the power imbalances between institutional/mainstream practices and new learners can affect engagement, providing consequences for transition. Edwards (2005, cited in Thorpe *et al*. 2005: 3) acknowledges the complexity involved when noting that 'however delicately treated or even disguised', pedagogy implies inequality both in expertise and in contexts.

Methodological approaches

The chapter draws on data derived from two methodological approaches. The methodology employed to investigate the HE learning context comprised a longitudinal case study conducted at a regional Australian university. It explored the experiences of alternative entry students as they strived to access and participate at the University of Southern Queensland (USQ) located in Toowoomba, Queensland. The study took a meta-disciplinary perspective, applying critical discourse theory, constructivism, communication and cross-cultural theories to contribute insights into the experiences of the students as they engaged and negotiated the university culture. It sought to determine how these students constructed their means of persevering, and succeeding, at university. The methodological structure of the research comprised a collective case study design (Yin 2003) encompassing critical ethnography (Carspecken 1996; Geertz 1973) and action research (Kemmis and McTaggart 1988). Participant observation and semi-structured interviews were conducted with 17 participants over the duration of their degree studies with the interviews first audiotaped, then transcribed, and finally analysed using a thick layered approach (Martin-McDonald 2000).

The second methodology constituted a critical discourse analysis of conference papers presented at the *Transformations Conference* held at the Australian National University in Canberra, the Australian Capital Territory, in December 2006 (*Transformations: Culture and the Environment in Human Development*

2006). Discourse analysis, when used together with a multidisciplinary approach to the study of language, provides the critic with a tool for studying communication within socio-cultural contexts (Van Dijk 1995). Ideology also plays a critical role as in this methodological approach it is viewed as an interpretation framework that organizes sets of attitudes about other elements of modern society. Ideologies, therefore, provide the cognitive foundation for the attitudes of various groups in societies, as well as the furtherance of their own goals and interests (ibid.). The *Transformations Conference* was selected as its goal was cultural transition and transformation:

> [to shift] the understanding and practice of multiculturalism within the Australian context, to explore how cultural diversity should be seen as both an asset and as an issue that should be integrated into all policy, planning and programs whether this happens at the precinct, or the global levels.
>
> *(Transformations* 2006: 4)

Fourteen papers were analysed along with two keynote addresses.

Critical discourse analysis is also the methodology selected to investigate the workplace learning context and the ways in which new employees learn how to work confidently and competently in a workplace setting. This analysis is in its initial stage. The literature review confirms, however, that it is an area that warrants further research (Thorpe *et al.* 2005). Fuller *et al.* (2005) argue for example that further in-depth studies of workplace learning in a wide a range of contexts are required if all the issues affecting learning and their interrelationships are to be fully understood and theorized. This is especially important, Fuller *et al.* (2005) note, because complex settings such as workplaces play a crucial role in the configuration of opportunities and barriers to learning that employees encounter.

The deficit-discourse shift

The application of CDT and the reconceptualization of the processes of transition generated a theoretical shift: the deficit-discourse shift. The shift draws on the primacy of discourses and literacies in a learning context. It characterizes new learning contexts as dynamic and embodying a multiplicity of discourses/literacies. Transition can be depicted as a journey of gaining familiarity, and ultimately mastery, of these discourses and literacies. Lankshear *et al.* (1997) contend that to feel comfortable in and perform with competence within a culture means becoming literate in that culture – becoming familiar with the multiplicity of new discourses in the culture. To Thorpe *et al.* (2005), pedagogy is the expertise enabling non-discourse speakers to participate within the discourse and become increasingly confident speakers and writers within it. They argue (2005: 4) that a key aspect is that it does not adopt a deficit model of the learner. Instead it recognizes learners as experienced meaning makers within their own discourse communities, 'with the

the highly developed skills adults possess for meaning making through inter-subjectivity – the sharing of frames of reference through which utterances make sense and develop the discourse taking place'.

The new learning framework

The deficit-discourse shift can be illustrated in a conceptual model, the New Learning Framework (see Figure 9.1). The framework illustrates the new learning context and its multiplicity of mainstream, often implicit, discourses, literacies and practices. A new learner's transition is represented as a journey: as the processes of being familiar with, engaging, mastering and, ultimately, demonstrating these literacies and discourses.

As the framework is essentially process-orientated it is applicable to a range of learning contexts. The chapter will next outline its application to HE, workplace and inter-cultural contexts.

Higher education learning contexts

Among the first of the discourses/literacies students need to engage and demonstrate in a HE learning context are their first semester subjects or courses – each of which encompasses specific cultural knowledge and practices. As the following list shows these are extensive and many may not be explicit. Each subject, for example, has its specific prerequisites and/or assumed entry knowledge; subject matter (content or process orientated, text-bound, oral or

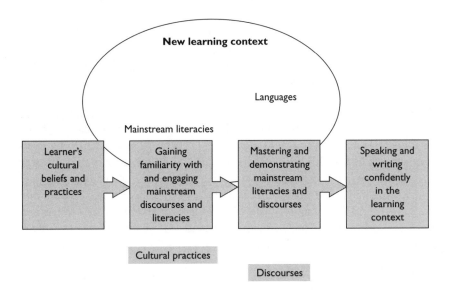

Figure 9.1 New Learning Framework (source: adapted from Lawrence 2004).

computer-mediated); language; texts (study packages, lecture notes, Power-Point notes, Web CT documents, CD-ROM); cultural practices (ways of dressing and showing respect – professor, first names); attendance (lectures, tutorials, practical sessions, clinical sessions); study mode (external/internal/online); behaviours (rule-governed/flexible, compulsory/optional attendance, consultation times, electronic discussion groups); class participation (passive, interactive, experiential); rules (about extensions, participation, resubmissions, appeals); theoretical assumptions (scientific/sociological); research methodologies (positivist/interpretive/critical, quantitative/qualitative); ways of thinking (recall, reflective, analytical or critical, surface or deep); referencing systems; ways of writing; structure (particularly in relation to assessment); tone and style; formatting; and assessment. To pass the subject, students need to become literate in all these practices.

Their subject is not the only discourse that students need to master. Each discipline area, section, faculty, group of students and staff group has their own discourses. As Figure 9.2 demonstrates, these can include administrative discourses; academic and/or tertiary literacies; academic numeracy; research discourses/paradigms; computer systems; communication and information technologies; library and database literacies; faculty, department, discipline and subject discourses; learning and teaching environments; student discourses (school leaver, mature age, international, on-campus, external, online); and learning styles (independent and self-directed learning styles). A nursing student explains the complexity involved:

> I found learning to use computers, the web, and referencing, technical jargon (anatomy and physiology), academic writing, medical calculations and maths so overwhelming that I wanted to leave. It wasn't helped that I had to get along with many younger students and get used to different methods of learning and teaching.[1]

A plethora of social and personal transitions are also involved. Students need to balance and master the study/work/family/life discourses that are often critical to their perseverance (Tinto 2005). These discourses include inter-personal and financial literacies (as university study becomes more expensive in many countries and as greater numbers of students are engaged in paid work), time and stress management practices as well as the accommodation of a range of 'life's demands', for example the need to engage and to learn to balance work, social and personal demands. A mature-age psychology student explains the difficulties involved:

> I haven't got the support that I thought that I had. So that made study-ing a lot more difficult. It comes down to the nitty gritty of how much work that you need to put in and how much sacrifice you need to make in your personal life. Others around me didn't comprehend that I was going to be so involved and have so little time for them.

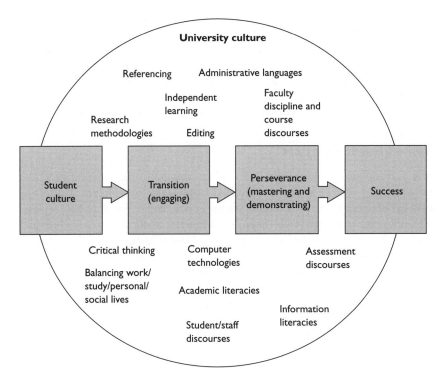

Figure 9.2 The New Learning Framework applied to HE (source: adapted from Lawrence 2005).

Workplace learning contexts

The framework is also relevant to new workplace learning contexts. Thorpe *et al.* (2005) confirm, for instance, that pedagogy is explicit in the formal training that might be given around technically complex job roles, both on and off the job. They argue that:

> Workplaces may at first sight appear pedagogy free, but, as Unwin *et al.* suggest, 'the extent to which workplaces exhibit the formal trappings of the traditional educational institution can certainly be surprising', in a reference to artefacts that codify knowledge and act as boundary objects between practices.
>
> (2005: 3)

In a new or unfamiliar workplace, learning contexts, such as languages and practices, may include organizational literacies, business planning and budgeting practices, culture building, performance appraisal and management systems, employment conditions, mental models, leadership practices and human resources practices like code of conduct protocols, promotion and professional development and training practices. As well, like HE, there are also the more informal discourses explicit in the new workplace. Unwin *et al.* (2005) identify, for example, strong relationships of association between individual learning opportunities, work organization and company performance. For example, in Britain, the current emphasis on employee involvement (EI) as a strategy for increasing performance is assumed to foster learning and play a strong role (ibid.).

Inter-cultural contexts

Inter-cultural transitions embrace the identification of the cultural practices and discourses present in the new inter-cultural learning contexts. These cultural beliefs and practices include practices and languages that are explicit but also those that may be taken-for-granted, implicit, unconscious and hidden. They may include: verbal behaviours; non-verbal behaviours; naming, greeting, work, wellness/sickness and grieving practices, etc.; cultural rituals; daily practices in relation to food; communication practices; spiritual practices; myths, stories and heritage; approaches to conflict; value orientations (Ferraro 2002); and worldviews (Hall 2005) (see Figure 9.3).

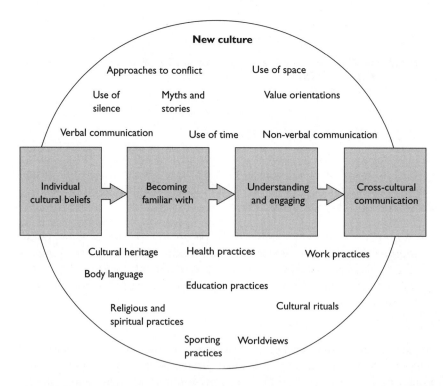

Figure 9.3 The New Learning Framework applied to intercultural contexts (source: adapted from Lawrence 2007).

New Learning Framework: implications

The New Learning Framework thus provides a means of identifying and making explicit the practices and languages present in a new learning context. The framework also reveals the complexities and nuances inherent in transition. The first complexity is the recognition that the same practice/behaviour may have different meanings in different contexts. A second complexity is that each time we communicate in a different context new learners do so from the viewpoint/worldview of their own understandings and background: that they embody and bring with them their own cultural knowledge/worldview/discourses and these may – or may not – be in tune with those in the new context. The processes of gaining familiarity include, then, the awareness that learners may interpret a new context's practices and behaviours from the basis of their own understandings and capital.

The conceptualization of transition embodied in the shift and the framework assists new learners to identify the (often less explicit) discourses and literacies in a diversity of new learning contexts, including new HE, workplace and inter-cultural contexts. This is an important first step in helping new learners raise their awareness of the context's mainstream discourses and literacies. It also alerts new learners to the importance of engaging and mastering mainstream literacies. However, the shift and the framework, in themselves, do not provide recipes for actively empowering learners. They don't encompass, for example, practical strategies that learners can integrate into their 'modus operandi' to assist them to master new discourses and literacies.

The Model for Transition Practices

A second model, the Model for Transition Practices presents three practical, dynamic strategies that can assist learners to make an effective transition. The three practices, which also stem from the application of theoretical perspectives, include reflective, socio-cultural and critical practice.

Reflective practice

The notion of reflective practice, as it is understood in this chapter, emerges from both educational (Boud and Walker 1990; Schön 1987) and sociological (Giddens 1996) literature. Reflective practice gives emphasis to learners' capacities to observe, to watch and listen to the cultural practices occurring at the site. The understanding of reflective practice also encompasses the concepts of 'reflection in action' and 'reflection on action' (Schön 1987) as well as 'reflection before action' (Boud and Walker 1990). Through these processes of reflection, learners continually reshape their approaches and develop 'wisdom' or 'artistry' in their practice.

The power of observation and reflection in both inter-cultural and workplace contexts was illustrated in the critical analysis of the *Transformations Conference* (2006) papers. For example, Beaumont (paper 54) discusses the value of spiritual reflection in relation to inclusivity in workplace contexts. Chiswell

(60), meanwhile, advocates the use of reflection in three areas: to help young Mexican Australians engage in an exploration of their own sense of cultural identity; to help her reflect on her experience of presenting her research; and to assist conference participants to engage in a mini exploration of their own sense of cultural identity through their reflections on her research video. Fialdo (67) notes the power of reflection when she described how an enquiring, self-reflective process committed to organizational transformation informed the Workforce Diversity Strategy at the University of Western Australia.

Testaments by HE learners also verify the efficacy of observation and reflection in relation to their learning practices: 'I basically asked a lot of questions. I talked to other people I knew out here and I also just listened and just basically figured it out' (Psychology student).

> Each semester, I further refined my method of attack to succeed in my studies. I analysed what my weak points were and worked on them to improve. Overall, I discovered that the transition is a continual on-going process throughout the degree on a daily basis. Each new subject requires some level of transition from the previous subject, and each year makes you stretch just that bit further than the previous year, and so the growing pains never stop.
>
> (Education student)

Socio-cultural practice

Socio-cultural practice stems from both constructivist approaches and cross-cultural communication theory (CCT). Constructivism, developed from the Piagetian individual development paradigm, accommodates the Vygotskian paradigm of cognitive development within a social setting (Azzarito and Ennis 2003). Its application to new learning contexts raises awareness about how social setting and context influence the individual cognitive process, and thus meaningful learning, and suggests that new learning contexts can be viewed as communities of learners (Plourde and Alawiye 2003). From this perspective, learning can be seen to take place in a social setting and occur through peer interactions, learner ownership and learning experiences that are authentic for students (Azzarito and Ennis 2003). Wenger accommodates this understanding when discussing the *horizontality* of learning, a process involving negotiation among learning partners (cited in Crossan and Mayes 2005). Research also documents the benefits of developing learning relationships where learners learn from, or through, others. Edwards (2005) reflects that the workplace, home and community are all held to be domains of learning. Duncan *et al.* (2004) value authentic learning sites that include, potentially, much of what is recognized in formally prescribed learning opportunities but they also include much that is not prescribed such as home, peer group and personal relations, accidents, career and other aspirations, and even sleep.

Socio-cultural practice also emerges from CCT. CCT is usually applied to international or English-as-a-second language learners adjusting to an unfamiliar host culture or context (Bandura 1986; Ferraro 2002; Hofstede 1997). CCT contends that, in order to reap maximum benefits from an unfamiliar context, learners need to establish interpersonal relations and communicate effectively in the new context. Integral to these learning processes is an individual's self-efficacy, the belief that he or she can successfully perform social behaviours in academic and everyday situations (Bandura 1986). Bandura's social learning model is utilized as the basis of a cross-cultural communication programme, *ExcelL: Excellence in Cultural Experiential Learning and Leadership Program* (Mak *et al.* 1998). *ExcelL* enables learners who have recently arrived to be competent and effective in dealing with members of the host context. *ExcelL* not only emphasizes the role of socio-cultural competencies in helping new learners adjust to an unfamiliar context, it also prioritizes specific socio-cultural competencies. These are seeking help and information, participating in a group, making social contact, seeking and offering feedback, expressing disagreement and refusing requests.

A major thread emerging from the *Transformations Conference* analysis, for example, was the pivotal role played by the competency of accessing sources of help and information. Papers prioritized its benefits and/or used the conference to announce sources of support in the process of being developed. Cunningham (paper 63), for example, discusses a resource location tool, *My Language*, which enables new and emerging communities to access web-based services and information sources. Cooke (62) emphasizes the importance of seeking help and information in relation to the judicial environment whereas Mosford and Trudinger (79) outline the value of two community projects conducted by Fairfield City Council.

Presentations also discuss the role of group participation and making social contact in helping people from both diverse and mainstream cultures become more familiar with 'other' cultures. The competencies' use facilitates the development of mentors, networks, learning communities, communities of practice, friendship groups and increased access to resources/sources of help. The *Transformations Conference* analysis demonstrates the power and efficacy of these twin socio-cultural practices: as a collaborative process; as a context for lobbying and public relations; and as an opportunity to network and build collaborations.

The socio-cultural practices of providing (negative) feedback, expressing disagreement and refusing requests are 'risky' in that there is a potential for offence; however, their use is essential if learners are to master and demonstrate unfamiliar literacies/discourses. The analysis of *Transformations Conference* presentations demonstrates the effectiveness of the practices in both inter-cultural and workplace contexts. Their use encouraging cultural diversity (Calma: 57); fostering sustainability and protected area management (Cater and Dyer: 58); bridging gaps between cultural diversity, community engagement, organizational/professional health cultures and policy development (Chalmers: 59); facilitating moves towards self-determination (Zagala: 92); and overcoming barriers to workforce participation by skilled migrants (Weeraratne: 91).

An essential feature of the socio-cultural practices is that they are socially and culturally appropriate or fine-tuned to the particular context, literacy or discourse being engaged. The specific verbal and non-verbal means of asking for help or refusing a request differs in different contexts, cultures, discipline and workplaces. For example, in terms of verbal communication, learners need to consider the appropriate words to use: whether to ask directly or indirectly or include explanations or reasons or not. In the HE context a nursing student notes:

> It's not a good idea to just walk in and say 'Look this is crap'. You can't bulldoze your way through: you have to be tactful about it.... 'Look, I agree with this, but I think I've been hard done by with this bit for this reason.'

When making social contact, some topics are 'taboo' in some contexts but acceptable in others (for example, in many contexts it would be considered 'rude' to discuss personal information on first acquaintance). In terms of non-verbal communication, learners need to think about body language – whether their non-verbal behaviours like posture, eye contact, tone of voice, pace, volume and pitch, how close they stand, etc., are appropriate to the situation and to the task.

The use of the competencies is also more complex than it first appears, dependent on the capital and belief systems and understandings each learner embodies and brings to the new context. Seeking help, for instance, may not be 'culturally' valued (in individualist self-reliant cultures), or an indication of weakness or a lack of confidence in others. Some learners may feel they do not have the right to ask, or equate help as 'remedial', or perceive it as a sign of 'sucking up', or 'uncool'. In HE, for example: 'I don't feel confident enough to speak to my tutor about the essay question because they might think I am stupid or something' (Psychology student); 'When I went to school it [asking for help] was a sign that you weren't coping or you weren't achieving. If you asked for help it wasn't looked on as a very good situation' (Nursing student). The *Transformations Conference* analysis also acknowledges the reticence/reluctance of some communities to request help or access sources of support. Allenby (52) argues that 'Australian arts/multicultural organisations must encourage cultural dialogues with an (Australian/Palestinian) community which has lost faith in the processes of (multi) cultural community support, and provide assurance that their voice is not being silenced.' The use of refusing a request, expressing disagreement and offering negative feedback can also be problematic, dependent on culturally appropriate strategies and on being fine-tuned to the particular context engaged. Khan (71) outlines the use of development processes to work with disadvantaged groups to overcome exclusion from community life and services. Lawrence (74) documents the difficulties of giving (negative) feedback to a high status lecturer in a HE context.

Critical practice

Critical practice encompasses twin capacities: people's capabilities for a self-awareness of their own belief systems and cultural practices (critical self-awareness) and their awareness of power configurations impacting on the processes of transition/retention (critical discourse awareness). This awareness includes students' capabilities for language critique including 'their capacities for reflexive analysis of the educational process itself' (Fairclough 1995: 1). Kelly (2003: 3) suggests that critical self-awareness requires a 'continued attention to the place from which we speak' whereas Gee (1999) describes it as the need to make visible to ourselves who we are and what we are doing. It incorporates people's capacities for unpacking their own cultural perspectives and belief systems (their socio-cultural capital), as well as their readiness to challenge these and to transform them if the need arises.

Critical discourse awareness differs from critical self-awareness in that it concentrates on the power configurations operating in the context or setting and underscores the role of social/cultural critique of the discourses operating at the educational site (Fairclough 1995). Learners provide evidence of the importance of applying critical practice (of both self and discourse) in an HE context: 'I've always worked in jobs where I've told people what to do. Now I'm in a role where I'm being told what to do and that is hard' (Business student).

> I asked for help and was told that 'No, I'm not giving you the lecture notes, because I don't know whether you went to lectures or not, and you'll just give them to your little network of friends that didn't go, and that will help them pass the exam'. Their idea assumes that not coming to the lectures means you were going down to the pub drinking beer or something ... There are implications for a mature-age person with a job.
>
> (Arts student)

The *Transformations Conference* analysis also provides evidence of the importance of applying critical practice (of both self and discourse) in both intercultural and workplace contexts. Lillian Holt, in her address as Conference Patron, refers to these practices as 'to look within' and 'to look without' and invoked Nelson Mandela's challenge 'to change ourselves'. Lillian Holt also maintains that 'to label was to limit'. The Conference Convenor, Professor Galla, appealed for a 'conceptual shift' to overturn negative views of diversity, calling for a new paradigm of human development to make the acceptance of difference (diversity) a part of everyone's life, common to humanity. Other presentations petitioned for a redefinition of the way government bodies and individuals respond to diversity (Khan: 71; Lawrence: 74).

Dynamic practices

The three practices are dynamic. The successful use of one of the practices often depends on the use of another and, if implemented together, they can be more effective in assisting learners to make a successful transition and to achieve their learning goals and objectives. For example, observation and reflection are prerequisites for fine-tuning the socio-cultural competencies to the particular context being engaged. Likewise, the socio-cultural properties of the competencies rely on learners' capacities to reflect and provide (appropriate) feedback about the mainstream practices. The socio-cultural properties of the practices also depend on learners' capacities to appraise not only their own cultural assumptions and expectations but also the external, and often hidden, assumptions and power configurations impacting in the new learning context. The capacities of learners to challenge and, where it is possible, to transform the unhelpful policies and practices operating in the context also rely on learners' use of the socio-cultural practices of offering feedback, expressing disagreement and refusing a request.

Conclusion

The two models conceptualize the processes involved in making effective transitions to new learning contexts. The first model identifies and makes explicit the specific literacies and practices learners need to engage with if they are to communicate confidently in the new context. The second model provides three practical and dynamic strategies that assist learners to accomplish these transitions. Together, the two models provide learners with a means of transforming their practices, of integrating into their 'modus operandi' practical capabilities for lifelong learning in a diversity of new learning contexts.

The analysis provides implications for our understanding of transitions to post-school learning contexts. The first is the need for any new learning context to identify and make explicit its discourses. This means making explicit the practices and artefacts through which learning is mediated as well as acknowledging the idea that objects may be part of many contexts. The second implication is that while this process of learning should not be seen as one of deficit there may be discourses resonating both within the learner and the new context that may intervene against learners making comfortable transitions. If the learner is unfamiliar with the worldviews and discourses of the new learning context, such as coping with mismatched levels of social capital, the role of critical self and discourse awareness then becomes vital. This implies that transition can involve a process of negotiation between the new learner and the context. The final implication is that the need to make transitions into new learning contexts is becoming relentless in our progressively more complex and multifaceted world. Thus transition skills are becoming essential: lying at the heart of lifelong learning.

Note

1 The student quotes cited in the chapter stem from the HE case study.

References

Azzarito, L. and Ennis, C.D. (2003) 'A sense of connection: Toward social constructivist physical education', *Sport, Education and Society* 8, 179–198.

Bandura, A. (1986) *Social Foundations of Thought and Action: A social cognitive theory*, Englewood Cliffs, NJ: Prentice Hall.

Boud, D. and Walker, D. (1990) 'Making the most of experience', *Studies in Continuing Education* 1, 61–80.

Bourdieu, P. (1999) *The Weight of the World: Social suffering in contemporary society*, Cambridge: Polity Press.

Carspecken, P.H. (1996) *Critical Ethnography in Educational Research*, New York: Routledge.

Cope, B. and Kalantzis, M. (2000) *Multiliteracies: Literacy learning and the design of social futures*, New York: Routledge.

Crossan, B. and Mayes, T. (2005) 'Learning relationships in community based FE, contexts, communities, networks: Mobilising learners' resources and relationships in different domains', Centre for Research in Lifelong Learning, Glasgow Caledonian University and the University of Stirling, February.

Duncan, B., Gallacher, J., Mayes, T., Smith, L. and Watson, D. (2004) 'Understanding learning cultures in community based further education: Working together towards enhancement', Centre for Research in Lifelong Learning, Glasgow Caledonian University and the University of Stirling, November.

Edwards, R. (2005) 'Contexts, boundary objects and hybrid spaces: Theorising learning in lifelong learning'. Paper presented at the SCUTREA Annual Conference. 35th Annual SCUTREA Conference, University of Sussex, UK, 5–7 July.

Eraut, M. (2004) 'Informal learning in the workplace', *Studies in Continuing Education* 26, 247–274.

Fairclough, N. (1995) *Critical Discourse Analysis: The critical study of language*, London: Longman.

Ferraro, G. (2002) *Knowledge and Competencies for the 21st Century*, New York: Intercultural Associates Inc.

Fuller, A., Hodkinson, H., Hodkinson, P. and Unwin, L. (2005) 'Learning as peripheral participation in communities of practice: A reassessment of key concepts in workplace learning', *British Educational Research Journal* 31, 49–68.

Gee, J.P. (1999) *An Introduction to Discourse Analysis: Theory and method*, London: Routledge.

Geertz, C. (1973) *The Interpretation of Cultures*, New York: Basic.

Giddens, A. (1996) *In Defence of Sociology: Essays, interpretations and rejoinders*, Cambridge: Polity Press.

Hall, P. (2005) 'Interprofessional teamwork: Professional cultures as barriers', *Journal of Interprofessional Care* 1, 188–196.

Hofstede, G. (1997) *Cultures and Organizations: Software of the mind*, London: McGraw-Hill.

Kelly, P. (2003) 'Responding to diversity in tertiary teaching and learning'. Presentation to the USQ Academic Staff Development Program, University of Southern Queensland, Toowoomba, 20 November.

Kemmis, S. and McTaggart, R. (eds) (1988) *The Action Research Reader* (2nd edn), Geelong: Deakin University Press.

Lankshear, C., Gee, P., Knobel, M. and Searle, C. (1997) *Changing Literacies*, Buckingham: Open University Press.

Lawrence, J. (2004) 'University journeys: Alternative entry students and their construction of a means of succeeding an unfamiliar university culture'. Unpublished thesis submitted for the degree of PhD, University of Southern Queensland, Toowoomba.

Lawrence, J. (2005) 'Reconceptualising attrition and retention: Integrating theoretical, research and student perspectives', *Studies in Learning, Evaluation and Development* 2, 16–33. Online, available at: http://sleid.cqu.edu.au (accessed 10 November 2008).

Lawrence, J. (2007) 'Two models for facilitating cross-cultural communication and engagement', *International Journal of Diversity in Organisations, Communities and Nations*, 6, 73–82.

Luke, A. (1999) 'Critical discourse analysis', in J.P. Keeves and G. Lakomski (eds), *Issues in Educational Research*, Amsterdam: Pergamon.

Mak, A.S., Westwood, M.J., Barker, M.C. and Ishiyama, F.I. (1998) *The ExcelL Program: Excellence in experiential learning and leadership*, Brisbane: Lyonco.

Martin-McDonald, K. (2000) 'Finding meaning in being dialysis-dependent: A constructivist perspective'. Thesis submitted for the degree of PhD, University of Southern Queensland, Toowoomba.

New London Group (1996) 'A pedagogy of multiliteracies: Designing social futures', *Harvard Educational Review* 66, 60–92.

Plourde, L.A. and Alawiye, O. (2003) 'Constructivism and elementary preservice science teacher preparation: Knowledge to application', *College Student Journal* 37, 334–342.

Schön, D.A. (1987) *Educating the Reflective Practitioner: Toward a new design for teaching and learning in the professions*, San Francisco, CA: Jossey-Bass.

Thorpe, M., Miller, K. and Edwards, R. (2005) 'The situatedness and mobility of learning: Pedagogical, theoretical and research issues'. Paper presented at the TLRP Annual Conference, Queens University, Belfast, 28–30 November.

Tinto, V. (2005) 'Foreword', in A. Seidman (ed.), *College Student Retention: Formula for student success*, Westport, CT: American Council on Education/Praeger, pp. ix–x.

Transformations 2006, Canberra: Union Offset Printers.

Transformations: Culture and the environment in human development 2005, Canberra: Union Offset Printers.

Unwin, L., Ashton, D., Butler, P., Clarke, J., Felstead, A., Fuller, A. and Lee, T. (2005) 'Worlds within worlds: The relationship between context and pedagogy in the workplace'. Paper produced for ESRC TLRP Thematic Seminar Series: 'Contexts, communities, network: Mobilising learners' resources and relationships in different domains', Glasgow Caledonian University, February.

Van Dijk, T.A. (1995) 'Discourse, semantics and ideology', *Discourse and Society* 6, 243–289.

Yin, R.K. (2003) *Case Study Research Design and Methods*, Beverly Hills, CA: Sage Publications.

Chapter 10

Worlds of difference

'Dual sector' institutions and higher education transitions

Ann-Marie Bathmaker and Will Thomas

Introduction

Differentiation and stratification are widely acknowledged features of mass higher education (HE) in England. The differentiation of provision to meet the needs of varied student groups, and the stratification of the system, whereby there is a division of labour amongst different institutions to meet the needs of these varied groups (Scott 1995), appear to run hand in hand (Gallacher 2006). A positive reading of this seeks to support new and alternative forms of HE, in order to embrace student diversity (see, for example, the collections edited by Duke 2005; Duke and Layer 2005). Literature concerned with inequalities in HE suggests a more critical reading of these developments, and points to how stratification may compound disadvantage whilst apparently widening opportunities (for example, Bhatti 2003; Bowl 2003; Reay *et al*. 2005; Naidoo 2004).

This chapter does not seek to reassert claims that mass HE brings inequalities along with diversity, but explores the tensions incurred through differentiation and stratification in practice, focusing on a growing area of higher education provision, that offered by 'dual' sector institutions (Garrod and Macfarlane 2006). By this we mean institutions that offer not just higher education, but what in England is referred to as 'further education' (FE), that is, a variety of forms of tertiary education at sub-degree levels. We are interested in how higher education in such contexts may be shaped, and also may work to shape understandings and experience of higher education in the twenty-first century. We do this through a focus on transitions, which we consider at three different, but interrelated levels: institutions in transition, transitions in institutions and students' experience of transition.[1]

The chapter comes out of work on a two-year study of widening participation in English higher education, the FurtherHigher Project.[2] This study used both qualitative and quantitative methods to investigate the changing shape and experience of HE in England. The fieldwork included interviews with 82 students, 35 course tutors and 11 senior managers in four case study 'dual sector' institutions, alongside documentary analysis, and the collection of fieldwork observation records. In this chapter we consider how transition worked at different levels to shape and construct meanings and identities in higher education in the context of one of the four case study institutions, East Heath College.

Our analysis draws on Bourdieu's concepts of field and habitus (Bourdieu 1986, 1990, 1997), and we discuss briefly, next, how these concepts have shaped our thinking. We then use the three levels of transition identified above to present data from East Heath College. We argue that the work that transition is doing involves processes of 'positioning', whereby both institution and individuals work at defining their place within higher education. Since such positioning both highlights and helps to create a differentiated and stratified system, which operates in the context of wider inequalities both within and beyond the education system, such work raises issues for social justice and equity. We conclude by pointing to the unsettling and complex issues this raises in relation to social justice and equity.

From elite to mass HE: institutions in transition

Following Trow's (1973) typology, the English HE system has been in transition from an elite to a mass and now nearly universal system since the Robbins Report of the 1960s (Committee on Higher Education 1963). However, as Scott's work (1995) suggests, it would be more accurate to describe the current system as an elite, mass and universal system all at the same time, with different parts of the system functioning in different ways.

A development in the mass part of the system is an increasing role for 'dual sector' institutions. These institutions work across overlapping but currently separate educational fields in the English system – further and higher education. They offer a range of HE qualifications, in particular two-year vocational sub-Bachelor degrees. As they become bigger players in the HE field, these institutions are undergoing processes of transition as they work to position and sometimes to reinvent themselves within the field of HE.

Such work may include the amalgamation of institutions, the formation of partnerships between institutions, the acquisition of new buildings and changes to the role of particular spaces and places, such as the creation of HE-specific teaching environments, or study centres for dissertation students. This shaping and forming of institutional cultures and identities has been connected to the notion of institutional habitus by Reay et al. (2005). They use 'habitus' to draw attention to how organizational cultures are linked to the wider fields in which institutions operate, whereby an institutional habitus embodies structures in the wider field, but there is also a process of mutual shaping and reshaping – an interplay of structure and agency, but always within the context of the power of the field. What our research has found is that dual sector institutions do not have one institutional culture. Instead they appear to have a culture and habitus that relates to the FE field, and a separate culture and habitus that relates to the HE field.

In using the concepts of habitus and field to develop a deeper understanding of institutional cultures, Reay et al. (2005) build on the work of Bourdieu, who studied the field of HE in the context of the French education system of the 1960s (Bourdieu 1990, 1996; Bourdieu and Passeron 1990). In *Reproduction* (1990, first published in 1970), Bourdieu and Passeron argued that the HE system contributes to reproducing and legitimating the social structure. They conceptualized HE as a sorting machine that selects students according to an implicit social classification and reproduces them according to an explicit academic classification, which in reality is very similar to the implicit social classification. Whilst Bourdieu's later work moved on to a more complex and nuanced understanding of reproduction (Harker 1990), the point they make in *Reproduction* is useful here. They emphasize that the role of individual institutions in the process of reproduction is due to their positioning in the system or field of HE. In putting forward this argument, they emphasize the need for a relational understanding of the field of HE, that is, an understanding of the networks within which particular forms of HE are placed, and the relationships between them, which create hierarchies of more and less valued/valuable HE. In the twenty-first century, and in the context of mass HE, we would argue that HE institutions are not just *placed* within the field of HE, but have to work increasingly hard at constructing a place for themselves within the field, which more and more resembles an HE market.

Student transitions in a changing world of HE

In a mass system, HE may be seen as a 'possible' future (Bourdieu and Passeron 1990: 227) for an increasing number of people in England, but this does not mean that all forms of HE can be taken for granted by all students (Bourdieu and Wacquant 1992). As Reay *et al.* (2005: 52) observe in their research: 'Students needed to be aware of particular segments of the higher education market depending on their own specific positioning within the field.'

In our study, it might be anticipated that there would be a convergence of interests between the institution, teaching staff and students, around transition from FE to HE provision within the same institution. However, what we found in the context of the case study college discussed below, were contradictory processes of positioning, where there was not necessarily a fit between students' expectations and horizons for action, the operation of the college in relation to HE and the strategic positioning of the institution by senior managers. In the next part of the chapter we look at FE/HE transitions as experienced in the context of East Heath College.

East Heath College in transition

East Heath College was one of the largest 'mixed-economy' colleges, combining further and higher education, in the country. It was formed in 1957 when various local institutions were brought together to form the 'Civic College'. In 1974, the name was changed to East Heath College of Further and Higher Education – the name reflecting the fact that the college had been delivering qualifications awarded by the Council for National Academic

Awards (CNAA)[3] since 1968. In the 1980s this provision grew significantly in partnership with a number of validating partners. A sole validating partner agreement with a nearby research-intensive university (University A) was signed in 1992.

However, in August 2007, the college's further and higher education provision were divided and two separate organizations formed. This split is interpreted here as a strategic 'repositioning' of the provision of post-compulsory education within the catchment of East Heath College. Rather than a blurring of the boundaries between the FE and HE sectors, the creation of New East Heath College (NEHC) and University Centre East Heath (UCEH) re-established the separation of the two sectors and underlined the existing stratification of the education system.

Table 10.1 provides a picture of structures in the three institutions (East Heath College, New East Heath College and University Centre East Heath), showing the reconfiguration that took place in August 2007. Broadly speaking, these new configurations reflect and reinforce existing sectoral boundaries, with all further education going to NEHC and almost all higher education going to UCEH. The only exceptions to this are small pockets of HE funded by the Learning and Skills Council (for example the Association of Accounting Technicians Level 4 qualification). In addition, NEHC acts as a UCEH delivery centre initially delivering some foundation degrees reflecting existing staff specialisms within the college. Foundation degrees are two-year (full-time) sub-Bachelor degree level qualifications that combine academic study with workplace learning.

What prompted this re-positioning of HE? In part, the creation of UCEH was a response to the lack of a university within the East Heath area, although HE has been available in the area for 40 years. Rhetoric surrounding the creation of UCEH makes it clear that the institution does not view its role as purely one of widening participation; the institution's website claims that its role is to 'staunch [East Heath's] brain drain which sees students migrate to other counties'. The new institution has a clear economic, as well as social and educational role.

Although the structures of the new institutions are somewhat complex, it is clear that the decisions taken to create two new institutions and formally to separate further and higher education in this way represents a strategic attempt to reposition both FE and HE within the East Heath area. This reflects benefits to be gained from allowing both institutions to create and develop their own identities.

UCEH is keen to define itself solely as an HE provider in a system that is stratified and differentiated at a policy and funding level. This strategy enables it to distinguish its provision from the old FE/HE college and from the new FE college. The latter distinction is particularly important; the success of UCEH is dependent on being able to show local people that it is an institution operating on a par with other universities and that it has moved away from the current perception of the 'Civic College'. The strategic repositioning of HE delivery in an institution aligned with (although not part of) the HE sector concerns the public perception of quality: that mixed-economy institutions provide lower-quality HE than institutions, which focus solely on HE delivery. Factually, provision at both East Heath College and now at University Centre East Heath is subjected to strict quality control mechanisms (as shown in Table 10.1).

Transitions in East Heath College

In the minds and actions of teaching and administration staff, HE and FE provision within East Heath College were split for some time before the formal separation, with boundaries and divisions between FE and HE work. During the 1997/1998 academic year East Heath College took the decision to split its FE and HE provision internally so that teaching and managerial staff no longer worked on both FE and HE courses.

Since this point, fewer and fewer members of teaching staff taught on both FE and HE courses. So, for example, one member of staff who was involved in the delivery of Media courses at the time reports that following the split, staff who had previously shared staffrooms no longer did so (and indeed the staffrooms may be in quite separate locations). As a result of this, staff who may have shared information, taught together and promoted transition from FE to HE within the institution in both formal and informal ways were less likely to do so. Communication between FE and HE tutors within the same subject area was severely limited by this split: there was no formal facility such as a subject area group for sharing information. In the case of business, the course tutor on the National Diploma (ND) Business did not have links with those teaching on HE business courses. Rather than having visits and teaching inputs from colleagues within the same institution, students visited business schools at other universities across the region.

A lack of communication between FE and HE staff was characterized in sports-related courses by a poor match between the content of the further education ND course and the HE Degree courses. Laura, course leader on the ND Sport (Sports Development and Fitness), commented in her interview that the Degree course offered at East Heath College focused too closely on sports science and that the students leaving the ND course tended to be more interested in sports management or sports development. In fact, FE provision had moved away from sports science type courses in response to the changing interests of their students.

Although progression routes existed through the East Heath College course provision, they were not necessarily encouraged either through actions of staff and students or institutional structures. Examples of possible routes included progression from the ND Business to either the BA Hons Business Management or the FdA Business Management; for students on the ND Sports, students could progress to BSc Sports Science, FdSC Sport, Health and Exercise or the BSc Science (foundation year). These routes, although *available* to students, were not *preferred* in the sense that students were

Table 10.1 A summary of the structural changes resulting from the repositioning of HE provision within the East Heath area

	East Heath College (EHC)	New East Heath College (NEHC)	University Centre East Heath (UCEH)
Formal status	Further Education College	Further Education College	Private Limited Company providing Higher Education, jointly owned by University A and University B (50/50 split)
Funding source	All HE numbers were directly funded through HEFCE, including significant NHS provision.	The LSC are responsible for funding all FE students.	Courses are indirectly funded through the two 'parent' institutions. Funding and student numbers will be split between these two institutions.
FE/HE balance	Approximately 60%–40%.	Entirely FE except for HE courses run at NEHC by UCEH.	100% HE with courses running at a number of centres across the East Heath area.
Franchise activity	EHC franchised out some provision to smaller FECs in the region.	NEHC does not participate in franchise activity.	UCEH formally franchises in its students from the 'parent' institutions – funding, numbers and validations runs through these institutions.
Quality arrangements	EHC was an accredited college of University A; Univ. A validated HE provision and retained ultimate QA responsibility but EHC retained significant autonomy.	All HE running at NEHC are UCEH courses, validated by Universities A and B.	Awards from UCEH are jointly validated by University A and University B. Univs A and B therefore retain and share formal QA responsibility for courses at UCEH.

Monitoring and reporting of data	EHC had an Academic Board: Quality Standards Committee, which dealt with both FE and HE matters. There were two Standards Committees of Corporation for HE and for FE. In December 2006, the Corporation resolved to disband the HE Academic Standards Committee. The functions of this committee were taken up by a corresponding committee of University Centre East Heath.	NEHC continues to have an Academic Board and an Academic Standards Committee and a Standards Committee of Corporation responsible for the monitoring of data.	UCEH operates its own internal data monitoring systems, including its own Academic Board. Formal monitoring of data and completion of HESES and HESA data occurs through Univ. A and Univ. B with students from UCEH being added to the returns regularly made by these institutions.
Non-prescribed HE	EHC ran a number of non-prescribed HE courses (non-HEFCE funded). Many of these were gradually converted to Univ. A validated courses in preparation for the split of provision in August 2007.	NEHC continues to run a very limited amount of non-prescribed HE – such as the Association of Accounting Technicians (Technician Level), which is a NQF Level 4 qualification.	UCEH does not run any HE provision with funding sources other than HEFCE. All courses which formally came into this category have now either been validated as Univ. A/B courses or will run as 'full-cost' courses without additional funding.

neither explicitly prepared for transition on to these courses nor were these options actively promoted to them.

As a result of these various factors, East Heath College may have been characterized as displaying two different cultures resulting from the split of internal structures in 1997/1998: one of FE study and one of HE study. The stratification within the education system was reinforced by staff and student attitudes, physical separation of teaching and administration spaces, and a lack of clear strategic commitment to promoting internal student progression. These cultures further complicated internal progression, requiring that students make the transition from one to another as they move from FE to HE within the college. For students, the experience of transition from FE to HE was similar to making the transition to another institution, both in terms of the process and in terms of the cultural differences.

Students' experiences of transition

The FurtherHigher research project focused on whether students chose to stay and progress within the same institution, where this was possible, or whether they chose to move elsewhere for the next level of study. At East Heath College there was little internal progression from Level 3 (FE) to Level 4 (first year of HE) with around 7 per cent of students making this transition each year. Instead of progressing internally, we found three patterns of progression amongst the students interviewed as part of this project: progression to other Higher Education Institutions (HEIs), progression to part-time higher level occupational qualifications while working and progression into work with no current or planned HE-level study.

Students on the ND Sports programme, generally speaking, progressed to HE at another institution. The ND course offered students the chance to try different types of sports-related study, from sports science to sports development. As a result of these opportunities, students looking to progress into higher education looked for different subjects or to progress in different ways. 'Some people have put in to go to university to do sports science because they like that area, and people want to become teachers and develop into a sporting role. Other people just go to work' (CX3004, interview 1, response 26). The primary motivation for choosing other locations to continue their studies was that they could not follow their chosen speciality at East Heath College (or at UCEH from 2007). In most cases, this choice was closely linked to their imagined future career and formed part of a plan for achieving their career goal. Other reasons cited included: wanting to move away or out of home, wanting a change or feeling that the course might be delivered better elsewhere. For students on this course who progressed to work rather than HE study various reasons were given, but most referred to the perceived cost of studying in HE or feeling that beginning full-time work offered a better vocational pathway.

Students on the ND Business showed a greater tendency to prefer a part-time mode of study, with most selecting an occupational higher-level qualification route (the Association of Accounting Technicians' Accountancy qualification). These students were no less committed to their anticipated careers, but they were happy to select this non-university route as one that was just as appropriate for their expectations and aspirations.

> I considered like university, but then I thought ... to get what I want I can do it through work and still get the same qualifications, get some experience in the workplace, and still get money. If you go to university you don't get none of the experience, as much, and you end up with loads of debt! ... And still wind up with the same thing.
>
> (CZ1001, interview 1, response 58)

'This way I don't get myself in debt and I still get paid for it. At university I'd have got myself in loads of debt for the same outcome really' (CZ1001, interview 3, response 19). Other students who were interviewed showed a similar aversion to debt and felt they could not afford or justify the expense of university study. Ryan, for example, stated that he 'probably would have considered it [university]' (CZ1005, interview 1, response 58) if it were not for the financial barriers. Ben also commented on the prohibitive cost of university study, saying, 'I've never been in debt in my life and I don't intend to' (CZ1003, interview 2, response 67).

Amongst students who did make the transition to HE, their interviews suggested three commonly experienced influences on the process of choosing a progression route following the conclusion of their FE studies: availability of information, the experience of making applications and finances. The ability to get hold of and to process information and advice about making the correct choice at a transition point was clearly important to students and made them very reliant on those who had the knowledge and experience to help them with this processing and positioning function. Many of the students we interviewed had limited experience of higher education within their immediate families or social groups. As a result, although family and friends were helpful to most students, many of them cited tutors as being particularly influential on their decision-making processes. One student, George, described what this meant for him. Although his family provided support and encouragement and he described them as 'really clever' and as working 'incredibly hard' in their schooling, none had studied at HE level before. The encouragement, but not pressure, from tutors was very important to him:

> Well the tutors were really good because they like didn't pressure you into like saying, 'oh you must go on for further education [sic]' or 'you must work', they gave you a choice. They asked you what you want to do ... like they asked what sort of course you wanted to do ... and then they go 'oh have you considered...?'
>
> (CX3003, interview 1, responses 70, 73 and 74)

His reliance on the advice and support of tutors reinforces the potential impact of structural divisions within East Heath College that served to keep further and higher education systems separate.

For students looking to make the transition between FE and HE, the UCAS application process marked the boundary between the two systems and highlighted the significance of the change. Once again, the process helped reinforce the reliance on experienced practitioners who were able to advise students on the application process and on how to write personal statements. One student, Craig, indicated how important tutors were in completing applications:

> Instead of having a tutorial for a month, we had like a sort of UCAS workshop-type session where if you were having problems with your forms, or with filling out the online thing you could go there and do. The tutor would sit down with you and say 'you need to be doing this' or help you with your personal statement ... putting in the right things, because I think when you're not used to writing things like that you can waffle a lot.
>
> (CX3006, interview 1, responses 39 and 40)

Most significant in the student interviews was the impact of finance on student perceptions of HE. Top-up fees played a key role in this, with many students in interviews commenting that they had trouble finding information and understanding how these fees might impact on them. Students needed to be proactive to find this information out, as Jessica explained:

> WT: Where did you get booklets about finance from? Were they available in college?
> JESSICA: No they weren't. I had to look at the internet to get a number and I had to ring up the local LEA to get it and then about a month later they were in college.
>
> (CX3004, interview 1, response 46)

The impact of financial considerations on student decision making is not straightforward and a variety of concerns were raised during the interviews: whether it might be cheaper to study nearby, whether there was a need to work part time and whether an HE course at university represented best value for money.

The above examples illustrate different patterns of positioning and repositioning at different levels that we found at East Heath College. At the structural level the separation of FE and HE provision as East Heath College split to form New East Heath College and University Centre East Heath can be interpreted as a response to a variety of pressures at local, regional and national levels. Primarily though, it serves to clarify the identity of the provision and to replicate and reinforce existing structures within the post-16 education system as a whole. At an institutional level, there is little evidence of the smooth transitions between further and higher education that supposedly might result from this type of mixed provision. Indeed, evidence from East Heath College suggests that within the college, making this transition required a cultural transition as great as that which might be experienced in moving to another institution. These cultural issues seem to limit internal progression despite the variety of possible routes open to students. At an individual level, the students we interviewed seemed to position themselves, through their choice of progression route, relative to their imagined future, their current circumstances and their family and social experiences. We have evidence of students making long-term plans and choosing between a variety of possible routes towards their intended goal. Influences on these decisions include family and social circumstances, finance and the availability of information.

Conclusions

In this chapter we have focused on transition at three different levels, and shown that student transitions take place in the context of a complex and moving field of HE provision. The work that transition is doing in the case study institution reveals processes of 'positioning', which are different and contradictory at different levels. The separation of FE and HE in the East Heath area can be interpreted as a repositioning of HE provision. This is justified on the basis that the new UCEH is acting as an economic driver for the area, but there is also evidence that UCEH is aiming to position itself in relation to two prestigious research-intensive universities, rather than maintain a close connection with FE. It could be argued that this may help potential students to gain more valuable cultural capital through studying at a higher-ranked institution.

However, the contradictory nature of this strategy is revealed in the unintended consequences of arrangements in the former East Heath College. Here, the strong boundaries between FE and HE within the institution meant that staff and courses were positioned in FE or HE, requiring students to negotiate the gap between these two 'worlds' just as they would if they moved to a different institution. In effect, the apparent advantage of offering both FE and HE in one institution was missed. This was despite the fact that the attitudes of students in the study towards HE were dominated by the sort of concerns that are associated with 'non-traditional' students from FE backgrounds, those of job goals and financial concerns (Widdowson 2005), which might lead them to consider seriously studying locally and in a familiar environment.

For students themselves, it turns out that transitions within the institution, and transitions to degree study did not necessarily match their imagined futures. The HE qualifications in sport did not necessarily reflect the specific interests of the Level 3 students, and the students studying Business recognized that an occupational qualification had more value than a degree in the jobs that they sought. It is unclear whether students' horizons for action were extended or limited by their experience of studying in a 'dual sector' institution, but there was certainly a sense in which students were positioning themselves in relation to higher-level study in ways that took account of and fitted in with their wider lives.

The various forms of transition taking place at East Heath College raise questions about the nature and impact of widening participation. What we found may be changing the current HE system, but does not appear fundamentally to challenge the power relations that are embodied in it. The work that transition currently appears to do is to create a more detailed nuancing of existing stratifications and inequalities within the system. How and whether this might relate to opportunities for greater access to the more powerful parts of the higher education field is unclear.

Notes

1 We have found a paper by James and Beedell (2006) very helpful in developing our ideas here. This is outlined in more detail in Bathmaker (2006).
2 The FurtherHigher Project was funded by the UK Economic and Social Research Council (Award Reference RES-139–25–0245) and was part of the ESRC's Teaching and Learning Research Programme. The members of the research team were Ann-Marie Bathmaker, Greg Brooks, Diane Burns, David Dale, Cate Goodlad, Liz Halford, Gareth Parry, Sammy Rashid, Andy Roberts, David Smith, Will Thomas, Anne Thompson and Val Thompson. Karen Kitchen was the research team administrator.
3 The Council for National Academic Awards (CNAA) was a degree-awarding authority in the United Kingdom from 1965 until 1992. The CNAA awarded academic degrees at polytechnics and other non-university institutions such as Colleges of Higher Education until they were awarded university status.

References

Bathmaker, A.M. (2006) 'Positioning themselves: Higher education transitions and "dual sector" institutions. Exploring the nature and meaning of transitions in FE/HE institutions in England'. Paper presented at the SRHE Conference in Brighton, 12–14 December. Online, available at: www.shef.ac.uk/furtherhigher/ (accessed 13 November 2008).

Bhatti, G. (2003) 'Social justice and non-traditional participants in higher education: A tale of "border crossing", instrumentalism and drift', in C. Vincent (ed.), *Social Justice, Education and Identity*, London: RoutledgeFalmer, pp. 65–82.

Bourdieu, P. (1986) *Distinction. A social critique of the judgement of taste*, London: Routledge.

Bourdieu, P. (1990) *Homo Academicus*, Cambridge: Polity Press.

Bourdieu, P. (1996) *The State Nobility. Elite schools in the field of power*, Cambridge: Polity Press.

Bourdieu, P. (1997) 'The forms of capital', in A.H. Halsey, H. Lauder, P. Brown and A. Stuart Wells (eds), *Education, Culture, Economy and Society*, Oxford: Oxford University Press, pp. 46–58.

Bourdieu, P. and Passeron, J.C. (1990) *Reproduction in Education, Society and Culture* (2nd edn), London: Sage.

Bourdieu, P. and Wacquant, L.J.D. (editor and translator) (1992) *An Invitation to Reflexive Sociology*, Cambridge: Polity Press.

Bowl, M. (2003) *Non-Traditional Entrants to Higher Education: 'They talk about people like me'*, Stoke on Trent: Trentham Books.

Committee on Higher Education (1963) *Higher Education. Report of the Committee on Higher Education* (the Robbins Report), Cmnd 2154, London: HMSO.

Duke, C. (ed.) (2005) *The Tertiary Moment. What road to inclusive higher education?* Leicester: National Institute of Adult Continuing Education.

Duke, C. and Layer, G. (eds) (2005) *Widening Participation. Which way forward for English higher education?* Leicester: National Institute of Adult Continuing Education.

Gallacher, J. (2006) 'Widening access or differentiation and stratification in higher education in Scotland', *Higher Education Quarterly* 60, 349–369.

Garrod, N. and Macfarlane, B. (2006) 'Scoping the duals: The structural challenges of combining further and higher education in post-compulsory education'. Paper presented at the SRHE Conference, Brighton, 12–14 December.

Harker, R. (1990) 'Bourdieu: Education and reproduction', in R. Harker, C. Mahar and C. Wilkes (eds), *An Introduction to the Work of Pierre Bourdieu*, London: Macmillan, pp. 86–108.

James, D. and Beedell, P. (2006) 'Transgression for Transition? Early reflections on the meaning of "transition" in the project Identities, Educational Choice and the White Urban Middle Class'. Paper presented at the TLRP Seminar Series 'Transitions through the Lifecourse', London, 16 May.

Naidoo, R. (2004) 'Fields and institutional strategy: Bourdieu on the relationship between higher education, inequality and society', *British Journal of Sociology of Education* 25, 457–471.

Reay, D., David, M.E. and Ball, S. (2005) *Degrees of Choice: Class, race, gender and higher education*, Stoke on Trent: Trentham Books.

Scott, P. (1995) *The Meanings of Mass Higher Education*, Buckingham: Open University Press.

Trow, M. (1973) *Problems in the Transition from Elite to Mass Higher Education*, Berkeley, CA: Carnegie Commission on Higher Education.

Widdowson, J. (2005) 'Implications for the mixed economy group of colleges', in C. Duke and G. Layer (eds), *Widening Participation: Which way forward for English higher education?* Leicester: National Institute of Adult Continuing Education, pp. 36–44.

Chapter 11

Improving transfer from vocational to higher education

International lessons

Gavin Moodie

Introduction

Researchers on Scottish higher education have expressed concern at the stratification of universities within a structurally unified sector and the bias of access by social class. Raab and Storkey (2001: 16–17) found that advantaged students were over-represented in the ancient universities, which are the most exclusive Scottish universities, in which they increased their enrolment from 1996–1997 to 1998–1999. McLaurin and Osborne (2002) and Osborne and McLaurin (2006) found that the ancient and old universities enrolled about half the proportion of students transferring from further education as the new, least exclusive universities. Morgan-Klein (2003: 351) reported that 'there is clear evidence that elite universities attract mainly middle-class students, while the post-1992 universities and the FE colleges are more successful in attracting students from lower socio-economic groups and from disadvantaged areas'. Field (2004: 12) concluded that 'The differential distribution of articulation arrangements, and of less formal arrangements for progression, has created a multi-track system' and further that 'articulation in Scotland may be producing a new binary divide' (ibid.: 10). Gallacher expressed the same concern, specifically about the prospects of further education graduates being able to transfer to elite institutions:

> However, if the 'elite' institutions do not provide access routes for non-traditional students, including those who wish to transfer from FE colleges with HNC/D qualifications, this can be viewed as a form of stratification, which limits opportunities. It must, of course, be recognised that many students will make positive choices not to apply for, or enter these institutions. However, it is important that appropriate opportunities are there for those who wish to pursue their studies in these institutions.
>
> (2006: 363)

Similar concerns have been expressed in Australia, which also has a formally unified higher education sector. But what effect does formal segmentation of higher education into tiers have on the ability of students to transfer from vocational education to the most selective higher education institutions? Is there less vertical stratification of universities in countries such as Scotland and Australia that do not formally segment their higher education systems than in other countries that formally segment higher education? It seems plausible that students may transfer from vocational education to the most selective higher education institutions more readily in formally unified systems than in stratified systems of higher education, and therefore that the formally unified systems of Scotland and Australia are less stratified than the formally segmented higher education systems such as those of some US states. This chapter tests that supposition by examining the rate at which students transfer from short cycle awards of non-university tertiary institutions into highly selective and moderately selective universities.

Student admission ratio[1]

Scotland has a formally unified university sector, but universities are informally grouped by age of establishment: ancient universities (those founded before the nineteenth century) are the most selective, old universities (institutions that had university status before the *Further and Higher Education Act 1992*) are the second most selective and new universities (the institutions that were redesignated as universities by the *Further and Higher Education Act 1992* or that were founded after the Act) are the least selective. Osborne and McMaurin (2006: 162) identified Scottish universities by category. I set out the universities and their categories in Table 11.1. I also show each university's rank in Shanghai Jiao Tong University's (2006) world university rank, currently the only credible world university league table. It will be noted that Labaree's (2006: 6) first rule for a highly stratified system applies in Scotland as much as the US: age trumps youth. But it will also be noted that this isn't invariant. The University of Edinburgh has a much stronger research performance than its older ancient siblings and the University of Dundee has a much

Table 11.1 Scottish universities by category and world rank

University	Founded	Category	World rank
St Andrews	1413	Ancient	151–200
Glasgow	1451	Ancient	102–150
Aberdeen	1495	Ancient	201–300
Edinburgh	1582	Ancient	52
Strathclyde	1964	Old	
Heriot-Watt	1966	Old	
Dundee	1967	Old	201–300
Stirling	1967	Old	
Napier	1992	New	
Paisley	1992	New	
Robert Gordon	1992	New	
Glasgow Caledonian	1993	New	
Abertay Dundee	1994	New	
Queen Margaret	2007	New	

stronger research performance than its old university siblings, at least on the heavily scientific criteria of research performance used by Shanghai Jiao Tong University.

Gallacher (2003: 12) reports the numbers and percentages of students entering higher education institutions in Scotland in 2000 for whom the higher national certificate or diploma or similar further education qualification was the highest on entry. He reports those for ancient universities (3 per cent), old universities that he called 1960s universities (8 per cent), new universities that he called post '92 universities (25 per cent) and art/music colleges (13 per cent), which I set out in Table 11.2.

Maclennan and colleagues (2000: 12) distinguish between selecting and recruiting universities, observing that 'Post-1992 HEIs often adopt a more promotion-based approach, consistent with a "recruiting" model. In contrast, pre-1992 HEIs have traditionally followed a softer approach, relying more on liaison activities with schools, and in certain cases, with FECs.' Gallacher (2006: 363) observes that the 1960s universities come somewhere in between the ancient and new universities: 'These universities continue to attract large numbers of well-qualified young applicants in many discipline areas, and in this sense are "selecting" institutions.' I therefore calculated Table 11.3 by classifying the ancient and the old universities as highly selective universities and the new universities as recruiting universities, or moderately selective institutions in this study. It will be noted that 5 per cent of the students entering the ancient and old universities that I categorized as highly selective had a short cycle further education qualification as their highest qualification on entry, whereas the corresponding proportion for the new universities was 25 per cent. The ratio of transfer student admission rates of highly selective and moderately selective universities is therefore 1:5 for Scotland.

Like Scotland, Australia has a formally 'unified national system' (Dawkins 1988) of higher education, in its case since 1988. Nevertheless, Australia's universities differ markedly by selectivity of student admissions. It is con-

Table 11.2 Number and proportion of entrants to Scottish universities for the higher national certificate or diploma or similar further education qualification as the highest on entry, by university category, 2000

University category	Number of entrants	Number of entrants with HNC/D as highest qualification	Percentage of all entrants
Ancient universities	10,000	303	3
Old universities	7,000	568	8
New universities	10,500	2,665	25
Art/music colleges	1,300	167	13
Total	28,800	3,703	13

Source: adapted from Gallacher (2003: 12, table 7): numbers and percentages of students entering HEIs in Scotland for whom HNC/D or similar was highest qualification on entry.

Table 11.3 Ratio of transfer student admission rates of highly selective and moderately selective universities, Scotland, 2000

Jurisdiction	Highly selective institutions	Moderately selective institutions	Ratio of highly selective to moderately selective
Scotland	5%	25%	1:5

venient to count as the highly selective institutions the group of eight universities that win the biggest share of external research grants and that have formed an association (Group of Eight 2003). Australia also allows a comparison with Prager's (1993) findings on transfer and articulation within US colleges and universities. Prager surveyed 408 chief executive officers of campuses that Peterson's *Directory* identified as sponsors of two-year tracks within a college, university or system also offering four-year curricula (Prager 1993: 541). She concluded:

> It appears that students from some two-year programs within four-year contexts may have as much, if not more, difficulty in 'transferring' within their institutions as do students who begin at a community college and seek to transfer to a senior one. Indeed, the findings explored here suggest that problems with internal student transfer and program articulation may be as pervasive within some institutions sharing a common institutional identity as external ones are for some from different sectors, such as community and senior colleges, that do not.
>
> (ibid.: 551)

Australia has five so-called 'dual sector universities' that comprise substantial student load in both Bachelor and sub-degree vocational programmes. The average transfer student admission rate for Australian dual sector universities is shown separately in Table 11.4. It will be noted that while the dual sector universities had a higher transfer student admission rate than the group of eight highly selective Australian universities, they had a lower rate than the other moderately selective institutions, thus replicating Prager's US findings in Australia.

Table 11.5 includes the dual sector universities with the other moderately selective universities. It shows that the difference in the ratio of transfer student admission rates between the highly selective and moderately selective universities is a high 1:4, although not quite as high as the ratio for Scotland.

California has segmented its higher education system since its master plan for higher education was enshrined in the Donahoe Act of 1960, and Douglass (2004: 11) points out that California had developed three distinct, geographically dispersed and multi-campus public segments as early as 1920. The master plan divides California's higher education institutions into three segments: the University of California whose intake is restricted by legislation to the top 12.5 per cent of high school graduates, the California State

Table 11.4 Proportion of undergraduate commencing students at the group of eight Australian highly selective and other moderately selective universities who were admitted on the basis of a vocational education and training qualification, 2000

Institution	Admitted on basis of VET	Total bachelor commencers	% of commencers who are transfers
Group of eight universities	1,028	45,359	2%
Dual sector universities	1,231	24,602	5%
Other universities	9,077	110,323	8%
Total	11,336	180,284	7%

Source: DETYA (2001) Higher education student statistics, 2000.

Table 11.5 Ratio of transfer student admission rates of highly selective and moderately selective four-year institutions, Australia, 2000

Jurisdiction	Highly selective institutions	Moderately selective institutions	Ratio of highly selective to moderately selective
Australia	2%	8%	1:4

University whose intake is restricted to the top 33.3 per cent of high school graduates and California Community Colleges that have open admission. The transfer rates calculated from data published by the California Postsecondary Education Commission (1998, 2000) are shown in Table 11.6.

Community College transfer students were 6.5 per cent of students at the highly selective University of California but were 13 per cent of students at the moderately selective California State University, giving a ratio of 1:2 between the two segments, which is shown in Table 11.7.

Other US states typically do not have as systematically or strongly segmented higher education systems as California's, although they may allocate them different amounts of general funds or research grants as a historical legacy or by a method in which all institutions ostensibly compete equally. Some 59 per cent of Colorado's higher education students start in four-year institutions, much higher than the US average (45 per cent) and very much higher than in California (34 per cent), so there are fewer students in two-year colleges seeking to transfer to four-year institutions in Colorado. Overall transfer student admission rates are therefore lower in Colorado than in California, which may also be partly due to differences in data definitions and collection methods. Colorado did not formally designate four-year institutions by selectivity of admissions at the time the data for this study were collected. However, the Colorado Commission on Higher Education (2003: 10) analysed institutions' selectivity to inform its new admissions standards policy from which it was possible to identify Colorado's highly selective four-year colleges as the Colorado School of Mines, the University of Colo-

Table 11.6 Proportion of students at the highly selective University of California and the moderately selective California State University who transferred from a community college, 1998–1999

Segment	Number of transfers	Total u/grad. enrolments	% of u/grad. enrolments who are transfers
University of California	10,161	155,412	6.5
California State University	44,989	336,803	13
Total	59,906	492,215	12

Source: California Postsecondary Education Commission (1998) Factsheet 98-1.

Table 11.7 Ratio of transfer student admission rates of highly selective and moderately selective four-year institutions, California, 1998–1999

Jurisdiction	Highly selective institutions	Moderately selective institutions	Ratio of highly selective to moderately selective
California	6.5%	13%	1:2

rado – Boulder and Colorado State University. Transfers were 3 per cent of enrolments at the highly selective institutions and 6 per cent of students at the moderately selective institutions. Despite Colorado's lower overall transfer student admission rate than California's, the differences in transfer student admission rates between Colorado's highly selective and moderately selective receiving institutions is the same as in California, which is shown in Table 11.8.

Texas does not have an explicit policy of distinguishing public four-year colleges by selectivity of student admission. A measure of the selectivity of institutions is the proportion of their first-time undergraduates who were in the top 10 per cent of their high school class and this was used to classify institutions as highly and moderately selective. Texas has a very strong transfer policy and consequently its four-year institutions have twice as many transfer students as California. But again, the different transfer student admission rates between highly selective and moderately selective four-year institutions is similar to, although a little less than in, California and Colorado. This is shown in Table 11.9.

These results are summarized in Table 11.10, which is ordered from Scotland and Australia where the difference in transfer student admission rates of the highly selective and moderately selective universities is relatively high, to California, Colorado and finally Texas where the difference in transfer student admission rates is much smaller.

It will therefore be seen that the formal segmentation of universities into sectors does not always structure opportunities for students as much as the informal differences between institutions. Clark's (1983: 52) explanation for highly differentiated student admissions practices is that the lack of formal

Table 11.8 Ratio of transfer student admission rates of highly selective and moderately selective four-year institutions, Colorado, 2001

Jurisdiction	Highly selective institutions	Moderately selective institutions	Ratio of highly selective to moderately selective
Colorado	3%	6%	1:2

Table 11.9 Ratio of transfer student admission rates of highly selective and moderately selective four-year institutions, Texas, 2000

Jurisdiction	Highly selective institutions	Moderately selective institutions	Ratio of highly selective to moderately selective
Texas	15%	26%	1:1.7

segmentation by tier drives systems to greater internal stratification, which at least in Australia and Scotland is by status, which in turn is strongly related to institutional age. What, then, may governments do to improve the rate at which further education students transfer to universities overall, and the rate at which they are accepted by the most selective universities?

Measures to improve student transfer

Gallacher (2005, 2006) has described several measures adopted by Scotland to improve student transfer from further to higher education. While these measures are fairly recent and should be given time to work before being declared ineffective, it is worth looking elsewhere to see what alternatives may be available. Student transfer has long been problematized in the US and has thus been the subject of government policy, which Clark (1983: 62) observed to be distinctive. In 2001 the Education Commission of the States (2001) found that of the 50 US states, 30 had legislation supporting transfer, 40 had statewide cooperative transfer agreements, 33 states regularly collected and reported transfer data, 18 states offered incentives and rewards to either transfer students or sending or receiving institutions and 26 states maintained a statewide guide to transfer. This is summarized in Table 11.11.

However, much of the US states' policies seem exhortatory (Moodie, 2008: 158). Of the 30 states with legislation supporting transfer, only six states specified minimum conditions for the transfer of students, ten states required a transfer agreement without specifying what it might contain, seven states exhorted cooperation in transfer and two states stated in legislation broad support for transfer. Anderson *et al.* (2006) furthermore found that the existence of a statewide articulation agreement did not increase the probability of students transferring within three years after the agreement was introduced.

Institutions in California, Ohio, New Jersey and other states have adopted dual admissions programmes, which are specialized transfer agreements that

Table 11.10 Ratio of transfer student admission rates of highly selective and moderately selective four-year institutions, selected jurisdictions

Jurisdiction	Highly selective institutions	Moderately selective institutions	Ratio of highly selective to moderately selective
Scotland	5%	25%	1:5
Australia	2%	8%	1:4
California	6.5%	13%	1:2
Colorado	3%	6%	1:2
Texas	15%	26%	1:1.7

Table 11.11 US states' instruments to support student transfer

Type of policy	Number of states
Legislation	30
Statewide cooperative agreements	40
Transfer data reporting	33
Incentives and rewards	18
Statewide transfer guide	26
Common core curriculum	23
Common subject numbering	8

Source: Education Commission of the States (2001).

guarantee admission and transfer of credits to specific four-year colleges and universities. Mercer County Community College, for example, has dual admissions agreements with six New Jersey colleges. Each requires completion of a specified programme and a minimum grade point average, which varies by institution and programme (Rifkin 1998).

Wellman (2002) studied six US states that rely heavily on transfer from two-year colleges to give low-income students access to the baccalaureate degree. She (ibid.: vi) selected three states that received high grades and three states that received low grades on retention and degree completion in *Measuring up 2000*, the state report card for higher education released by the National Center for Public Policy and Higher Education (2000). Wellman (ibid.: 38) characterized state policies as structural and academic. She understands structural polices to be those that affect the overall approach to post-secondary education: governance, institutional and sector mission and differentiation, statewide information system capacity, funding, planning capacities and accountability mechanisms. Wellman argues that the preconditions of student transfer are determined by these structural policies and by demography, economic conditions and institutional histories. She understands academic policies to be those specific to transfer from two-year to four-year programmes. They are designed to influence the internal alignment of students, programmes and subjects within and across institutions. Academic policies concern admissions standards, curriculum requirements, articulation and transfer of credit (ibid.: 38).

Wellman (ibid.: vi–vii) found that the key difference between the three high-performing states and the others in her study seems to lie in the statewide governance structure for higher education. The low-performing states construct transfer as mainly an academic and institutional matter and grant institutions considerable autonomy, while the high-performing states of Florida, New York and North Carolina have a comprehensive, integrated approach to transfer implemented by stronger state governance or coordinating mechanisms. For example, the 16 public baccalaureate-granting institutions of North Carolina are part of the University of North Carolina and the state's 58 public community colleges form the North Carolina Community College System governed by the State Board of Community Colleges. In New York, public community colleges are part of either the State University of New York or the City University of New York and thus report to the same governing board as the four-year institutions, which Wellman (ibid.: 39) says may facilitate transfer within those sectors. However, Prager (1993: 551) found in her study that transfer within 'dual sector' institutions can be as difficult as transfer between segmented institutions.

Wellman (2002: vii) also found that all three of the high-performing states also use data better to improve transfer performance, including reporting to campuses about their performance relative to others. This echoes Rifkin's (1998: 6) finding that:

> Effective transfer programs benefit from a well-developed technical infra- structure that includes statewide student information and tracking systems, articulation databases and research on transfer. The most effective programs have all three and often are found in states where higher educa- tion is closely coordinated at the state agency level.

In contrast to the large differences in structures between the states, Wellman (2002: 39) found:

> There is a good deal of commonality between the states on the academic policy side of the equation, as they have all adopted similar approaches to core curriculum, transfer of credit, remediation and testing, and statewide articulation agreements and course catalogues.

However, she concluded that academic policy alone is not sufficient to achieve strong transfer.

Conclusion

This chapter opened by asking about the effect of formal segmentation of higher education into tiers on the ability of students to transfer from voca- tional education to the most selective higher education institutions. This led to the supplementary question of whether there is less vertical stratification of universities in countries such as Scotland and Australia that do not formally segment their higher education sectors than in other countries that formally segment higher education. The results reported here show that having a unified higher education sector does not of itself provide strong student transfer from short cycle sub-degree programmes: quite the contrary. The chapter has shown that the formally unified higher education sectors of Scotland and Australia are informally stratified more steeply than the formally segmented higher education systems of the US states studied. This contradicted the supposition (held by the author at the outset of the study) that students may transfer from vocational education to the most selective higher education institutions more readily in formally unified systems than in stratified systems of higher education and that therefore the formally unified systems of Scotland and Australia are less stratified than the formally segmented higher education systems such as those of some US states.

Following Clark (1983: 52) the single most effective measure a government may take to improve student transfer may be to reintroduce or reinforce the formal segmentation of higher education into tiers or sectors since this would reduce institutions' perceived need to differentiate themselves informally, including by different student admissions policies and practices. However, maximizing student transfer is unlikely to be the most important reason for governments' structuring of higher education, so it is worth considering what else governments may do to improve student transfer. Merely having a policy promoting student transfer is not effective. Also apparently largely ineffectual are government policies on academic matters such as admissions standards, curriculum requirements, articulation and credit transfer.

Strong student transfer in the US seems to be associated with governments' structural arrangements and policies for higher education. This starts with a strong higher education coordinating commission or statewide governance board that has the resources and expertise to monitor student transfer. Next, there needs to be a strong information system and systematic data collection and reporting on student transfer. The state higher education commission or board typically reports publicly institutions' relative performance on student transfer. Some but not all states with strong student transfer include institutions' performance on student transfer in their institutional funding formula. Finally, the states with strong student transfer actively research student transfer, often conducted or sponsored by the state higher education commission or board.

Note

1 This ratio and the problems with other measures of student transfer are discussed in Moodie (2007).

References

Anderson, G.M., Sun, J.C. and Alfonso, M. (2006) 'Effectiveness of statewide articulation agreements on the probability of transfer: A preliminary policy analysis', *Review of Higher Education* 29(3), 261–291.

California Postsecondary Education Commission (1998) *Factsheet 98–1: Composition of higher education in California*. Online, available at: www.cpec.ca.gov/FactSheets/FactSheet1998/fs98–01.pdf (accessed 23 October 2008).

California Postsecondary Education Commission (2000) *Performance Indicators of California Higher Education, 2000*, Commission report 01. Online, available at: www.cpec.ca.gov/completereports/2001reports/01–03.pdf (accessed 23 October 2008).

Clark, B.R. (1983) *The Higher Education System: Academic organization in cross-national perspective*, Berkeley, CA: University of California Press.

Colorado Commission on Higher Education (2003) *Admissions Standards Policy*. Online, available at: http://highered.colorado.gov/Publications/Policies/Current/i-partf.pdf (accessed 23 October 2008).

Dawkins, The Hon. J.S., MP (1988) *Higher Education: A policy statement* ('the White Paper'), Canberra: Australian Government Publishing Service.

Department of Education, Training and Youth Affairs (2001) *Students 2000: Selected higher education statistics*. Online, available at: www.dest.gov.au/sectors/higher_education/publications_resources/statistics/selected_higher_education_statistics/students_2000_revised.htm (accessed 23 October 2008).

Douglass, J.A. (2004) 'The dynamics of massification and differentiation: A comparative look at higher education systems in the United Kingdom and California', *Higher Education Management and Policy* 16(3), 9–33.

Education Commission of the States (2001) *Transfer and Articulation Policies*, Denver, Education Commission of the States. Online, available at: www.ecs.org/clearinghouse/23/75/2375.htm (accessed 23 October 2009).

Field, J. (2004) 'Articulation and credit transfer in Scotland: Taking the academic highroad or a sideways step in a ghetto?' *Journal of Access Policy and Practice* 1(2), 1–15.

Gallacher, J. (2003) *Higher Education in Further Education Colleges: The Scottish experience*, London: The Council for Industry and Higher Education. Online, available at: www.cihe-uk.com/publications.php (accessed 23 October 2008).

Gallacher, J. (2005) 'Differentiation and stratification in Scottish higher education', in I. McNay (ed.), *Beyond Mass Higher Education*, Buckingham: SRHE and OU Press, pp. 28–43.

Gallacher, J. (2006) 'Widening access or differentiation and stratification in higher education in Scotland', *Higher Education Quarterly* 60(4), 349–369.

Group of Eight (2003) *Welcome to the Group of Eight*. Online, available at: www.go8.edu.au (accessed 23 October 2008).

Labaree, D.F. (2006) 'Markets and American higher education: An institutional success story'. Vice presidential address (Division F, History of Education) at annual meeting of the American Educational Research Association, San Francisco.

McLaurin, I. and Osborne, M. (2002) 'Data on transfer from FECs in Scotland to HEIs in Scotland', in M. Osborne, J. Gallacher and M. Murphy (eds), *A Research Review of FE/HE Links: A report to the Scottish Executive Enterprise and Lifelong Learning Department*. Online, available at: www.scotland.gov.uk/about/ELLD/HESP/00016640/annexe2p1.pdf (accessed 23 October 2008).

Maclennan, A., Musslebrook, K. and Dundas, M. (2000) *Credit Transfer at the FE/HE Interface*, Scottish Higher Education Funding Council/Scottish Further Education Funding Council. Online, available at: www.sfc.ac.uk/information/info_circulars/sfefc/2001/fe3301/fe3301a.pdf (accessed 23 October 2008).

Moodie, G. (2007) 'Do tiers affect student transfer? Examining the student admission ratio', *Community College Journal of Research and Practice* 31(11), 847–861.

Moodie, G.F. (2008) *From Vocational to Higher Education: An international perspective*, Maidenhead: McGraw-Hill.

Morgan-Klein, B. (2003) 'Scottish higher education and the FE-HE nexus', *Higher Education Quarterly* 57(4), 338–354.

Osborne, M. and McLaurin, I. (2006) 'A probability matching approach to further education/ higher education transition in Scotland', *Higher Education* 52(1), 149–183.

Prager, C. (1993) 'Transfer and articulation within colleges and universities', *Journal of Higher Education* 64(5), 539–554.

Raab, G.M. and Storkey, H.R. (2001) 'Widening access to higher education in Scotland: Evidence for change from 1996–97 to 1998–99'. Report commissioned by the Scottish Higher Education Funding Council, Edinburgh, Scottish Higher Education Funding Council. Online, available at: www.sfc.ac.uk/information/info_circulars/shefc/2001/he3601/he3601annex.pdf (accessed 23 October 2008).

Rifkin, T. (1998) 'Improving articulation policy to increase transfer', *ECS Policy Paper*, Education Commission of the States, cited in R.J. Coley (2000) *The American Community College Turns 100: A look at its students, programs, and prospects*, Princeton, NJ: Educational Testing Service. Online, available at: www.ecs.org/html/Document.asp?chouseid=2775 (accessed 23 October 2008).

Shanghai Jiao Tong University (2006) *Academic Ranking of World Universities – 2006*. Online, available at: http://ed.sjtu.edu.cn/ranking2006.htm (accessed 23 October 2008).

Wellman, J.V. (2002) 'State policy and community college-baccalaureate transfer', *National Center Report #02–6*, The National Centre for Public Policy and Higher Education. Online, available at: www.highereducation.org/reports/transfer/transfer.shtml (accessed 23 October 2008).

Chapter 12

Imagined transitions

Social and organisational influences on the student life cycle

Muir Houston, Yann Lebeau and Ruth Watkins

Since the 1990s, there has a been a significant expansion in the numbers of students attending university in the UK, with a measurable shift towards gender equality (Egerton and Halsey 1993) and a range of initiatives to broaden the social composition of higher education. This has coincided with the conversion of polytechnics and colleges to universities resulting in an increasingly institutionally and socially diverse higher education (HE) system (Houston and Lebeau 2006). Within this disparate system, there has also been a range of other changes including a proliferation of degree programmes, changes in funding regimes, increased flexibility and modularisation, an increased emphasis on employability and a shift to a highly competitive market where students theoretically have more choice.

It is within this dynamic context that the authors of this chapter took part in a four-year research project (SOMUL) funded as part of the Teaching and Learning Research Programme, looking at the social and organisational mediation of learning processes and outcomes in higher education. More specifically, this UK-wide project aimed to identify how variations in institutional organisation, curriculum design, the social and spatial context of study and informal learning experiences mediate student conceptions of their learning and identity (Brennan and Jary 2005). The 15 SOMUL case studies, involving surveys and interviews with first- and final-year students, in addition to staff interviews, reflect the diversity of the undergraduate experience in three contrasting subjects (business studies, sociology, biosciences).

Drawing on a subset of data from the SOMUL project,[1] this chapter focuses particularly on choice and expectations at times of transition and explores the student perspective on transitions at different stages; from the choices made before entering HE and the transition between first year through to final year.

There are many transitions and choices to be made throughout a student's educational career but it is usually only in the post-compulsory sector that students begin to make independent decisions whilst simultaneously considering potential changes in their personal lives, and their social and financial circumstances (Foskett and Helmsley-Brown 2001). These transitions and choices are made within a highly diverse education system (as described above).

It is perhaps useful to define more fully the concept of transition as applied in this chapter. A dictionary defines 'transition' as 'the process of changing from one state or condition to another... or, a period of such change' (AskOxford 2008). Shildrick and MacDonald (2007) have provided an overview of the recent sociological use of the concept of transition as applied in relation to the journey from youth to adult and note that it is an increasingly contested field (Wyn and Woodman 2006; Stokes and Wyn 2007; Roberts 2007). While recognising the large amount of work that reports differentiation in transitions on the basis of class, gender, ethnicity and education (e.g. Furlong and Cartmel 2007) they suggest that recent changes in society have resulted in a more blurred and fuzzy notion of the concept. These changes include:

> [T]he virtual collapse of the youth labour market and the sharp decline in the supply of jobs and skill apprenticeships; persistent, regionally-concentrated, structural unemployment; the introduction of widespread youth training provision and employment preparation programmes; welfare 'reforms' that have reduced young people's entitlement to benefits; and the expansion of opportunities in Further Education (FE) and Higher Education (HE) for young people who might previously have been unlikely to continue in post-compulsory education.
>
> (Shildrick and MacDonald 2007: 590)

As a consequence of these changes, transition it is suggested is seen to be less coherent and more fractured than previously theorised and has resulted in young people staying in the parental home for longer; delaying entry to employment until after university and putting off cohabiting and starting families (Jones 2002; Wolbers 2007). However, this 'emergent adulthood' theory (Arnett 2004, 2006) is itself subject to critique (Bynner 2005). These debates notwithstanding, this chapter will apply the concept of transition in line with the dictionary definition provided above. When this is applied to individuals entering, experiencing and leaving university, the transitions an individual undertakes during the student life cycle may be seen as composed of three interlinked, multifaceted stages: that of becoming a student, moving from student to graduate and from graduate to employee.

Student life-cycle transitions

In the first stage, from application to entry, individuals are faced with a number of choices about what and where to study, both of which may involve transitions in relation to location, accommodation and living arrangements and which are often conditioned by economic considerations. There has been substantial work on pre-entry student choice at the level of institution and programme including early work on choice in HE by Roberts and Allan (1997) and a more recent investigation by Connor et al. (1999); the latter indicating that student choice was primarily dictated by a

Table 12.1 Contextual information on case studies cited

	Student characteristics	Institutional context	Principles of curriculum organisation
Warthill	Socially and educationally homogeneous. School leavers. Entry requirements: 320 tariff points.	Elite pre-92, selecting and residential, research intensive. Situated in county heritage city.	Closed at level of discipline, but relatively open within through operation of common core. Placements available.
Ulleskelf	Socially relatively homogeneous and ethnically heterogeneous. Mixed age. Entry requirements: 200 tariff points.	Post-92 inner city campus, ex-industrial with ongoing regeneration. Recruiting with mix of residential and commuting.	Generally closed at level of discipline with common core. Placements available.
Fridaythorpe	Some social and ethnic heterogeneity, generally school leavers. Entry requirements: 320 tariff points.	Pre-92 city centre campus, ex-industrial yet with vibrant social scene. Research intensive. Selecting and generally residential.	Closed at level of discipline, common core. Placements available.
Givendale	Some social and ethnic heterogeneity, generally school leavers. Entry requirements: 320 tariff points.	Redbrick pre-92 in regenerated ex-industrial city with expanding social scene. Research intensive. Selecting and generally residential.	Closed at level of discipline, common core. Placements available.
Tockerington	Socially and educationally homogeneous with predominantly middle-class national school leaver recruitment.	High reputation, pre-92, selecting and residential, research-intensive campus university, but relatively modest research reputation in sociology.	Traditional relatively closed single honours curriculum but within a department shared with applied social studies and some combined studies.
Holme	Relatively homogeneous in terms of age and social origin. Entry requirements: 300 tariff points.	Research-led selecting university, with strong international research reputation but local and national recruitment to its undergraduate courses.	Non-modular relatively traditional sociology single honours structure. Also more market-oriented joint honours courses but these mostly under the strong hegemony of sociology
Fenton	Predominantly local recruitment, including some ethnic minority students. Entry requirements: 160 tariff points.	Inner city post-92 recruiting university with small relatively insecure sociology group. Limited research.	Open modular structure but students mostly make traditional disciplinary choices.

combination of the subjects available, image and location of the institution and its teaching reputation. Reay *et al.* (2001, 2005) focused their research on the experience of 'non-traditional' students and non-applicants and suggested that the decision-making process was heavily influenced by both racial and class inequalities with many minority ethic groups and working-class students selecting from a limited number of options and within a number of constraints.

Once the early choices have been made, the individual is then subject to other potential transitions, including social transitions, as existing social networks are displaced or marginalised through the formation of new and expanding networks. In some respects, this will either be enhanced or inhib-ited as a result of choices in relation to discipline studied, location of study and the resultant impact on pre-existing living arrangements. In addition, there are usually academic transitions in relation to forms of teaching and assessment. These early transitions into university are often labelled as the 'first year experience', which cover research into the academic and social transitions faced upon entry to university (Houston 2008).

In the second stage, students undergo both personal and intellectual devel-opment as a result of their experiences as a student. It is suggested that the student experience is mediated by the social, institutional and organisation context (Brennan and Jary 2005; Brennan and Osborne 2005; Houston and Lebeau 2006; Richardson and Edmunds 2007). Social interactions may be influenced by, for example, living arrangements, the organisation of the cur-riculum and the presence of term-time employment, while personal develop-ment as a result of increasing independence may be expected to take place.

The expected third transitional stage is that of graduate to employee. Exiting from HE into employment or further study is also a time when many of the social, economic and spatial transitions are repeated with changes or adjustments in social networks and living arrangements. In addi-tion, post-university transitions and opportunities to enter graduate employ-ment or post-graduate study are influenced by gender, class, ethnicity, disability and university attended (Moreau and Leathwood 2006).

Following Houston's analysis of the third transitional phase (Houston 2008), we are focusing here on the first two transitions of a cohort of stu-dents surveyed throughout their student life cycle between 2004 and 2007. Our analysis draws on narratives and questionnaire responses of students studying in contrasting institutional environments and in subjects located in disciplinary groupings supposedly reflecting cognitive as well as social and cultural differences (Becher 1989). Largely based on students' perceptions, the results seek to report on how students analyse their choices and transitions and relate them to disciplinary and institutional/social contexts. More specifically, they draw upon preliminary findings to explore:

1   How students justify the choice of subject and institution they make and how they relate it to issues of pre-university trajectory, prestige and professional prospects.

2   How students' views of what they learn, their conceptions of learning and learning styles are influenced by the social and organisational context of their studies.

Choice of subject and institution

The data focus only on the perspectives of students who were in their first year. A total of 342 first-year questionnaires were distributed (and returned). Questionnaires included sections on demographic data and on 'student choice'; the latter including 12 factors that could influence choice listed against a Likert scale of one to five (one being of no 'importance' and five representing 'of great importance'). Forty-seven student interviews (semi-structured over 30–40 minutes) concentrated on the social contexts of study but also included a section that encouraged students to reflect upon the choices they had made prior to entry. These interviews have been drawn upon to provide exemplars.

Figure 12.1 summarises the relative importance of influential factors as determined from the survey data. Only those scores of four and above on the scale are reported.

It is acknowledged that these data present an apparent picture of rationality and logical reasoning and it has to be recognised that in reality students make choices within a framework of dynamic options and competing demands. The options are not always so obvious and the reasoning is not always rational; this is where interview data can provide some elucidation of the individual nature of the decision-making process. As Reay *et al.* (2001: 860) remind us, 'individuals applying to do higher education courses are

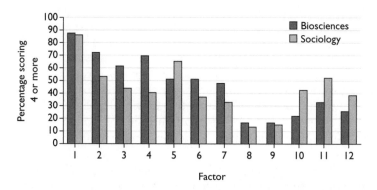

Figure 12.1 Factors influencing choice (Source: adapted from custom HESA dataset).

Notes
Key: (1) It was a subject that interested me; (2) It was a subject I had done well previously in; (3) The job prospects seemed good; (4) The reputation of the course or institution seemed high; (5) The geographical location suited me; (6) Social life seemed good; (7) Suitable accommodation was available; (8) I felt the standards expected would not be too high; (9) I already knew some people here; (10) It meant I did not have to move house; (11) I could remain close to my family; (12) I could obtain work while studying.

making very different kinds of choices within very different circumstances and constraints'. It is not possible in this chapter to explore the full range of interrelated influences that operate and so particular highlighted issues have been highlighted around subject choice, reputation, location and emotional constraints.

For many students the choice of subject area comes before the final choice of institution and has a significant impact on which institutions will then be considered. Personal interest in the subject of study was a major factor in degree choice with over 85 per cent of respondents acknowledging that interest was of 'some' or 'of great' importance when thinking about which degree to study, with over 70 per cent of bioscience entrants and over 50 per cent of sociology entrants indicating that they had previously done well in the subject. One student expressed an intrinsic interest as the primary motive for studying.

> So it sort of opened up this whole new world of ways of looking at things and stuff and I was just so interested in that, I wanted to learn more. So it isn't really – like my degree for me isn't really about a career at the end of it.
>
> M. (Holme)

The importance of subject interest is highlighted in the literature. Connor *et al.* (1999) indicated that offering a particular discipline was the primary influence in initially narrowing down choice of potential institutions and Young's (2000) study, across a broad range of institutions, showed that 49 per cent of his sample chose their course for interest and enjoyment. Within Young's study there were, however, significant variations by gender, age and subject area. Indeed, although not reported here, differences within subjects on many of the factors influencing choice were apparent often on the basis of some aspect of institutional context.[2] Those in the social and physical sciences were more likely to choose out of interest, which would support the higher figures obtained in this research. Scott's (2006) work, which focused specifically on the biosciences, found that over 70 per cent of participants said that enjoyment of the subject was the most important criterion for studying bioscience. In our interview data there is evidence that once a subject had been chosen factors such as employment prospects and reputation then became primary considerations. This would appear to be supported by the relatively high percentage (61 per cent) of bioscience entrants who agreed that job prospects after graduation were an important consideration. Interestingly, and perhaps given the less obviously vocational nature of sociology, only 43 per cent rated this of at least some importance. In interviews reference to interest in the subject were common but when spoken about in the context of choice of institution it was often tied to other issues such as reputation and employment.

Course or institutional reputation was important to over 70 per cent of bioscience entrants yet only 41 per cent of sociology entrants rated it of importance. In interviews, reference to league tables and reputation were especially prominent amongst students who attended more traditional universities; many students at these universities spoke about league tables without prompting and referred to them as a mechanism for narrowing down their initial choices. For example, 'he said universities in the north were better at sciences. So I looked at the league tables to try and get an idea' A. (Givendale). Others already knew which university they were interested in based on institutional reputation: 'And this university because it was one of the best universities' M. (Tockerington). Students were therefore taking 'reputational capital' into account when formulating their choices. The concept of institutional reputation was often linked with potential employment prospects, particularly amongst the bioscience students: 'That's part of why you come here because when you leave it's the reputation that the people in the city will turn round and go "Well yes we'll take a Warthill graduate"' C. (Warthill). However, the data suggest that for many students, institutional reputation was not sufficient and they were more clearly focused on the departmental or course reputation: 'I was interested in Givendale at the start because it was high up in the league tables for molecular biology' M. (Givendale).

Issues of geographical location were also regularly commented upon and the quantitative data indicate that this was important to 66 per cent of the sociology and 52 per cent of bioscience entrants. Location appears to be a more important factor in making a choice compared with the reputation of course and institution; however, the qualitative data give some insight into the diversity of issues that location presents for the individual.

A number of students indicated that their choices were severely constrained by locality either through economic factors or family responsibilities. This was more noticeable for students attending less prestigious institutions but was still a factor for some at more traditional universities. J. (Fridaythorpe) commented that she had strongly considered going south to study, 'but the financial things stopped me. I couldn't have afforded that.' This theme was echoed by many students indicating that potential debt had forced them to consider staying at home as a viable option: 'I didn't want to get into a lot of debt when I went to university. . . . So I decided that I'd live at home' N. (Warthill). For some it was a combination both of economics and family responsibilities that limited the geographical area that a student could consider: 'no I live nearby, I can't travel. I have children in the home. So it's a 20-minute walk to get to here' K. (Holme).

Reay *et al.* (2001) identified the issue of 'localism', which exerted a significant influence on the choices that working-class students made. Localism is induced by financial constraints that prevent travel and moving away from home. In Reay *et al.*'s study, 'localism' was identified as a class and race issue that then intersected with issues of identity. Connor *et al.* (1999) also investigated the impact of financial issues on the choice process and indicated that 50 per cent of students had considered applying to an institution close to home for economic benefit. This figure, however, was higher (66 per cent) for older students but slightly less for those under 21 years old. In this research there were students who did not consider finance to be an issue but few were as optimistic as M. (Givendale):

> Money had nothing to do with my decisions. Obviously I mean like I said that I'm not from a rich family … but come on, it's money, if you want to do something you do it, money's got nothing to do with it really.

A relatively high number of students (mostly female) deliberately chose to stay within easy travelling distance from home but give no indication of feeling constrained by this choice. For these students their choice of institution was a compromise between leaving home and becoming independent; a way of minimising the risk of going away. For example: 'I wanted somewhere that was kind of a, a nice distance away from home' V. (Fridaythorpe). In contrast there was a minority of students who viewed the transition to university as an opportunity to distance themselves from their local communities. J. (Holme) was one such student who saw a move to the south as an opportunity for a fresh start: 'So I just thought, you know, I want a totally clean start, new people, nobody knows me. I'll come down south and Holme was the first choice.' There is a hint in this text of 'dis-identification' with socio-cultural background (cf. Reay et al. 2001) but no clarification to suggest this was seen as a shift to a more privileged status.

There was evidence to indicate that some students focused on the facilities within the host city rather than just the university. The perception of a good social life was important for 37 per cent of sociology students and 51 per cent of bioscience students and it would appear from interviews that many students were keen to participate in the social life provided by the city rather than the institution. For example, R. (Fridaythorpe) indicates that: 'so it was quite an exciting place to be. Things changing all the time. Good night life. Cheap to live, well relatively cheap to live.' Connor et al. (1999) indicate that perceptions of an active social life were of particular importance for young male students and Young's (2000) study of institutions in the north west found that over 50 per cent were attracted by a large city location.

Location is therefore an issue for all students but it manifests itself in different ways. In this work it can be seen that there are contrasting perceptions on location and distance. Some students have little choice and cannot travel far whereas others appear to have choice but prefer to stay a 'safe' distance from home. A minority are keen to move away and the reputation of the host city as a lively destination was an important factor in their final choice.

This brief review of data on early choices and transitions indicates the many factors that impact on student choice. These are multifaceted and interrelated with students expressing their attempts to negotiate a rational path through their options but with many alluding to emotional constraints or parental influences, which are more difficult to express and cannot be quantified. The data suggest that many students 'play safe' and minimise the risks (cf. Roberts and Allen 1997) when considering their transition into higher education. The key issue is how to elucidate the implications of these initial choices on student perceptions of their university experience.

Changes during the student life cycle

This part of the chapter seeks to capture the changing perceptions students have of their subject and course as they go through their undergraduate studies. Our approach draws on three dimensions of the student experience that are said to structure perceptions of outcome and learning strategies in massified higher education systems: the level of integration in a student environment, the intellectual engagement with the subject studied and the professional project (or goal) (Dubet 1994, 2000).

Using data from four institutions (Givendale, Holme, Ulleskelf and Fenton), we explore the extent to which changes in student perceptions of what they learn, their project or goal and their engagement with their subject are gradually influenced by the subject culture, by organisational factors such as the curriculum and departmental structure, and by social factors such as their level of integration in students' activities and their activities and commitments outside the university sphere.

Valuing the impact of the student experience

Exploring the impact of the student experience on the formation of ideas, attitudes and networks suggests that the transition process in HE is neither reducible to predetermined choices and conditions nor simply the result of rational and autonomous decisions made by students at key stages of the process.

We suggest that transitions take multiple intended and unintended forms in a massified HE system, reflecting inherited constraints and opportunities as well as the contingencies of student lives in institutional environments with various (but overall diminishing) levels of control over the student experience.

If, as Dubet suggests, universities tend to be both massified (larger numbers suggesting lower impact on student behaviour and strategies) and 'atomised' worlds (diversity of origins, trajectories and projects), then sociologically analysing student attitudes and expectations on the sole basis of pre-entry data inevitably generates caricatured oppositions between 'non-traditional' students doing vocational subjects in 'new' universities and the others (young, white, middle-class, 'traditional' students).

We would like to explore the range of options, of behaviours and trajectories generated by the presence of the transitional process. We will then proceed to subject-based as well as institutional comparisons of the social experience of learning, and suggest the possibility of a complex *dual process* of diversification and individualisation (of experiences, expectations and identities) on one hand but also a degree of commonality of learning experiences and outcomes (via shared conceptions of 'graduateness' still prevalent in UK higher education) in all types of institutions.

First-year perspective on subject and institutional differences

Choice and motivation

As suggested above, most students surveyed in first-year sociology (Y1 Sociology) and biosciences (Y1 Bioscience) stressed the importance of their personal interest in the subject in their choice of course (+85 per cent in both cohorts), but results show that Y1 Bioscience students generally paid more attention to questions of course and institutional reputation compared with Y1 Sociology students for whom issues of location played an important role. We found interesting exceptions to this, but generally sociology students showed a more homogeneous attitude to choices and expectations than bioscience students whose multiple paths tend to reflect more or less carefully planned strategies.

Subject engagement and work-related socialisation

Both cohorts signalled an interest in the discipline area pre-dating entry to university with the chosen subject studied at A level by a majority of students. Y1 Sociology students tend to read more in relation to their course and to spend more time engaging in informal conversations with their lecturers compared to the bioscience students, but overall students of both groups express an interest in their course that contrasts with the attitudes of consumerism and instrumentalism commonly reported by their lecturers.

However, this interest manifests itself in different forms of engagement and again subject differences, driven by curriculum content, are worth noting: 62 per cent of Y1 Bioscience students surveyed spent 16 hours or more a week in the classroom or laboratories, while 62 per cent of sociology students spent less than ten hours in class. This sharp contrast in the number of contact hours not only impacts on the knowledge acquisition process but also on socialisation within the discipline. Bioscience students indicate a greater propensity to socialise with other students on their course compared with their sociology counterparts (20 per cent of Y1 Sociology never socialise with students from their course).

In their first year, biology students are drawn into forms of peer socialisation that remain largely institutionally driven, but this seems to be related more to the specific requirements and mode of delivery of their course than to a broader 'college experience'. Indeed, this comparatively high level of integration is observed across contrasting environments: 38 per cent of the bioscience students never socialise with people outside the university (19 per cent in sociology), but if they do, they spend very limited time with contacts external to the university world.

As the above example indicates, the identity formation process associated with the student experience remains largely (and probably increasingly) subject related. The patterns of subject differentiation that we found by far exceed the cognitive dimensions and curriculum content to encompass broader social issues. For example, generally sociology students were drawn from the local community (compared with bioscience students), which probably impacts (as much as workload) on their social life outside university and explains why these students retain these pre-existing social networks for longer periods.

Expected outcomes

Unsurprisingly on such courses, students from both cohorts tended to emphasise the importance of generic skills and placed a great importance on interpersonal skills (68 per cent in bioscience; 77 per cent in sociology). However, we found more significant institutional differences within Y1 Bioscience on this issue suggesting course content-related levels of expectation at the more vocational ends of the bioscience spectrum.

Also worth noting, is that both cohorts seemed to have unspecified ideas of their future career prospects (45 per cent of both cohorts had an idea of future careers) and were fairly open to the prospect of postgraduate studies (in both cases the proportion of first-year students aiming for a postgraduate qualification was around 67 per cent).

The time factor: final-year students looking back and forward

Overall and considering the three dimensions of our analytical framework the early university experience within the two disciplines seems to impact more sharply on levels of student integration and interactions with the non-university environment than on the level of engagement with the subject or on student anticipations and expectations regarding learning outcomes and professional prospects.

A brief longitudinal overview (gained through the review of Y3 students) on these issues offers useful information towards an understanding of the multiple transitions of the student life cycle.

Choice

Retrospectively Y3 students seemed happy with choices made (only 3 per cent of bioscience and 2 per cent of sociology said they 'sometimes wondered why they ever decided to come here'). Expectations remained fairly general (a manifestation of the non-vocational nature of these courses, except for specific applied bioscience programmes).

Workload and subject engagement

A greater engagement with the studies is evident, overwhelming time across subjects. Differences in number of contact hours between the two subjects increase over time but overall students in both groups felt they had more work in their third year. Y3 Bioscience students seemed more engaged with wider reading around their subject and showed a slightly greater propensity to discuss course-related issues with staff outside the class. These two dimensions remained constant for sociology students. However, Y3 Sociology students showed much more course-related forms of socialisation in their final year, now exhibiting a profile close to that of the bioscience students (35 per cent of both groups never socialise with non-university friends). The longitudinal data suggest that the student experience is creating a clear divide between the students and their pre-existing life, although this takes different forms according to subjects and institutional contexts

Skills and prospects

For both subjects, data are consistent with the fairly high level of satisfaction reported above. Both final-year cohorts indicated low levels of variation between expected and acquired skills. Career plans do not appear to be finalised at the end of bioscience students' final year while 66 per cent of Y3 Sociology students (45 per cent in Y1) now have an idea of potential employment opportunities. In both groups the prospect of a postgraduate course remains unchanged at nearly 70 per cent (considering this as a possibility). However, interviews in sociology show that students do not often consider postgraduate studies as an option immediately after their first degree. This may be a consequence of the accumulation of debt during their undergraduate experience, which appears to be increasingly influential on the transition process.

The weight of institutional matrices in the transition process

This part of the chapter has so far paid more attention to subject differences than to institutional contexts. This is not to suggest that institutions have no influence on student integration or expectations. Differences between institutions can sometimes be more subtle but are nevertheless observable on every issue relating to choice and motivation in both disciplines. What is less clear at this level is the impact of institutions over the transitional processes. Differences between Y1 and Y3 within each participating institution were usually found insignificant as if institutional contexts were primarily reflecting and confirming pre-existing socio-economic differences among students.

However, on the basis of a more detailed look at our four subsample institutions (Table 12.1), differences within biosciences appear to be more contrasted and the most extreme polarisation concerns the attention paid to reputation as a choice criteria. While Givendale recruits almost exclusively through A Levels, 8 per cent of entrants to Ulleskelf enter through access courses.

Institutional differences on engagement indicate that more time is spent in class/laboratory in the two teaching-oriented institutions of our subsample (Ulleskelf and Fenton), but that more time is dedicated to course work (reading in particular) in institutions where emphasis is more clearly on critical thinking and research-led teaching (e.g. Holme).

On skills acquisition and future prospects, the main institutional differences were again recorded between the two bioscience sites, with more emphasis placed on generic skills and subject expertise by Givendale students than by Ulleskelf students. Givendale students also show a greater propensity to embark on postgraduate studies. No discernible institutional effect was found in sociology on ideas of future career; while in bioscience, Ulleskelf and its more vocational focus attracts more career-oriented students.

Overall, stronger institutional contrasts were found in bioscience where very limited changes were recorded over time. Generally speaking, gradual changes observed at subject level in the student experience and forms of engagement can hardly be associated with specific types of institutional context; except in relation to the specific nature of programmes of study. The picture is more nuanced in sociology where the greater homogeneity of the curriculum and of student profiles allows a better grasp of institutional factors in identity changes.

Overall in both subjects, we found that changes reported by students were very close to expectations and those expectations tended to vary a great deal according to socio-economic identities.

Conclusion

This chapter provides a brief overview of the choices that students make prior to the transition into a higher education institution and how these choices may then influence the student experience throughout the life cycle. These choices are perceived by students as being predominantly linked to course and institutional reputations, employment prospects and also location and economics. However, as Young (2000) points out, there is rarely one overwhelming reason for a student to choose an institution and final decisions are based upon a combination of multifaceted factors that vary with the individual. There are also still stark contrasts between those who have apparently a broad range of choices and those who are heavily constrained by economic or practical considerations. Reay *et al.* (2001: 871) suggest that the process of choice-making for working-class students is 'qualitatively different to that of the more privileged middle-class counterparts'. There are hints of this in this early work. What is important is that these early choices and their influencing factors have consequences for student expectations and experiences for the duration of their undergraduate study. Socio-economic factors that are influential on initial choices are still influential in the way in which university life is experienced.

The second main focus in this chapter was to provide insight into how social and organisational mediation impacts on the perceptions of students over time. It is suggested that while elements of the traditional student experience are still viable, they are coming under pressure as institutions admit a far more diverse student body; with different perceptions and expectations of what university is about. Moreover, while curriculum organisation and the number of contact hours are seen to have positive benefits for student social integration for some students, the university experience tends to distance them from pre-existing social networks.

Finally, this chapter has allowed only a brief overview of some of the rich longitudinal data on the student life cycle (from entry to employment) that the authors have at their disposal and that is subject to ongoing analysis. It is expected that detailed analysis might provide further insights into the ways in which social and organisation mediation influences all stages of the life cycle identified in this chapter.

Acknowledgements

The authors of this chapter acknowledge the significant contribution of other members of the SOMUL project team (J. Brennan, D.W. Jary, Y. Lebeau, J.T.E. Richardson, M. Osborne, R. Edmunds and M. Houston). The ESRC/TRLP grant number was RES-139–25–0109.

Notes

1 We have decided to focus on the two subjects (biosciences and sociology) on which we have done most of the data collection and analysis. The illustrations provided originate from institutions presented in Table 12.1.
2 In general, differences within subjects existed for all influencing factors.

References

Arnett, J.J. (2004) *Emerging Adulthood: The winding road from late teens through the twenties*, Oxford: Oxford University Press.

Arnett, J.J. (2006) 'Emerging adulthood in Britain: A response to Bynner', *Journal of Youth Studies* 9, 111–123.

AskOxford (2008) 'Ask Oxford: transition'. Online, available at: www.askoxford.com/concise_oed/transition?view=uk (accessed 12 December 2008).

Becher, T. (1989) *Academic Tribes and Territories*, Buckingham: Open University Press.

Brennan, J. and Jary, D. (2005) 'What is learned at University? The Social and Organisational Mediation of University Learning: A research project'. Working Paper 1, Higher Education Academy and Open University/CHERI.

Brennan, J. and Osborne, M. (2005) 'The organisational mediation of university learning'. SOMUL Working paper No. 2. York: HEA and OU/CHERI.

Bynner, J. (2005) 'Rethinking the youth phase of the life-course: The case for emerging adulthood?' *Journal of Youth Studies* 8, 367–384.

Connor, H., Burton, R., Pearson, R., Pollard, E. and Regan, J. (1999) *Making the right choice. How students choose universities and colleges*. Online, available at: www.employment-studies.co.uk (accessed 1 March 2007).

Dubet, F. (1994) 'Dimensions et figures de l'expérience étudiante dans l'université de masse', *Revue Française de Sociologie* 35, 511–532.

Dubet, F. (2000) 'The sociology of pupils', *Journal of Education Policy* 15, 93–104.

Egerton, M. and Halsey, A.H. (1993) 'Trends by socio-economic group and gender in access to HE in Britain', *Oxford Review of Education* 19, 183–196.

Foskett, N. and Hemsley-Brown, J. (2001) *Choosing Futures: Young people's decision-making in education, training and careers market*, London: RoutledgeFalmer.

Furlong, A. and Cartmel, F. (2007) *Young People and Social Change* (2nd edn), Maidenhead: Open University Press.

Houston, M. (2008) 'Tracking Transition: Issues in asynchronous e-mail interviewing' [55 paragraphs], *Forum Qualitative Sozialforschung/Forum: Qualitative Social Research* 9, Art. 11. Online, available at: www.qualitative-research.net/fqs-texte/2-08/08-2-11-e.htm (accessed 9 February 2009).

Houston, M. and Lebeau, Y. (2006) 'The social mediation of university learning'. SOMUL Working Paper No. 4, York: HEA and OU/CHERI.

Jones, G. (2002) *The Youth Divide*, York: Joseph Rowntree Foundation.

Moreau, M.-P. and Leathwood, C. (2006) 'Graduates' employment and the discourse of employability: A critical analysis', *Journal of Education and Work* 19, 305–324.

Reay, D., David, M.E. and Ball, S. (2005) *Degrees of Choice, Social Class, Race and Gender in Higher Education*, Stoke on Trent: Trentham.

Reay, D., Davies, J., David, M. and Ball, S.J. (2001) 'Choices of degree or degrees of choice? Class, "race" and the higher education choice process', *Sociology* 35, 855–874.

Richardson, J.T.E. and Edmunds, R. (2007) 'A cognitive-developmental model of university learning'. SOMUL Working paper No. 4. York: HEA and OU/CHERI.

Roberts, D. and Allen, A. (1997) *Young Applicants' Perceptions of Higher Education*, Leeds: Heist.

Roberts, K. (2007) 'Youth transitions and generations: A response to Wyn and Woodman', *Journal of Youth Studies* 10, 263–269.

Scott, J. (2006) *Why am I here? Student choice in the Biosciences*. Online, available at: http://biosciences.heacademy.ac.uk/journal/vol.7/Beej-7-4.htm (accessed 1 March 2007).

Shildrick, T. and MacDonald, R. (2007) 'Biographies of exclusion: Poor work and poor transitions', *International Journal of Lifelong Education* 26, 589–604.

Stokes, H. and Wyn, J. (2007) 'Constructing identities and making careers: Young people's perspectives on work and learning', *International Journal of Lifelong Education* 26, 494–511.

Wolbers, M.H.J. (2007) 'Employment insecurity at labour market entry and its impact on parental home leaving and family formation. A comparative study among recent graduates in eight European countries', *International Journal of Comparative Sociology* 48, 481–507.

Wyn, J. and Woodman, D. (2006) 'Generation, youth and social change in Australia', *Journal of Youth Studies* 9, 495–514.

Young, Z. (2000) 'Undergraduate choice and decision-making', *Labour Market Information Briefing* 11. Online, available at: www.lmi4he.ac.uk/Documents/Undergrad.doc (accessed 1 May 2006).

Chapter 13

Accumulating knowledge in researching technology-enhanced learning

Going with the flows

Uma Patel, Nicky Solomon and Laurence Solkin

Introduction

In this chapter we take up the problematic of the coexistence of two constructs, 'knowledge cumulation' and 'interdisciplinarity'. This problematic came to our attention as we worked on an 'interdisciplinary' research project funded as part of the Technology Enhanced Learning (TEL) Programme in the UK. The project is called 'Personalization of learning: constructing an interdisciplinary research space' and appropriately the research team was a multidisciplinary one. In this chapter we focus on just one of the project aims: 'researching the discourse processes, practices, opportunities and management challenges of interdisciplinary collaboration' as well as on the concept of 'knowledge cumulation'. Both 'interdisciplinarity' and 'knowledge cumulation' are two terms that are embedded in the TEL Programme documentation. From the early stages of our research collaboration we have become puzzled by the ways in which the idea of 'knowledge cumulation' is both present and absent in our interdisciplinary conversations. In order to work with the tensions around the coexistence of the two seemingly incompatible concepts of 'interdisciplinarity' and 'knowledge cumulation', this chapter draws on actor-network theory.

Collaborations between disciplines and institutions are a key characteristic of contemporary knowledge production and professional practice. These collaborations are symptomatic of a blurring of boundaries between disciplines and institutions, which partially reflects the current emphasis on 'practice' and 'working knowledge' (Symes and McIntyre 2000), as well as on the complexity of 'real world' questions that contemporary research is responding to. In addition, new technologies, such as digital repositories and virtual collaboration environments foreground the changes in practices around knowledge creation, where educational institutions and learners are not simply consumers but also knowledge creators (Carmichael 2007).

However, while the concept of interdisciplinarity 'makes sense' its realisation is often fraught and problematic. Each discipline area is located within a particular set of discourses and histories, within specific social structures using particular kinds of language – all of which inform particular kinds of research interests and questions. Therefore, at times the dialogue between disciplines occurs within a contested space requiring a considerable amount of negotiation as the participants work around various stakes, theoretical perspectives, investments and power relationships (Carmichael 2007; Scheeres and Solomon 2000). As a consequence of these negotiations, the interdisciplinary outcomes are part of the capacity-building process (Newell 2001).

Not surprisingly, interdisciplinary research is understood to be an important way of approaching research in TEL. TEL crosses subject and theoretical areas including technical domains (e.g. computer science, technology), design disciplines (e.g. system design, human computer interaction design), learning fields (e.g. education, lifelong learning, cognitive psychology) and disciplines concerned with communication, communities and discourse (e.g. social sciences, linguistics). Furthermore, the emergence of technologies and their use for knowledge construction means that one or two disciplines can no longer adequately provide the breadth of vision and practices that work with the complexities of contemporary life, work and learning. Appropriately (in our view) the 2006 UK TEL Programme invited a reconfiguration of TEL research in terms of the *new collaborations* (interdisciplinary) and *new accountabilities* (users and others). This is recognisable as part of the contemporary emphasis on modes of knowledge production, which indicate cross discipline, cross-sector collaborations and doing relevant research (Gibbons *et al.* 1994).

As indicated earlier the research team was an interdisciplinary one. The team was made up of 12 collaborators working in the same university. They were located in different disciplines and fields (social sciences, education, human computer interaction design, computer science, informatics and business). Included in the group were three professors, three programme directors and two learning technologists. Identified in a different way there were four educationalists, five technology designers and three people linked with user groups. While interdisciplinary research and interdisciplinary higher education academic programme may be increasingly understood as desirable, the disciplinary homes of academics together with the disciplinary structures of universities help to sustain disciplinary identities and silo-like practices. Therefore, it is unlikely that this group would have come together for an extended research project without the specific interdisciplinary conditions set by the TEL Programme and by the cross-disciplinary interest in the topic 'Personalization of Learning'.

In the Programme call for research proposals, the conditions for investigating 'interdisciplinarity' and cross-sector collaborations deploy a particular discourse that frames success, and excellence in terms of 'cumulation of knowledge'; the term accumulation is adopted as a synonym (*Understanding, Creating, and Exploiting Digital Technologies for Learning* 2006: 6). It is possible to recognise this as a response to pressure for accountability in educational research. For example, Whitty writes:

> Although the overall picture was not entirely bleak, politicians reading the headlines and press reports could perhaps be forgiven for believing that UK education research as a whole was characterised by the follow-

ing features.... Failure to produce cumulative research findings....
Theoretical incoherence.... Inaccessibility and poor dissemination....
Poor cost effectiveness.

(2005: 2)

This rhetoric invokes the language of 'value for money', 'results for investments' and 'evidence-based' practice, drawing attention to the current focus
on the economic benefits of education.

In response, the public face of the TEL Programme foregrounds the values
of 'authentic interdisciplinarity' and equal 'engagement of users, stakeholders and potential beneficiaries' (*Understanding, Creating, and Exploiting Digital
Technologies for Learning* 2006: 5, 6). However, at the same time, there is an
implicit construction of 'cumulation' as hierarchical, incremental, additive
and progressive; and 'knowledge' as a commodity with fixed quantifiable
characteristics. The form and content of the outcomes are predefined. We
suggest that there is a risk that the TEL vision will be undermined if the
requirement for demonstrating 'knowledge cumulation' is regarded as
unproblematic rather than as a construct that for the time being does rhetor-
ical work for reconfiguring TEL research.

What follows is a discussion of our use of a particular theoretical frame to
explore the workings of our TEL research project. We use actor-network
theory as it allows us to explore the complexities that we describe as a *messy*
landscape of interdisciplinary research practices. Exploring our research in
this way challenges the more idealised accounts of knowledge cumulation
practices.

Setting the stage

Actor-network theory (ANT) is increasingly influential in education (Fox
2005; Nespor 1994), the social sciences (Latour 2005; Law 2004) and
technology design (Suchman 2007), and 'part of a shift from individualized, psychological approaches to understanding of knowledge-building
to more social and cultural interpretations' (Edwards and Nicoll 2007:
187). The ANT frame offers a way of understanding this transition, which
is not fixed in time or space but is distributed and enacted so that 'when
we act we're simultaneously interacting with the people and things in
the immediate environment *and* with people and things spatially and
temporally removed from us, but none the less present in the situation in
some way' (Nespor 1994: 3).

Theorising learning transition in interdisciplinary research entails tracking reconfiguration of research practices and changes to the relations of
power and knowledge. Interdisciplinarity implies boundary transgressions
and challenges disciplinary training, habits and even identities (Barry *et al*.
2008).

We find ANT is useful in examining eddies and whirlpools in the flows
of reconfiguration. In our analysis, we use four ideas from ANT:

- *What becomes important?* The activity of constructing the world as textured relationships (networks), which include actants that are human, physical artefacts (e.g. computers, reports) and semiotic (e.g. the idea of 'knowledge cumulation').
- *How does the stable state come to be?* The occasional stabilisation of networks that produce regimes of truth and embody rules of engagement and rituals, ways of thinking and understanding and language practices.
- *What is invisible?* A stable network is understood as a black box that is treated as a 'fact' – where 'facts' and 'explanations of closure' suggest certainties that put aside contradictions and complexities that might otherwise become problematic.
- *What is forgotten or simplified?* The performative activity in unstable networks that are characterised by controversies and uncertainties in the way people talk and write about groups, actions, objects and facts.

The remainder of this chapter is divided into four. The first three parts start with an observation and a theoretical lens that is then used to deconstruct our collaborations in terms of: 'Becoming a TEL project', 'Doing TEL project work' and 'Performing on a TEL project' (respectively). We conclude with some insights into how ANT makes the invisible more visible, and how the performative activity (including the unspeakable) can scaffold a network in creating research practices that are somewhat different from the idealist public narrative.

Becoming a TEL project

Our first observation is on the black boxing of the 'knowledge cumulation' construct. The term black box is used in engineering and software design whenever a piece of machinery or code becomes very complex, and the complexity is represented as a black box about which nothing needs to be known except its input and output. The black box denotes confidence in what is inside. What is inside is finished and no longer part of the research. TEL assessment criteria construct 'authentic interdisciplinarity' as the subject and object of research but in contrast, 'knowledge cumulation' is black boxed. Latour writes about the effect of black boxing: 'no matter how controversial their history, how complex their inner workings, how large the commercial or academic networks that hold them in place, only their input and output count' (1987: 3).

Looking inside the black box (in the context of our TEL project) consider for example a flashback to March 2006.

Uncertainty, relationships at work, pressure, lack of time, competition, conjecture, intuition, hearsay, risks and costs, search for clues, controversies – this is what is inside the black box. Evidence of 'knowledge cumulation' had to be gathered, and constructed as part of the interdisciplinarity collaboration.

Following the town meeting a pragmatic decision was made to 'locate'

Story 1. Behind the scenes

On a sunny Tuesday in March 2006, I went to Brunei Gallery Lecture Theatre at SOAS in London for the TEL Programme town meeting. Before going I had some snatched conversations with colleagues, here are some snippets: 'Why technology enhanced – what happened to e-learning', 'It is probably about building demonstrators'; 'You need a track record of technology funding, it is hard to go in cold, who do you know?'; 'Yes, xxx is shrewd, she thinks it's techie more than education'; 'Interdisciplinary won't count in the RAE'; 'Use your intuition if it feels like a dead end drop it'; 'Makes me tired just thinking about it'; 'You go for it – but I haven't got much time'; 'Think of it as part of constructing our research identity'.

The briefing was organized formally in an auditorium with comfortable seats and dimmed lighting. The stage was set with corporate backdrop; this was big, real, and exciting. I came away thinking there is a shift – it felt like a new kind of questioning. It might be worth having a go if we can come up with the right story. On the other hand, questions from the floor came from people who where known to the speakers (who used their first names). Those on the outside signalled – 'what is in it for my business', 'my University is new realistically we are not going to get a look in, are we?' I did not stay for the networking workshops (it was too late to build partnerships) but I did go back to the office and forage for clues on the web on where this had come from, to work out where it might go.

(Constructed from researcher's diary and quotes: 10 March 2007)

researchers from different disciplines within the same university. Most of the people approached had at some time been on an internal mailing list for an 'Open and Distance Learning Special Interest' group. At least five of the final group had significant research funding in their own field and regarded her/himself an e-learning expert. Everybody had heard of the TEL call, but nobody knew 'much' about it. The approach was bottom up in the words used to persuade the group: 'we do e-learning, we do e-learning research, personalization of learning is relevant to what we do, how do we become funded researchers?' The first meeting was all about mobilisation of individual assets for a common purpose.

The 'game' was to submit a credible bid for funding. Who was best placed to lead? What technology should we focus on? Who are the users? What about financial arrangements? What level of commitment? What key papers to reference? What collaborations to highlight? And the 'game' had to be 'played' under pressure: not enough time! Not enough admin support! Exam marking! What about my sabbatical coming up? How to work around access to Je-S? Partially convinced players needed to be persuaded. Each member of the group agreed to contribute two sides of A4 text and provide a list of their relevant references (own and others). That was as far as anybody was prepared to commit to a venture that would be too good to miss (if it turned out to be a win) but also a risky waste of time (felt like a likely loser)!

Story 2. Nothing ventured anything gained

PERSON Y: So how are we going to do this, there are some big egos here?
PERSON X: The only way this is going to work is if we make everybody a Co-principal investigator.
[Refers to printed emails covered with highlighter and exclamation marks.]
PERSON X: I have everybody's texts. Can't believe everybody had the same brief! We are all over the place or in different places.
PERSON Y: Don't try to integrate it. Use it as data and quote. Play up the 'University of business the professions' branding.
PERSON X: We'll have to make the links between the publications (from the group). How do we show cumulation? The call puts a lot of emphasis on the reference list.
PERSON Y: References depends on who we think the referees are going to be. Include a reference to funded output from each of the agency listed in the call – don't want to hurt anyone's feelings.
PERSON X: Ok so tactics! And how are we interdisciplinary?
PERSON Y: That's what we are going to research but we also have to be it now [laugh].
(Constructed from researcher's diary and quotes: 18 March 2007)

This heterogeneous account is not an arbitrary prelude to the real work. The proposal physically emerged from a series of localised contingencies, last-minute decisions and workarounds. As in other accounts of constructing research, context and contents merge (Latour 1987). The idea of temporal issues opens up a nexus of meanings. There is the sense of academics teaching time, career aspirations as in life time, and project time with deadlines, all of which compete for attention and priority.

This raw account of becoming a TEL project challenges more sanitised versions of rational, methodical 'knowledge cumulation'. It works around the need to demonstrate 'knowledge cumulation' in a certain way by co-constructing potential collaborators, materials like the 'reference lists', and ideas like 'the University brand' – as coherent indicators of 'knowledge cumulation'. Does the co-construction of coherence change or influence the practices of people who take part or does the straitjacket of constructs like 'knowledge cumulation' result in public stances with particular audiences in mind? The performative nature of ANT networks means that activity is closest to the ebb and flow of what is changing so we now turn to the 'doing' of our TEL project.

Doing a TEL project

The second observation is that disciplines work through actants that are carriers of the discipline. Actants include people, artefacts and particular research practices. Disciplines are disciplinary and so regulate how we

Story 3. In search of method

PERSON X: I really like the ANT metaphor of research as travelling on foot, at a slow pace, as a way of experiencing and seeing culture and landscape (backpacking), compared to the rapid freewheeling on the superhighway towards a fixed destination (driving).

PERSON Y: So that makes you a backpacker when you say here: 'From the project's inception (during bid writing) the group has collectively and individually generated discursive texts. The conversations in our meetings have been recorded. In addition we have also assembled quotes and thick accounts from online and face-to-face communications and field notes from observation.'

PERSON N: The project needs more structure a super highway to travel on?

PERSON X: No point in building one let's pick a motorway a kind of 'Route 40' that people know about.

PERSON Y: You mean carefully select DELPHI [Lempert *et al.* 2003] as a tool for structuring our conversations. 'The group began by asking what are our research questions, and how can we build on current theoretical frameworks, issues and findings?' Drawing on discussions at face-to-face meeting a questionnaire was developed. The questionnaire was distributed online and extended textual responses were collected for 12 questions.[1] This was followed up with discussion, abstraction and refinement of various positions and changes.

PERSON X: Doesn't sound like ANT except DELPHI becomes an actor...

(Constructed from quotes, technical reports and DELPHI questionnaire 29 March 2007; metaphor from Latour 2005)

I The questionnaire included the following questions: What do you understand by 'interdisciplinary'? What do you understand by 'knowledge cumulation'? (DELPHI questionnaire round I: II December 2007).

framed our activity and purpose – even as it is enacted in the coming together of different discourses.

Some terms are a common part of the research world even though uses, customs and practices vary radically, e.g. methodology, research questions and data. This is not the case with the phrase 'knowledge cumulation'.

Story 4. Never heard of it

PERSON X: I'm looking at the responses to the question: 'What do you understand by knowledge cumulation?'

PERSON Y: It seems people have things to say about 'research questions', 'methodology' etc., but when it comes to 'knowledge cumulation' it is a blank.

PERSON X: Yes comments like: 'I simply don't use this term'; 'I don't know the term', and 'This is not a term I am familiar with'. Some people link it to interdisciplinarity for example: 'Is this meant to refer to the interdisciplinary dimension? The

whole better than the parts? Or longevity, the older the wiser?' and 'Does it refer to
the fact that bringing people from different disciplines together means that the overall
body of knowledge is enhanced?'
PERSON Y: It might be because the question is at the end, but saying nothing at all
is different to saying what does it (knowledge cumulation) mean. Most people just
aren't familiar with the phrase.
PERSON X: Some of the group want us to get on with it ... you know knowledge
cumulation.

(Constructed from quotes; responses to questionnaire round
1 March 2007, and quotes 12 March 2007)

So is 'knowledge cumulation' a new idea or new to some people in the
group? At some level, in the bid writing, we responded to national and
international discourse around what counts as cumulative knowledge, and
how this is negotiated, represented and warranted (James and Brown 2005).
This was constructed on behalf of the group by the application writers. On
the other hand, 'knowledge cumulation' may have other labels and no label
at all and still be embedded in discourse. The question of *what is* 'research'
and 'progression' for our TEL project is a localised version of the multiple
coexisting discourses around 'knowledge cumulation' and 'interdisciplinarity' in the governance of the TEL Programme. This is evident in controlled
conflicts in story 5, and account of how interdisciplinarity is understood in
story 6.

Story 5. Getting on with research

At the first meeting people in the room divided broadly but not cleanly into two
camps. C1 is tentatively called 'applied technology science' (the e in e-learning),
and C2 is even more tentatively called 'learning/education'. C1 came with
artefacts (laptop, PDA) their mobiles were visible and ready. In-between times
the conversation revolved around devices, hints and tips on 'must have' technologies, and can't wait for (this or that) technology. C1 people 'demonstrated' and
'explained' to C2 people, who responded with (forced) ohs and ahs.

(Researcher's diary 9 December 2006)

At one stage availability of the domain name 'ourspace.org' was checked before we
could discuss this as a possible short name for the project. The response via wireless
was not questioned even though the initial answer (yes) was inaccurate. The technology empowered those in possession of the technology to influence the act of naming.

(Researcher's comment 24 November 2008)

Frustrations became to surface as the group struggled to understand itself.

'Is this about interdisciplinarity or is it about Personalization of technologies',
'what are our research questions', 'when are we going to start', 'what are the
milestones', 'Shouldn't we be using technology on a technology project'.

Technology solutions to the 'problem' of slow progress were offered; 'I use a really good online project management site and it is free'. 'We need to be pushy and show visibility what about a streaming video of our meetings'.

This jarred with voices from elsewhere, 'we have already started – this conversation is part of the research', 'this is not only a technology project'.

Back again: 'but what do we do with this stream of text and talk, how does it answer real research questions not just exploring'.

(Constructed from quotes 20 March 2007)

It seems that in the doing of our TEL project we rejected the label 'knowledge cumulation' but different senses of this emerged in our activities anyway. The activity is not so much consensus, synthesis and integration but more like speaking different languages, identity assertions and conflict management. Or going with the flows. Disciplines do not frame research questions in the same way so framing common research questions is a stumbling block even when the topic (in this case personalization of learning) is shared.

Performing on a TEL project

The third observation is the uncertainties around the meaning of actions, objects and facts when different people and people in groups are acting out (performing) interdisciplinary activity.

Each researcher expressed strongly that their involvement in the project was part of an existing identity coming out of a personal history that provided them with relevant research capabilities. In many different acts online, in face-to-face meeting, formally and informally, they reiterated a simple faith that interdisciplinarity made sense. Everyone in the group saw her/himself as a person who has crossed boundaries, for example between different types of work, between academia and industry, across sectors and disciplines. However, interdisciplinary identity work brings into play disciplinary identities that go beyond subjective border-crossing skills to include particular kinds of research interests, questions and languages. We observed that the very construction of interdisciplinarity is regulated by the disciplines. Consider for example the differences between the three positions in story 6.

As a group we accepted and embraced the label 'interdisciplinarity' but seem to interpret this from particular disciplinary perspectives. The juxtapositions in the story suggest at least the potential for irreconcilable conflict, but there are other performances, which contain the situation. In particular interpersonal alliances contained frustrations behind the scenes. In the collective forum (i.e. face-to-face meetings) care was taken to avert open confrontations through the use of humour, the sharing of chat and personal details and the use of the terms 'we' to suggest group cohesion. The key driver for this reserve and discipline came from a shared commitment to work together.

Story 6. I do interdisciplinary (already)

A postmodernist position:

> Knowledge cumulation and interdisciplinarity is just another way of talking about research, we can move the idea about and use it in different situations for different purposes, for example: public narrative (presenting ourselves); gathering (appropriating ideas to fit our frames of reference); entrenchment (I'm right); and identity work (this is what I am).

Applied science position:

> Interdisciplinary means the bringing together of two or more disciplines to work on a problem of shared interest and importance. For example in project xxxxx environmentalists, engineers, and software developers worked together in an interdisciplinary team. The environmentalists were concerned with accuracy and amount of knowledge and information available. The software developers were concerned with efficiency and architecture, and the users (expert or novice) were concerned about the simplicity of the search interface and general ease of use.

Entrepreneurial position:

> If people work together they soon co-develop... for example as a result of the national teaching fellowship scheme, genuine interdisciplinary partnerships have arisen. I am working closely with a professor of drama. Xxxxx in Law has been working with an expert in dance. We have called this: extreme collaboration.
>
> (Constructed from quotes, technical reports, meeting notes and DELPHI questionnaire 20 March 2007)

But there was multiplicity in enactment and understanding of the shared commitment. Consider the diversity in the small sample in story 7.

Story 7. Sure I'm committed

Funding. 'I know the meeting (was) challenging ... but at the same time re-affirming our commitment to work towards the larger bid.'

Research. 'Between us we have got to go to every TEL seminar event and make contacts with the other capacity building projects – this is our chance.'

Career. 'Can you give me the Ourspace project website address I'm applying for promotion.'

Enterprise. 'The spin-off company is interested in extended inter-company collaboration.'

Institution. ' *"Now It's Personal" Learning Futures week* around the themes of Personalization of learning and the future for educational institutions in 2020.'

(Email 10 December 2006; conversations 20 January 2007, website 2 May 2007)

Law writes: 'Realities are not explained by practices and beliefs but are instead produced in them' (2004: 59). Considering how our TEL project was performed demonstrates the uncertain and complex lives of people, physical artefacts and semiotics.

Conclusions

Interdisciplinary research is influenced by all the personal, historical and cultural practices that shape disciplinary research. The ANT way of 'looking' makes the invisible more visible and shows that stipulating 'interdisciplinarity' and 'knowledge cumulation' is not enough to reconfigure the landscape of TEL research.

In the final report for our project we made two claims: (1) interdisciplinarity is about understanding and enabling a strong and sustained commitment to work together; and (2) TEL interdisciplinarity is about working with disciplinary differences rather than battling though them. While we stand by these findings, this chapter demonstrates that these claims are relative.

In spite of the complexities and tensions in working as an interdisciplinary team we continued to work together until the project ended. Why was this? Is it that: 'The "coming together" seems to work best when it is not imposed but rather when it is motivated by a shared need – be it a research question or a concern with professional practice' (responses to questionnaire 1 March 2007). At times, the shared purpose is questionable (see story 7).

Perhaps another answer is that in spite of the irreconcilable interdisciplinary conflicts, there is the potential of another project. We cannot ignore other actors on our institutional stage, and those actors are 'income' and 'academic prestige'. Funded research carries status and power. If we dig deeper into the black box of 'knowledge cumulation' what will we find? The unspoken – that, perhaps 'knowledge cumulation' is warranted by an accumulation of research income?

We show in this chapter that 'cumulation of knowledge' is constructed in a particular way. This, however, is not a revelation because everything is socially, culturally and historically constructed. Rather the issue is that the actor 'cumulation of knowledge' makes (or implies) contestable claims about its relationship to another actor called the 'TEL Programme'.

Acknowledgement

The authors would like to thank our colleagues and collaborators who agreed to take part in the research reported here. This work is part of the TEL Project Grant reference RES-139–25–0368, funded by ESRC in partnership with EPSRC and the e-Science Core Programme, and managed as part of the ESRC's Teaching and Learning Research Programme (TLRP).

References

Barry, A., Born, G. and Weszkalnys, G. (2008) 'Logics of interdisciplinarity', *Economy and Society* 37, 20–49.

Carmichael, P. (2007) 'Introduction: Technological development, capacity building and knowledge construction in education research', *Technology, Pedagogy and Education* 16, 235–247.

Edwards, R. and Nicoll, K. (2007) 'Action at a distance: Governmentality, subjectivity and workplace learning', in S. Billett, T. Fenwick and M. Somerville (eds), *Work, Subjectivity and Learning*, London: Springer, pp. 179–193.

Fox, S. (2005) 'An actor-network critique of community in higher education: Implications for networked learning', *Studies in Higher Education* 30, 95–110.

Gibbons, M., Limoges, C., Nowotny, H., Schwartzman, S., Scott, P. and Trow, M. (1994) *The New Production of Knowledge: The dynamics of science and research in contemporary societies*, London: Sage.

James, M. and Brown, S. (2005) 'Grasping the TLRP nettle: Preliminary analysis and some enduring issues surrounding the improvement of learning outcomes', *Curriculum Journal* 16, 7–30.

Latour, B. (1987) *Science in Action*, Cambridge, MA: Harvard University Press.

Latour, B. (2005) *Reassembling the Social: An introduction to actor-network-theory*, New York: Oxford University Press.

Law, J. (2004) *After Method Mess in Social Science Research*, London and New York: Routledge.

Lempert, R.J., Popper, S. and Bankes, S.C. (2003) *Shaping the Next One Hundred Years: New methods for quantitative, long-term policy analysis.* Rand Pardee Centre, Boston University, MA: RAND Research Centre.

Nespor, J. (1994) *Knowledge in Motion: Space, time, and curriculum in undergraduate physics and management*, London: Falmer Press.

Newell, W.H. (2001) 'A theory of interdisciplinary studies', *Issues in Integrative Studies* 19, 1–25.

Scheeres, H. and Solomon, N. (2000) 'Whose text? Methodological dilemmas in collaborative research practice', in A. Lee and C. Poynton (eds), *Culture and Text*, Sydney: Allen & Unwin, pp. 114–131.

Suchman, L. (2007) *Human–Machine Reconfigurations Plans and Situated Actions* (2nd edn), Cambridge: Cambridge University Press.

Symes, C. and McIntyre, J. (eds) (2000) *Working Knowledge: New vocationalism in higher education*, Milton Keynes: Open University Press.

Understanding, Creating, and Exploiting Digital Technologies for Learning (2006) Research on Technology Enhanced Learning, Call for Research Proposals. Online, available at: www.tlrp.org/manage/documents/CALLTELfinal-1.pdf (accessed 30 March 2007).

Whitty, G. (2005) *Education(al) Research and Education Policy Making: Is conflict inevitable?* Inaugural Presidential Address British Education Research Association, University of Glamorgan, September 2005. Online, available at: www.ioe.ac.uk/directorate/BERA2005PresidentialAddress.pdf (accessed 30 March 2007).

Part III

Transitions through working life

Chapter 14

Working out work

Integrated development practices in organizations

Clive Chappell, Hermine Scheeres, David Boud and Donna Rooney

Introduction

Employees when asked to nominate where they learn how to do their job overwhelmingly point to their workplace as a major site of learning (Skule and Reichborn 2002). Researchers, policy makers and practitioners have taken up this idea to understand how and to what extent workplaces are sites for learning, and how work and learning can be better integrated to benefit both individuals and organizations (Ellström 2001). For the most part, these endeavours have either focused on examining structured learning at work leading to a qualification or tailored to the specific skill needs of the organization (e.g. Griffiths 2004; Fuller and Unwin 2003), or they have focused on understanding the significance and facilitation of learning that can occur during the normal activities of work (e.g. Billett 2002).

This contemporary focus on the integration of work and learning in organizations has resulted in a re-examination of learning theories in terms of their usefulness in the context of learning at work (Hendry 1996). There is growing acceptance among educational thinkers that understanding learning at work challenges learning theories that have informed traditional education and training pedagogies commonly deployed in organizational and workplace contexts. New understandings of learning are emerging as a result of the uncoupling of learning from the dominant learning theories that have operated in the field of education and training (OECD 2003). Contemporary views on learning in relation to work explore practices that are outside formally prescribed learning situations, have no instructional metaphors and do not employ traditional pedagogical activities (Bereiter 1994; Saugstad 2005; Hager 2003; Fuller *et al.* 2005). In other words, the practices are not explicitly named or described using teaching and learning discourses.

We suggest that we now need to look to other theoretical resources to understand the dynamic and complex relationships and transitions that characterize learning at work. For example, there are work practices that are specifically named, and often supplemented by explicit company documentation, that are part of the profile of the organization – integral to the way it 'works' – that are not usually seen as learning practices. Identifying and investigating these practices, as learning practices is the focus of the Australian

Research Council Discovery project *Beyond Training and Learning: Integrated Development Practices in Organizations*.

Integrated development practices

The importance of learning in and by organizations, and the integration of work and learning have increased in significance in order to manage the uncertainties and rapid changes that characterize workplaces operating in the contemporary global economy (Bonal and Rambla 2003; Ellström 2001). As Felstead *et al.* (2004) observe, in the twenty-first century workplace, learning by doing, workers organizing and checking their own work and, crucially, advice, understanding, coaching and counselling (rather than directives) from line managers, have emerged as keys to the development of effective and productive staff.

In this context, learning is embedded in practices beyond those traditionally understood as training or workplace learning. They include practices such as performance management, teamwork, succession planning, career development, coaching and mentoring, and more. These kinds of organizational practices, although not new, have recently come to the fore as important organizational discourses and practices. As such, the new spaces they take up are creating new meanings and understandings of what constitutes work and who people are at work. What employees learn and how they learn at work involve the production of different discourses and practices from those of the past. One way of characterizing these practices is as hybrid or transitional, bridging the binary between formal (course-based) and informal or incidental learning (Hodkinson *et al.* 2008). We argue that what distinguishes many of these contemporary practices is that they simultaneously (and often explicitly) perform organizational functions unrelated to learning; however, they almost always involve learning of some kind. Indeed, it is usually the function other than learning that is foregrounded in their representation, and any notion of a transition from working to learning work remains unacknowledged. These functions include such things as contributing to organizational effectiveness, developing new organizational relationships and creating new accountabilities and work roles. The commonality in almost all of these practices is that they are introduced as strategies to effect organizational development.

In the discussion so far, we have used the term 'practice' repeatedly, and particular kinds of practices are the focus of our research project. Our understanding of practices follows Schatzki (2006: 1864), who sees practices as 'structured, spatial-temporal manifolds of action such as political practices, cooking practices, recreational practices and religious practices'. Practices comprise both structure and action where structure includes understandings of the 'how to' of a practice, the rules, possible ends and goals as well as general understandings, and action is about the carrying out of a practice. Thus, practices encompass what 'goes on' in an organization on a day-to-day basis, as well as what makes these 'goings-on' possible (or not). We use the term 'integrated' to refer to practices that are part of what constitutes work, and 'development' to refer to some kind of positive consequence or outcome for the organization (and perhaps also for the employee).

We use the term *Integrated Development Practices* (IDPs) to mean organizational practices that are: independent of formal training programmes and are not defined in terms of training/learning/education; managed or implemented by those who do not have as their primary job function managing training or learning; and introduced as practices that attempt to invoke an organizational influence of some sort. In general, these are familiar practices in discourses of organizational management, but less understood in terms of learning. There has been little detailed examination of how these kinds of organizational practices construct and produce learning, and we suggest that researching these practices in terms of learning can contribute to understanding how particular work practices involve learning by workers. In our empirical work so far, we find that not only are organizations invoking these practices, but also staff create their own IDPs that operate in and on the organization. The identification of these employee-generated practices is not only extending the ways in which we are thinking about IDPs, but it is leading us to consider ways in which integrated development practices can be 'created' by employees to produce work satisfying for themselves as well as being consistent with the goals of the organization.

Learning in practice

Drawing on the work of early educational theorists such as Dewey, Piaget and Vygotsky, constructivist learning theories offer a view of learning in which learners construct meaning for themselves through the activities they undertake. This notion of learning has grown in significance in studies of organizations and other social settings in that it recognizes that much learning occurs without direct educational interventions (Saugstad 2005; Bereiter 1994). Saugstad (2005: 352) refers to this kind of learning as learning in practice and suggests that 'our contemporary understanding of learning is so closely tied to scholastic (school) learning that we are inclined to overlook the fact that learning in practice differs radically from learning in schools'. Further, practice should not be conceived as the isolated activities of the individual or as ritualized, bureaucratized and institutionalized activities based on general maxims or rules. Rather actions must be judged from case to case, and Saugstad notes the work on 'situated practice' by Lave and Wenger (1991) as an example of how learning in, and as practice, is being theorized.

Tensions remain within constructivist learning theory (James and Bloomer 2001; Hodkinson *et al.* 2008), largely to do with the relational dynamics that exist between the individual-socio-cultural dualism in the practices of learning. There is general agreement though that learning involves practice or activity in which individuals interact with their social world, changing both themselves and the social world at the same time. Ways of understanding practice(s) and activity(ies) in relation to learning have recently become a focus of research.

Practice theory

The focus on activity in contemporary constructivist learning theory is mirrored in social theory. Schatzki (2001: 2), for example, suggests that 'practices' have, for many contemporary social theorists become 'the primary generic social thing' and are seen as 'embodied, materially mediated arrays of human activity centrally organised around shared practical understanding'. For Schatzki, all social phenomena are aspects or components of the field of practices, which in turn is seen as the total nexus of interconnected human practices. This 'practice turn' is the latest attempt to transcend an ongoing dilemma in social theory illustrated by Barnes who writes, 'Practices are enacted by people, and simply because of this they are an insufficient basis for an understanding of the ongoing pattern of social life that they constitute' (2001: 29).

Disagreements continue concerning the relational connections between structure and agency, subjectivity and objectivity, individual and culture and theory and practice (Bretell 2002), with social and cultural theorists 'see-sawing' between these problematic dualisms. The weakening of the concept of agency and the strengthening of structure has been a feature of social theorizing since the time of Weber and Durkheim. More recently cultural theorists have problematized the essentialist notion of the individual, suggesting instead that the individual is constituted through a discursive process open to ongoing reconstruction. Bourdieu (1990, 2001) for example sees the subject as constructed through the twin concepts of habitus and field. That is, the subject is constructed as a durable but changeable set of dispositions derived from the mental and physical embodiment of the social by individuals (habitus), and the structuring (field) of social relations in which positions are derived relationally (James and Bloomer 2001). Post-humanist sociologists Callon (1991) and Latour (1992) go further, rejecting any distinction between human and nonhuman agency in social activity. Giddens (1979) and Ortner (1996) attempt to restore a degree of agency and the individual human subject within social theorizations. They suggest that although subjects can be understood as being structurally and culturally produced, there is always an element of agency in this production. For Giddens and Ortner subjects are therefore constituted as partly 'knowing' subjects capable of escaping overly deterministic cultural and structural production.

Despite these disagreements Schatzki (2001) suggests that there is general agreement that the 'practice approach' involves analyses that develop an account of practices, either the field of practices or a subdomain thereof and that treat the field of practices as the place to study the nature and transformation of their subject matter.

In the context of our research, practice theory is useful because it suggests that any analysis of learning at work must involve analysis of the field(s) of practice in which learning takes place. And as Saugstad writes, 'learning and activities in practice are closely connected, since learning is understood as changing positions in a changing social practice'. Learning can therefore be understood as being 'located within the context of activity and/or in a social practice' (2005: 351) and related somehow to change. Embedded in these ideas is that learning and practice involve relationships – among people, between people and systems and processes, and so on. Thus, work on networks of practices, or activities, is discussed in the next part of the chapter (Hodkinson *et al.* 2008).

Activity theory

With its origins in the work of Vygotsky, particularly his notion of mediating action through cultural artefacts, and Leont'ev's work on individual action and collective activity, activity theory has made an important impact in understanding the processes of learning. Engeström (2001) maintains the centrality of the interrelation between the nature of the individual subject's actions and the community in which the individual acts. He suggests that the weakness of Leont'ev's theory is that it fails to account for diversity in the context of community and the pluralist perspectives that inhabit contemporary communities. Thus, he argues that activity theory must develop conceptual tools that can account for multiple perspectives that can be used to understand how networks of activity systems interact with each other. He puts forward the view that the interaction of activity systems surfaces contradictions that become 'sources of change and development' (2001: 137).

Reeves and Forde (2004) deploy some of Engeström's ideas in their analysis of the impact continuing professional development has on the practice of Scottish teachers wishing to move into leadership roles. They use the concept of 'activity sets', suggesting that the concept foregrounds the ways in which different activity sets interpenetrate and create interference and interaction between them. They define the broad characteristics of an activity set as:

- centring around the pursuit of a particular objective or activity;
- having its own discourses and artefacts that are used by members of the set;
- embodying a particular point of view and hence a set of values;
- having a membership that is acknowledged by the people involved and forms an element, however minor, in defining their identities;
- being permeable so that members of the set belong to others;
- exercising the means for inclusion and exclusion in terms of membership;
- bounded in terms of time and space.

They also indicate in a similar way to Engeström that activity sets intersect and compete, creating tensions and contradictions that have the potential to change the activities.

Research project: integrated development practices in organizations

In our investigations of organizational practices in four diverse workplaces we are drawing on a number of the theoretical insights outlined. First, after

Schatzki, we use his notion of practice, and we see IDPs as subdomains of the field of practices that construct organizational life and our investigations focus on situated practices in particular organizations. Second, after Engeström, we understand organizational life as constituted by activity systems, which are often in tension creating the conditions for changing activity. Third, after Reeves and Forde, we make use of their characteristics of activity sets to analyse particular IDPs in the organizations we are investigating. We suggest that organizations are both domains of practice and activity systems where the playing out of IDPs involves complementarity and contradiction, as well as creativity and improvisation.

One starting point is that IDPs are often deployed in the pursuit of particular organizational objectives such as performance improvement, change management and organizational effectiveness, and therefore have many of the characteristics outlined. However, we also suggest that these practices are simultaneously examples of learning in practice. We therefore understand IDPs as being strong organizational change practices and weak learning practices. By this we mean they are understood either explicitly (named and documented), or implicitly (emerging from employees themselves) as organizationally focused. When learning is named or surfaced, it can be a 'value added'.

One of the tasks we have set ourselves in this research is to develop an account of the IDPs from the perspective of organizational change and learning, while at the same time identifying what and how learning occurs for employees within the organization.

The discussion above has outlined the theoretical approaches that we are finding useful in our research project, and it has also positioned our research in relation to some of the key ideas from these approaches. The chapter now goes on to present some of the data and findings; it focuses on how and why particular organizational practices are IDPs, and it offers some ways in which we are beginning to frame these IDPs as learning practices. We do not take up all of the theoretical ideas here, rather we concentrate on how this kind of exploration and understanding of practice(s) can draw out and add to knowledge about work and learning.

Research sites, methods and initial observations

At the time of writing we have undertaken empirical work in two organizations: one in the community sector (community college), the other in the public sector (local council). The college is a not-for-profit community sector organization located in the inner-city suburbs of the city of Sydney. It provides community and adult education, ranging from adult literacy, language, business skills and computing courses to weekend hobby courses. The college employs about ten full-time employees, ten casual employees and over 300 sessional tutors. The management structure of the college has few hierarchical levels. The Principal is responsible for the day-to-day management and reports to the college board. Reporting to the Principal are three Faculty Managers, the Customer Service Manager, the Bursar and a Marketing and Promotions Manager. These managers lead small work teams comprising both full-time and casual employees.

The council is a large local council in the Sydney metropolitan area. Local councils represent the third layer of government in Australia and are responsible for service provision and governance at a local level. The council provides a vast number of diverse services to its local community. These include the provision of library and community services, road maintenance, waste collection, development assessments, parks and community centres as well as health and regulatory services. The council employs approximately 600 people. Its structure is hierarchical, with the General Manager overseeing all operations across the council's four divisions. Reporting to the General Manager are four Group Managers who are responsible for the day-to-day running of specific parts of the council's operations. Within each division the structure includes a Group Manager, business unit managers, team leaders and workers. The General Manager reports to the elected council that comprises 12 politicians who are either independent candidates or affiliated with a political party. The role of the elected council is to make strategic policy decisions.

Notably, both organizations are in the midst of reconstructing, or adding to, their organizational identities: the college is becoming more business oriented through developing 'user pays' ways of operating, while the council is introducing competitive business practices between its own divisions and departments.

Research methods include workplace observations, semi-structured taped interviews and analysis of organizational documents from each site. Forty semi-structured interviews were conducted with workers across hierarchical levels and functions of both organizations. All interviews were recorded using a digital voice recorder. We analysed organizational documents including annual reports, business plans, policy and procedure documents and job descriptions from both organizations.

The semi-structured interviews have enabled a focus on the experiences of workers as they enacted and extended a number of newly introduced organizational practices. The document analysis has enabled us to understand the formalized descriptions of these organizations, the practices and the jobs within them. The data generated from these methods have enabled various accounts of practice and jobs to emerge. Observations of the worksites were taken prior, during and after the interviews. These enabled us to gain a 'feel' for each workplace.

The interviews constitute our primary data source and the questions are designed to elicit accounts of what people understand as their jobs; how they 'do' their jobs and how they know how and what to do. Further, there is a focus on the organization's processes and experiences of organizational change. Discourses are emerging that link employees' work practices and organizational practices in various ways. We are finding that employees' accounts of their practices – what they are, how they know how to do their work, including new work, how they engage with particular organizational IDPs and so on, raise ways of working and learning that require engagement with understandings of practice from perspectives of both organizations and employees. Some of our initial findings are outlined below in a discussion of three IDPs – performance appraisals, 'acting-up' and an employee-generated IDP – making up one's job.

Performance appraisal

Performance appraisal processes appear explicitly in organizations' accounts of themselves and they are promoted as important development practices for the organization and the individual. However, they are not necessarily regarded as significant practices by employees or their managers. Thus, an organization may portray performance reviews as strong organizational (change) practices, but these may not be experienced by participants as either strong organizational processes or strong learning processes. For example, another council employee comments that she doesn't 'think much of [performance appraisals] for all sorts of reasons – don't think they give much direction about how you're going'. When asked why she thought performance appraisals were an organizational practice in her workplace she answered 'I really don't know – well it's not to do with anything … but there's no direction from the team leader'. In the same organization another employee states 'yeah performance appraisals we do them once a year – they tend to be – they're getting similar each year and it's easy just to repeat each one – feedback we do get feedback there to an extent'. Neither of these workers presents performance appraisal as important in terms of development, although the statement regarding feedback introduces a qualified – 'to an extent' – awareness of the developmental purpose of these practices.

On the other hand, a number of people from both the college and the council gave more complex responses regarding performance appraisal. For example, a council employee sees performance appraisal as part of his everyday work rather than as a separate organizational practice to be 'done' once or twice a year. He thinks that appraisal practices are there 'to keep you on track and to make sure that you're doing what you're meant to and vice versa – to look at training you would need or like'. Thus, he combines notions of surveillance and professional development. A manager from the college similarly refers to the accountability purposes and even though he doesn't see performance appraisal as too onerous, he outlines the 'official' organizational processes that emphasize formality and structure. He uses a discourse of accountability – terms such as 'benchmark' and 'judge' – thus recognizing that accountability is inherent in the appraisal practices, while at the same time offers some notion of employee development or 'moving forward':

> it doesn't happen very frequently – I think we're talking officially supposed to happen … we're talking about structured appraisals where two parties come together with a pre-planned set of questions where they discuss their views on these various criteria and make a – some external benchmark – judge against – make some plan about moving forward.

A more collegial view comes from a council manager, who describes practices around performance appraisal as:

> they say have you done your performance appraisal in June – I say I do it everyday – I call for people – I call people in just do it daily – just a cup of coffee with them – still got to do the formal thing at the end – but I'm sure all the staff realise by now that there's going to be no surprises – I must admit I do – we do joke about it – I get them to fill in the forms and say no-one is to give themselves a five this year – or you'll get my job – and they'll give themselves fours and I don't even care what they give themselves ... if they've given themselves a two I say 'why would you do that?'

Notable in this response is that this manager too uses a discourse of organizational accountability, here characterized by the numerical values ascribed to items of performance, coupled with a mentoring discourse where talk about employees' work practices is integral to everyday work and is characterized by informality and supportive suggestions and advice. His response can be understood as an approach to performance appraisal that fits it in as part of creating and maintaining a collegial work environment. Even though there are competing discourses in his comments, he demonstrates that his practices around performance appraisal are more to do with people's positive sense of themselves – their identities – than any kind of accounting.

'Acting up'

Work reorganization, promotion, resignation or other movements of employees give rise to practices such as 'acting up', a familiar activity in bureaucracies in which individuals temporarily take on a different, usually more senior, position. The position is not normally advertised and the employee reverts back to their substantive position at a later date. It is seen by the organization as a process to ensure work continues smoothly. The existence of the position is not prompted by developmental concerns, nor is it usually formally articulated in terms of either organizational or individual development.

However, the opportunity 'acting up' creates can be useful for individual employees. One council employee's explanation of 'acting up' demonstrates that it can be of benefit to the organization and to her own career as she 'wants to put in place new things' while she is 'there', and she also sees the potential opportunity to 'go for a higher job'. Interestingly, this employee invokes an explicit learning discourse as she adds that this provides 'an opportunity to multi-skill'. Another worker at the council also emphasizes the learning he sees as coming from 'acting up' when he says 'currently I'm acting manager and Team Leader at the front counter... I'm learning heaps as I go along'.

Coaching is an organizational discourse and practice that can be seen as related to learning. One interviewee, a senior council manager, makes this connection explicitly, while at the same time demonstrating how 'acting up' is developmental for both the individual employee and the organization:

> I think there's a lot of coaching happens in this part of the organization every day. A couple of the opportunities are opportunities for people to act in different roles – really big, really big ... we had a vacancy for a community safety officer with the support of a manager, we commandeered her, got her to suspend her uni for six months and gave her full time, an opportunity in the job. So, we were building on her own skill and pinching her to do a job, and she's done a brilliant job.

The allocation of acting positions was not based on natural succession and sometimes the acting roles are spread amongst a number of employees. One manager told us that 'there's never a single person [acting] in the role'. She adds that she was confident that when she was away her duties were carried out 'because any one of [her] managers can act in [her] role'. Within this view is a confidence that regardless of staff movements the organization's operations are protected from significant disruption. Spreading acting roles around or sharing them between various employees could achieve this.

For workers, acting positions mean working in ways that are unfamiliar or unanticipated until they are called on to perform them. Thus, performing in these uncertain and unanticipated ways presents a challenge to the acting workers. Many accounts of acting practices express similar notions of challenge to the one expressed below:

> I have been Acting Manager of the Strategy and Policy Unit and so that's very different to the work that I do on a day-to-day basis, which I still have had to continue with. So that's been quite interesting, it's been a bit of a challenge.

Heightened by uncertainty, another employee account went further as she recounted that 'acting up' was 'a lot of hard work, it was petrifying that you'll do something wrong and the consequences of those decisions that you'll make'. This feeling was often coupled with one of having no time to reflect, consider and consciously learn new practices:

> I just had to sort of feel my way to actually manage the role of hiring and firing staff, dealing with staff issues, and there was no help of learning, it was just fly by the seat of your pants.

What we see here are organizational practices where employees engage with new work and new responsibilities, yet construe their experiences as exciting and challenging with learning embedded within their practices. In other words, while we suggest that 'acting up' is an organizationally generated practice that manages and maintains 'business', it is also a practice that produces a 'significant stimulus for learning' (Hodkinson 2005: 527). In all, these accounts of 'acting up' concur with Hodkinson's point that, 'people learn because their existing practices are challenged by crossing the boundary into a new situation' (ibid.: 527).

'Making up' your job

The final IDP we include here is 'making up' your job. Organizations and their immediate agents in, say, human resource departments, do not have a monopoly on creating IDPs. We have observed practices that meet our criteria of IDPs yet are ones that are invented by employees themselves as they 'read' the organization and identify priorities that they believe fit the directions in which it is moving. From this they use the opportunities they have to influence their own work to construct practices to their own liking. We have identified several practices, such as 'making up one's own job', in which individuals creatively interpret, and in some cases modify, their own job description and have this validated by their managers.

For example, one employee who is a manager in the council told us that her main job was policy development and analysis, and that everyone was now part of a work team that met every two weeks. She decided to plan and implement team-building exercises. She now sees this as an integral part of her work and would like this kind of activity to increase and continue.

Another worker, this time from the college, made up a job that was more meaningful for her. This worker saw her job as a career and broadened her original job to include greater variety, scope and responsibility. Employed originally as a team leader in the administrative support staff, this worker currently reports her job as:

> Customer Service Manager, which I kind of made up myself because there wasn't that job before – as Customer Team Leader – I saw a need for increasing the customer service and also looked at my progression in the company – so I put together a package for [the Principal] to look at a role that managed the whole of Customer Service.

She had come to the college with a history working in a large corporation and it is likely that this history contributed to her understanding (and possibilities) of her work. Furthermore, the making up of the Customer Service Manager job also impacted on the jobs of others. In making her job up she also remade the jobs of her direct reports: the site coordinator role was remade from being a job responsible for opening and closing venues, to a customer service role representing the college, and servicing students and tutors. This practice created new development spaces that other workers could chose to engage in (or not) – and even these remade jobs were open for further remaking by the incumbents.

On the other hand, we also found examples of employees who had to make up their jobs as there were no clear or specific roles, tasks, activities and so on given to them. A college employee was literally handed a job description with four broad headings: 'VET and compliance, business development, professional development and management of tutors – I only got this recently – from management – I get those four headings – and he says can you just flesh this out for me.' Although our initial interest was in investigating induction and job orientation practices, we have developed a focus on making up jobs. We now want to investigate further the sub-field of working out what to do at work and who to be as a worker. Our path into the employee-generated IDP of making up one's job is leading us to analyse organizationally created practices and employee-produced ones associated with learning (at) work. Awareness of making up your job practices has led us to reframe the third of our criteria for identifying IDPs so as not to imply that they are necessarily organization led.

Earlier in this chapter we linked IDPs to change in organizations. In various ways, the above examples can all be understood in relation to change. Overall, the organizations are consciously instigating identity shifts – from more traditionally understood notions of what a community college is and what a local council is – to constructing themselves as organizations that are customer service focused and competitive. For both organizations this shift can be partly attributed to neo-liberal mandates that have seen publicly owned and managed organizations not only becoming more accountable, but also taking on discourses and practices of 'business'. However, business discourses and practices are open to local interpretation and enactment by managers and employees, and they are always also subject to a complex array of compliances and resistances. In this chapter, we have discussed some of these local interpretations through our exploration of IDPs. How discourses and practices are interpreted and what meanings are ascribed to them also affect learning. For instance, the community college, with its past histories of working to teach, develop and empower a broad cross-section of people and communities, represents itself as an organization where learning to transgress is acceptable as part of its changing identity. Thus, business practices in the college seemed sometimes to be 'performed' – in talk and action – for public accountability and financial accounting purposes. At the same time, older practices were maintained, albeit in new and different ways (Rooney *et al.* 2007). The council, although also a community organization in many senses, has always had business as part of its ethos, and learning to become more of a business seemed to be taken up with fewer explicitly stated subversions. The council appears more eager to introduce new practices to replace older ones, and employees talk openly about creating a new organization (Rooney and Scheeres 2008).

In both cases the wider economic climate has prompted conditions for learning through its promotion of change. However, as can be seen from our discussion, the practices that constitute performance appraisal, 'acting up' and making up one's job are not easily able to be characterized as simply transgressive or compliant with 'new' business agendas. Furthermore, they are not easily characterized or captured in (rational and ordered) documentation, protocols, rules, descriptions and so on. These practices, as both instances of action and enactments of the combination of know-how, effects, understandings and rules that are brought to, and integrated with the action, can therefore be understood as creative and dynamic.

Further directions

The practices we are uncovering in this project range from the more well-known and named practices to ones that are extending our original views of IDPs to include the opportunist and the unpredictable. As we identify, name and map IDPs across the research sites, we are grappling first with how and why some practices in organizational life can be acknowledged as development practices. In other words how we can analyse practices such as those discussed above as subdomains of the field of organizational practice(s). As the examples above demonstrate, this entails more than an investigation of organizationally sanctioned practices, or ones cited in management/organizational publications. Second, we are looking at what characterizes organizational practices as developmental in terms of the organization and in terms of particular employees. An IDP such as *performance appraisal* may not be recognized as developmental by employees, so there may be a mismatch between the intention of the organization and the experiences of employees. This kind of contradiction or tension (as well as other examples of complementarities) will be examined in terms of interrelationships and intersections of activities – activity systems in the organization. Third, building on these analyses we will take up notions of learning in practice, investigating how IDPs are, and who sees IDPs as, learning practices. This involves exploration of the use of learning discourses and how these discourses are related to broad development discourses as in the 'acting up' example above. Already emerging from our research concern with learning, are issues about teasing out the relationship between development and learning, and the importance (or not) of a 'learning intent' as integral to an IDP. In other words, how IDPs produce learning, and what are the similarities and differences across different kinds of organizations, is a central problematic and focus of our work.

References

Barnes, B. (2001) 'Practices as collective action', in Schatzki, T. (ed.), *The Practice Turn in Contemporary Theory*, London: Routledge, pp. 25–36.

Bereiter, C. (1994) 'Constructivism, socioculturalism and Popper's world', *Educational Researcher* 23(7), 21–23.

Billet, S. (2002) *Learning in the Workplace: Strategies for effective practice*, Sydney: Allen & Unwin.

Bonal, X. and Rambla, X. (2003) 'Captured by the totally pedagogised society: Teachers and teaching in the knowledge economy', *Globalisation, Societies and Education* 1(2), 169–184.

Bourdieu, P. (1990) *The Logic of Practice*, Stanford, CA: Stanford University Press.

Bourdieu, P. (2001) *Practical Reason: On the theory of action* (trans. Polity Press, 1988), Cambridge: Polity Press.

Bretell, C. (2002) 'The individual/agent and culture/structure in the history of the social sciences', *Social Science History* 26(3), 430–445.

Callon, M. (1991) 'Techno-economic networks and irreversibility', in J. Law (ed.), *A Sociology of Monsters: Essays on power, technology and domination*, London: Routledge, pp. 132–161.

Ellström, P.E. (2001) 'Integrating learning and work: Problems and prospects', *Human Resource Development Quarterly* 12(4), 421–435.

Engeström, Y. (2001) 'Expansive learning at work: Toward an activity theoretical reconceptualization', *Journal of Education and Work* 14(1), 133–156.

Felstead, A., Fuller, A., Unwin, L., Ashton, D., Butler, P. and Lee, T. (2004) *Better Learning Better Performance: Evidence from the 2004 learning at work survey*, Leicester: NIACE.

Fuller, A. and Unwin, L. (2003) 'Learning as apprentices in the contemporary UK workplace', *Journal of Education and Work* 16(4), 407–426.

Fuller, A., Hodkinson, H., Hodkinson, P. and Unwin, L. (2005) 'Learning as peripheral participation in communities of practice: A reassessment of key concepts in workplace learning', *British Educational Research Journal* 31(1), 49–68.

Giddens, A. (1979) *Central Problems in Learning Theory: Action, structure and contradiction in social analysis*, Berkeley, CA: University of California Press.

Griffiths, P. (2004) 'New approaches to work experience', *New Perspectives for Learning Briefing Paper 3*, Brussels: European Commission.

Hager, P. (2003) 'Changing pedagogy: Productive learning', *OVAL Research Working Paper* 3(16), 1–16.

Hendry, C. (1996) 'Understanding and creating whole organizational change through learning theory', *Human Relations* 49(5), 621–641.

Hodkinson, P. (2005) 'Reconceptualising the relations between college-based and workplace learning', *Workplace Learning* 17(8), 521–532.

Hodkinson, P., Biesta, G. and James, D. (2008) 'Understanding learning culturally: Overcoming the dualism between social and individual views of learning', *Vocations and Learning* 1(1), 27–47.

James, D. and Bloomer, M. (2001) 'Cultures of learning and the learning of cultures'. Cultures of Learning Conference, University of Bristol. Online, available at: www.education.ex.ac.uk/tlc/publications.htm (accessed 15 August 2007).

Latour, B. (1992) 'Where are the missing masses? The sociology of a few mundane artefacts', in W.E. Bijker and J. Law (eds), *Shaping Technology/Building Society: Studies in sociotechnical change*, Cambridge, MA: MIT Press, pp. 224–258.

Lave, J. and Wenger, E. (1991) *Situated Learning: Legitimate peripheral participation*, Cambridge: Cambridge University Press.

OECD (2003) *Beyond Rhetoric: Adult learning policies and practices*, Paris: OECD.

Ortner, S. (1996) *Making Gender: The politics and erotics of culture*, Boston, MA: Beacon Press.

Reeves, J. and Forde, C. (2004) 'The social dynamics of changing practice', *Cambridge Journal of Education* 34(1), 85–102.

Rooney, D. and Scheeres, H. (2008) 'An enterprising phoenix: Learning through challenge and excitement in times of change'. Paper presented at the International Conference on Organizational Learning, Knowledge and Capabilities (OLKC), Denmark, March. Online, available at: www.olkc.net/ (accessed 2 November 2008).

Rooney, D., Rhodes, C. and Boud, D. (2007) 'Performing organization: An adult education college as drag king', SCUTREA 2007, Belfast, Northern Ireland, July, in Armstrong, P. (ed.), 'Proceedings of the 37th Annual Standing Conference on University Teaching and Research in the Education of Adults (SCUTREA)', Belfast: SCUTREA, pp. 380–387.

Saugstad, T. (2005) 'Aristotle's contribution to scholastic and non-scholastic learning theories', *Pedagogy, Culture and Society* 13(3), 347–366.

Schatzki, T. (2001) *The Practice Turn in Contemporary Theory*, London: Routledge.

Schatzki, T. (2006) 'Organizations as they happen', *Organization Studies* 27(12), 1863–1874.

Skule, S. and Reichborn, A. (2002) *Learning-conducive Work: A survey of learning conditions in Norwegian workplaces*, Luxembourg: CEDEFOP.

Chapter 15

'Drifting', 'desperate' or just 'diverse'?

Researching young people in jobs without training

Jocey Quinn, Robert Lawy and Kim Diment

Introduction

This chapter focuses on young people in jobs without training (JWT), young people who are everywhere around us but often neglected and almost invisible. This is a group that has been identified as an area of priority concern by policy makers and is targeted within the 14–19 agenda. Whilst these young people are not placed at the bottom of the hierarchy of social concern, like those who are totally NEET (not in education, employment or training), they are seen as having low levels of life and vocational skills and pose a threat to the government's expressed aim that all young people be in education and training up to the age of 18. According to the DfES they 'may be difficult to contact and identify' (2006, p. 2), are often unaware of statutory training entitlements and are sometimes reluctant to discuss them with their employers. The chapter draws on a longitudinal qualitative research project conducted from 2006–2008 that sought to locate the problem of JWT within its broader social and educational context (Quinn *et al.* 2008). The research was funded by the Learning and Skills Council (LSC), the European Social Fund (ESF) and also by the Connexions service, whose personal advisers (PAs) worked directly with young people to provide them with information, advice and guidance in respect of learning and employment opportunities.

The research project had a regional flavour being concerned specifically with young people in the south west (SW) of England. The aim of the project, based within the University of Exeter, was to explore issues and questions relating to young people's lack of participation/involvement in work and training, from the perspective of the young people themselves and of policy makers and other stakeholders. A second but no less important strand of the project has been to raise capacity and promote improved understanding and practice amongst front-line delivery staff. In both strands it draws upon participative methodological approaches previously developed by Quinn and colleagues (2006). The research charted patterns of transitions amongst young people and explored and analysed their meanings and the implications that arose from them. It investigated how young people perceive themselves and are perceived by those who advise them.

Methodology

The key assumption of our methodological approach was that the issues, questions and concerns of young people cannot be easily represented, and indeed are often misrepresented. Although there is an emerging body of research concerning young people in the NEET category (e.g. Yates and Payne 2006; Maguire and Rennison 2005; Bynner and Parsons 2002) little has been written about young people who are in JWT. The project drew on our previous experience of research with young people: Quinn *et al.*'s (2006) work on provincial working-class masculinities, Lawy's (2006) work on young people and connective learning and young people and risk taking (Lawy 2002b) and Diment's work with colleagues on vocational habitus (Colley *et al.* 2003). We sought to maintain a research design grounded in the day-to-day interests and concerns of the young people themselves. The four key research questions were:

1   What are the characteristics of young people in JWT? How can these be best theorised and understood?
2   What are the interests and enthusiasms of young people in JWT?
3   How can Connexions services best understand and respond to these diverse interests of young people in JWT?
4   At what points in their careers and in what ways are young people in JWT most receptive to moving into learning opportunities?

In addressing all of the *four* questions we exemplified the iterative relation between policy interests and practices and the interests and concerns of young people. We have incorporated a longitudinal dimension to chart any changes in the views and attitudes of the young people over the duration of the project.

Young people in JWT are a difficult group to categorise and to reach. One of our early problems was deciding who to interview. For example, whilst young people who take a gap year between school and university are not engaging in level-2 training/education, we did not wish to over-represent them within the cohort that we interviewed. Likewise there are many jobs where young people are engaged in training but their qualifications are not formally recognised, hence they are/should be represented in the JWT statistics. Many young people in the JWT category move into and out of employment and are also likely to hold down two or more part-time jobs at the same time. We did not seek to exclude these categories but saw them as being integral to our work. Despite the emphasis on tracking young people (Connexions partnerships had to produce regularly updated databases of all the young people they were in contact with), young people in JWT can be hard to find because of high job turnover (DfEE 1988) and local disparities in the collection of statistics. Government proposals to create an electronic database of all children leaving school seek to address this problem but seem likely to cause other complexities and resistances.

Methods

The research involved a sample of 114 young people aged between 16 and 21 years and who were identified by Connexions as not having level 2 qualifications and as being in jobs that did not provide accredited training. The study was longitudinal and involved initial interviews with follow-up interviews conducted some months later. A total of 182 interviews were conducted, 27 in person by the Research Fellow and 155 by telephone by Connexions PAs, plus a focus group with three young people and a participative stakeholder seminar, both conducted by the research team. One of the interesting, and in some respects problematic, aspects of the research was its role in capacity building. The research aimed to involve front-line staff (PAs) in conducting the telephone interviews from various Connexions offices in the SW region (Cornwall, Devon, Somerset, Dorset, Gloucestershire) in order to build capacity across the region and lead to discernible improvements to service afforded to young people. Involving the PAs in this way, which was partly a condition of Connexions funding, obviously posed some issues for the research. Part of the purpose of the research was to explore the nature of the advice and guidance offered to the young people and to take a critical perspective on this issue. As researchers, we insisted on combining the telephone interviews with a series of individual in-depth interviews conducted by the project Research Fellow. By combining the two types of data in the research we were able to trace the prevalence of certain themes across a larger cohort as well as explore a richer account amongst a smaller number. Most importantly, it enabled us to sustain a critical perspective on Connexions and its work. In practice, as would be expected, these face-to-face interviews tended to be more discursive and more personal. However, there is mirroring between the researcher and PA interviews, indicating that participants did feel able to raise issues in both contexts and were not necessarily silenced by their official relationships with the PAs.

The ability of the PAs to take an active and, it seems, a successful part in the research was facilitated by a participative approach to their involvement. We organised 'training days' for the PAs where they were involved directly in developing the interview specifications and questions and interpreting the data. We also used this opportunity to explore how the PAs positioned young people in JWT and also to trace how being involved in the research might change or refine attitudes. During the first training day we asked them to identify the problems facing young people, the problems of advising young people and, finally, the reasons why the young people are high on the government's agenda. Some of the words that they used to describe the young people in JWT were *potential, motivation, varied, achievement, disparate, desperate, drifting, sorted, accessibility, trapped, unmotivated, knowledge*. The most interesting aspect of this discussion was the paradoxical way in which young people in JWT were viewed, which allowed for some highly negative views, as well as recognition of the possibility of other stories. The young people were simultaneously desperate and drifting but also sorted and possessing knowledge. The PAs, having proceeded to conduct a first round of interviews then discussed their findings at the university-based second training

day. The third workshop gave the PAs the opportunity to devise and structure the follow-up questions. From these discussions and from a small
number of reflective journals that they kept, it was evident that there had
been a shift in understanding and that more positive views of these young
people and their potential were emerging. This was based on what the PAs
recognised as a growing knowledge that there were distinctions to be made
between this group and those without any job at all.

> I have learned of the apparent importance of young people getting work,
> work without training doesn't necessarily mean a dead end for these
> young people, it appears to be a springboard ... those whom I inter-
> viewed appeared to have a happier more independent view on life and all
> had aspirations. This is not always the case with NEET clients.
>
> (PA reflective journal)

The PAs faced real difficulties in securing both the time and the young person
to interview and this was even more problematic when it came to organising the
face-to-face interviews. Our researcher undertook many long and wasted journeys across the SW during the first round of interviews, but, having developed
good relationships, found this process much easier in the second round. We also
organised one small group session where the three young people who attended
contributed to a discussion about the issues facing young people. However, a
further event organised with Connexions, where we hoped to involve young
people in peer interviewing could not take place because no young people turned
up. We also invited stakeholders involved with young people in the SW to a
participative seminar where we sought their comments on our preliminary findings. This proved extremely helpful in both supporting and challenging our
interpretations of data and enabled us to strengthen and refine our research.

Analysis of findings

This chapter draws on an analysis of the first 70 telephone interviews produced by the PAs and on five of the first in-depth interviews conducted by
the Research Fellow. The researcher interviews are with George, John, Jo,
Rick and Draco and all other quotations are from PA interviews. The young
people all have pseudonyms, chosen by themselves. They are involved in a
range of jobs, such as retail, clerical work, gardening, farming and branches
of the leisure industry. Having considered how the PAs themselves perceived
young people in JWT, we were particularly interested in tracing how this
was reflected or contested in the accounts of the young people themselves.

Fragmented narratives of the self

The emphasis on individuation in contemporary society (Beck and Beck-
Gernsheim 2002) and the idea that we are all engaged in making sense of
our lives through reflexive narratives of the self (Giddens 1991) is both

widely influential and strongly contested. It has been argued that this is a luxury most open to white middle-class metrosexuals with most to gain from the process of individuation (Ribbens McCarthy *et al.* 2002); that it does not reflect the realities of provincial living, and that trauma and alienation make it impossible for many people to create such narratives (Quinn 2003). The accounts of the young people in our research are very interesting in this regard. Many seem unable and unwilling to give any coherent narrative of themselves and their lives. Their accounts shift spatially and temporally, making them very difficult to locate.

> I lived in Swindon till I was 15 and then I moved away on my own
> Did you?
> Yeah moved down to Bournemouth and I lived with my girlfriend.
> Did you go to school there?
> No I went to work in a warehouse and got a supervisor's job there.
> What when you were 15?
> I got it when I was 16.
> So did you stay on at your secondary school in Swindon to take your GCSEs or not?
> I did GCSEs there. I was back and forth when I was in Bournemouth.
>
> (George)

They are vague about their job histories:

> How many jobs have you had since you left school?
> Between 8 and 10.
>
> (Nathalie)

and mystify their qualifications:

> What subjects did you take?
> GCSE Rural Science, Financial Maths and managing money.
>
> (Harry)

> What GCSE's did you do?
> English I got 2 Es – no that's Science I got 2 Es. I got English an E. Maths I did terrible. I got a D in Theatre Graphics and Design. Used to do Cooking but didn't actually take that but I could have done.
> So in total how many did you get then?
> That's a tough question. I wouldn't know.
>
> (George)

The lines between fantasy and fact are kept blurred, or crossed and recrossed. Ball *et al.* (1999) suggest many young people conjure an 'imagined future' that bears little or no relation to the reality of their lives. For many of those in our study, the *present* itself was imaginary, in that facts were highly malleable and roles and relationships were fantastic as much as they were real.

Little wonder therefore that formal transition points such as leaving school or interviews for jobs are slipped over and have little meaning.

All research that relies on 'voice' faces this problem, because there is no true and authentic self only multiple narratives that are culturally shaped. Similarly, as Quinn (2009) has argued elsewhere, conceiving of transition as a fixed point in a linear life is wrong: we are all permanently lost in transition and flux. Indeed, as Lawy (2002a) has shown, identity is not simply a product of change, but is itself an input into the processes that produce change. This was demonstrated where young people continuously reconstructed themselves and their vocational identities. The sheer refusal to make a convincing narrative is particularly marked in young people: this is not peculiar to the young people in the JWT cohort (Lawy 2006). However, we would argue that it is exacerbated by their negative social positioning. Our explanation for this is not that they have some individual pathology, but that no socially validated narrative exists that will allow them to make their case. Moreover, whilst we recognise that society sees the problem as an issue of risk (Yates and Payne 2006), the young people themselves do not necessarily view their lives in the same way (Lawy 2002b). In a society where the onus is on gaining school-level qualifications, continuing in education, getting a respectable job with training or somehow circumventing the system and gaining celebrity, those who do not do any of these things are losers, and no one wants to hear their story. Being vague on the details enables the young people to slip some of these constraints and evade being fixed.

Wasted potential

The dominant discourse concerning such young people is that they have 'potential' but are wasting it through lack of 'motivation'. Potential tends to be defined as the ability to study and train and the waste is the perverse refusal to take up this opportunity. Turning to the young people themselves, we find a rather different story. Although to some extent they did position themselves as 'the thick bunch' (John), who were channelled towards Connexions advice from school onwards, they were also able to recount many forms of informal ability and interests. They had skills with computing or mechanics, developed at home rather than school, skills looking after animals, creative skills. Making a bridge between these informal interests and work and training opportunities could be done; for example, Rick was carving out a successful working life as a magician:

> I like to do something different, I'm more of a people person really. I like to get there and chat to people, there's so many interesting people out there you know ... I'm really lucky because I've got a residency in a nightclub in Weymouth and I'm working for them every Saturday evening and that's brilliant as well.
>
> (Rick)

However, he was unusual in our sample as coming from a relatively mobile and middle-class family. Most of our participants did not appear to have the confidence to forge a vocational trajectory from their informal interests, and they did not appear to be encouraged to do so by those who were advising them. They also made a dichotomy between practical and book learning: 'I've got a practical mind ... give me a book to learn, I can't learn it, tell me to do something, if I do it wrong, I know what I've done wrong straightaway, I can fix it like that' (John). 'Things at home that came to pieces, I could put them back together again' (Draco). Moreover, these skills had legitimacy for them even without formal accreditation or even being part of paid employment.

Street wise and victimised

Young people in JWT are commonly presented as 'dead end kids' simultaneously both street wise and victimised, 'drifting' but also 'trapped'. In the accounts of the young people and the way that they presented themselves, we can also trace such polarities. They acted streetwise in trying to play mind games with the researcher and the PAs. They detailed how they responded to threats and slights in their localities and had the kind of street knowledge needed to survive: 'Someone I know nicked my bike, but he didn't know me at the time and he didn't know who I knew' (John). At the same time they frequently gave detailed and convincing accounts of bullying at school and its impacts on their educational progression:

> When I got to secondary school it all went downhill ... it was just bullying and the teachers just chose to ignore us. The way I saw it in my experience is that they knew about the problem, they knew what was going on, they'd seen it happen and they did nothing about it.
>
> (Jo)

The difference is that official accounts and media portrayals essentialise these factors: young people are othered as dangerous victims, because of their fundamental lack of the qualities necessary to be successful citizens. In the accounts of the young people themselves, it is structural inequalities and inadequate systems that produce personal trauma and failure. At the same time it is possible to create a persona that enables them to handle and negotiate the past and 'navigate the future'. Although they are positioned as needing support, they themselves have developed relevant stores of knowledge that they deploy with maturity to help others:

> A lot of people struggle.... A few people I've met say they've broken up with their families, they've hated their life and they've tried to do stupid things ... I don't know why they do it but they've cut themselves. ... One of the people I know I got them to promise not to cut themselves or drink.
>
> (George)

A job without training, not a job without learning

A significant number of the young people whom we have interviewed face many difficulties and disadvantages, often living in families struggling with poverty, in areas that are poorly resourced, where employment opportunities are very limited and where they have little likelihood of owning or even renting their own home. Commonly, being in JWT is seen as simply compounding and entrenching these problems and certainly there were young people interviewed who saw their jobs as boring, frustrating and pointless. However, the research indicates that this is not the whole story. As one of the PAs noted in her reflective diary:

> each young person is different, even though they are seen to be in a job with no training, he is happy with this and content with his life. This will make me more aware ... so not to get caught up in the 'thought' that they should move on to get a better job.
>
> (PA reflective journal)

Many of the young people stressed that they did not want to learn in a classroom: 'I like to learn at work without teachers' (Andrew). They took pride in their work:

> What do you do in a typical day?
> Strimming, hedging and planting people's gardens, not big work....
> It's good I enjoy it. It makes me feel proud when I stand back and look at the finished job.
>
> (Stephen)

'I love my job it's really varied and I like being outside, it's practical and every day is different. I like the animals too' (Ben), and felt they could learn far more that was of use through work activities:

> They didn't want no trainees. You just go in; you train as you do the job. I thought that sounded good. I like doing that sort of work because studying I never got the hang of, cause textbooks and that, it doesn't really register in my brain that much.
>
> (George)

They even compared the quality of learning they experienced with those learning formally and felt far better 'educated' via the workplace than their peers in college. For example, Richie working as a pig farmer and being trained on the job to be a manager asserted:

> I have thought about it [college] but when I look after the kids from college on day release I'm in the best position as I'm learning more and more each day and I don't need a classroom to learn it.
>
> (Richie)

Of course, these observations need not be taken strictly at face value, they may be justifications and obfuscations, but they certainly formed a consistent thread in the ways that the young people presented their relation to work. Concomitantly their ideas about training were extremely hazy and even distorted. For example, John claimed to want to go to Agricultural College but felt it was impossible because it would cost '10k a year on travel and tweed suits'. However, in some respects they were well informed: very many spoke of wanting full apprenticeships, but of the very limited chances of gaining them, and also of the likelihood that training does not lead to a job. Draco, for example, appeared to have spent two years in further education college training to be a mechanic only to end up valeting cars in one of only two small garages in his area, where further training was never discussed, only 'the events of the day'. Although they seemed aware that training was generally considered desirable, they knew from experience that small employers did not necessarily encourage it. Overall, their stance was evasive and their priorities more immediate: 'For me work means I can live here and I can save my money. I can get to Canada. So to me, work is brilliant' (Jo). As we have discussed they resisted being fixed, sometimes in very explicit ways: 'I want to pass on thoughts of college, I just want to float' (Abigail).

Similarly the emphasis on formal pathways into work was not relevant to these young people. Many of the jobs they were currently doing had come via informal contacts of families and friends: 'My mum is my boss in Asda' (Vicky), 'I stepped into my cousin's shoes' (Joe). Whilst we have noted the fragmentation of their identities and their learning lives, these informal networks suggest that for some there is integration into family and other networks that help hold them together. These networks also give access to multiple informal and transitory jobs: 'I get a bit of money here and there gardening, they come down to my house tell me to start work tomorrow morning 8 o'clock sharp' (John). Personal relationships were seen as more important than formal qualifications and mentor figures at work were crucial: 'If I can't get on with the person I'm working for I won't stay in the job, simple as that' (John).

Local contexts

It is interesting to note how the life courses of these young people were strongly shaped by local contexts and traditions in the SW. Their opportunities and choices were very different from those living for example in large metropolitan areas. Ranges of employment were limited and seasonal: 'Oh yes a lot of tourists come down here, but it's not very busy the rest of the time... they always try to get some extra staff then they're dismissed as soon as summer's over' (Jo), transport difficulties were common and mobility was restricted. However, rural pursuits like shooting and local activities, such as being in the Army Cadets, were important in shaping their activities, their work patterns and even their personal behaviour: 'I kept myself to myself... I had to walk away from trouble because I've got a shot gun licence and I don't want to lose it' (John). Our difficulties involving these young people in our research reflect their marginal position within national debates as provincial, rural and often sidelined.

Guidance

Although our research suggests that these young people are more 'sorted' than policy makers often assume, the need for someone to turn to was a prominent refrain. Moreover, someone who really listened rather than trying to impose their own agenda:

> When I was at school part of my depression was I was attacked ... I met this woman who came out, this volunteer who was an old lady with hearing aids in both ears and she didn't listen to a word I'd said cause when I'd said something to her she'd try and change the subject and she just literally wouldn't listen and if I had something to say she'd interrupt and talk about what she wanted to talk about.
>
> (Jo)

In this respect Connexions services seemed variable: for some Connexions had been their only valuable source of personal advice and guidance, for others Connexions was simply pushing a government agenda and failed to listen to the young people themselves. Our research took place at a time when the role of Connexions was being radically reconstructed and being placed under the remit of local authorities. There are many well-founded anxieties about loss of specialist knowledge under the new arrangements, but proposals to link Connexions with other forms of youth and social provision seem to have validity in the light of our findings. On one level the research alerted us to the tremendous difficulties faced by the PAs in developing consistent relationships with a group of young people who are extremely resistant to being pinned down. On the other hand it highlighted the limitations of providing advice and guidance on careers without attending to the holistic needs of the young person. The tick box agenda, whereby Connexions staff raced to meet their targets of getting young people into work, meant that it was only those PAs willing (and able) to go beyond their job remit and spend their own time on providing crucial extra support, who were able to do the job properly. Nevertheless, whatever the arrangements and however much energy they invest, they cannot hope to redress the structural issues of class, poverty and the limitations of the labour market, which are the main problems facing these young people.

Conclusion

Researching young people in jobs without training has been an extremely interesting challenge and has left us with a great interest in this hitherto neglected subject. The young people in our study are not a waste of space, nor should they be constantly defined in terms of what they lack. There are many positive features in their working lives and many ways in which they are learning. For most of them they are still exploring and finding their way in life. Nevertheless, we must be wary of overstating our case. What may now be transitional periods of liminality for these young people can all too easily solidify into low-waged and insecure futures. All three of us are parents of teenage children ourselves: would we happily accept for them a lifetime of working in a supermarket? However, as researchers we must be willing to have our assumptions about what are a worthwhile job and a worthwhile life course challenged. Undertaking this research has provided new perspectives on work, training and guidance for young people that we feel hold important messages for policy makers and other researchers. We believe that the research has also reached its objective of building capacity in advice and guidance for these young people. Undertaking the research has challenged the PAs to recognise that being in a job without training is not always a problem that they need to come in and solve, and that learning need not always come with a certificate. The findings also re-emphasise the fact that young people in JWT do need support and guidance, even though providing it can be frustrating and difficult. The question is what support will be most beneficial? It is almost a platitude that we need to listen to their own accounts and doing so is not easy given their attempts to shape shift and resist linearity. However, punishing them for not being linear, which the current highly structured and hierarchical educational system does, is anachronistic in this postmodern age, and also counterproductive. Failing to recognise and build on the skills they are developing at home and the workplace, in favour of accredited learning of dubious quality and relevance is not the answer either. Solutions seem to require significant changes to policy and provision of both training and advice and guidance, as well as economic and social change. Even in the relatively buoyant economy under which we conducted this research, these changes were not forthcoming. Prospects now seem even less likely, with the insecurities of the job market increasing dramatically. Although these young people are in many ways survivors not victims, it must be said that the future does not look rosy for them.

References

Ball, S.J., Maguire, M. and Macrae, S. (1999) 'Young lives, diverse choices and imagined futures in an education and training market', *International Journal of Inclusive Education* 3, 195–224.

Beck, U. and Beck-Gernsheim, E. (2002) *Individualization*, London: Sage.

Bynner, J. and Parsons, S. (2002) 'Social exclusion and the transition from school to work: The case of young people not in education, employment, or training (NEET)', *Journal of Vocational Behavior* 60, 289–309.

Colley, H., James, D., Tender, M. and Diment, K. (2003) 'Learning as becoming in vocational education and training', *Journal of Vocational Education and Training* 55, 407–422.

DfEE (1988) 'Young people in jobs without training', Research Brief no. 75, IFF Ltd, ISBN 0 85522 834 2.

DfES (2006) 'Understanding young people in jobs without training', 22 April, RR736/RB736.

Giddens, A. (1991) *Modernity and Self-Identity: Self and society in the late modern age*, Cambridge: Polity Press.

Lawy, R. (2002a) 'Transition and transformation: The experiences of two young people', *Journal of Education and Work* 15, 201–218.

Lawy, R. (2002b) 'Risky stories: Youth identities, learning and everyday risk', *Journal of Youth Studies* 5, 407–423.

Lawy, R. (2006) 'Connective learning: Young people's identity and knowledge-making in work and non-work contexts', *British Journal of Sociology of Education* 27, 325–340.

Maguire, S. and Rennison, J. (2005) 'Two years on: The destinations of young people who are not in education, employment or training at 16', *Journal of Youth Studies* 8, 187–201.

Quinn, J. (2003) 'Powerful subjects: Women students, subjectivity and the HE curriculum', Unpublished PhD thesis, Lancaster University, Lancaster.

Quinn, J. (2009) 'Rethinking "failed" transitions into HE', in K. Ecclestone, G. Biesta and M. Hughes (eds), *Transitions and Learning through the Life-course*, London: Routledge.

Quinn, J., Lawy, R. and Diment, K. (2008) 'Young people in jobs without training in south west England: Not just "dead-end kids in dead-end jobs"', Exeter University/Marchmont Observatory, Exeter.

Quinn, J., Thomas, L., Slack, K., Casey, L., Thexton, W. and Noble, J. (2006) 'Lifting the hood: Lifelong learning and young white provincial working-class masculinities', *British Educational Research Journal* 32, 735–751.

Ribbens McCarthy, J., Edwards, R. and Gillies, V. (2002) *Making Families*, York: Sociology Press.

Thomas, L., Quinn, J., Slack, K., Casey, L., Vigurs, K. and Flynn, N. (2004) 'Learning Brokers Research Project: Report 1', Learning and Skills Research Centre, London.

Yates, S. and Payne, M. (2006) 'Not so NEET? A critique of the use of "NEET" in setting targets for interventions with young people', *Journal of Youth Studies* 9, 329–344.

Chapter 16

The limits of competency-based training and the implications for work

Leesa Wheelahan

Introduction

Competency-based training is a feature of vocational qualifications in many Anglophone nations. National Vocational Qualifications (NVQs) in England, Wales and Northern Ireland are based on competency-based training (CBT) models of curriculum, as are Scottish Vocational Qualifications (Misko 2006). CBT is also a feature of many vocational qualifications in South Africa (Allais 2007). Australia is of particular interest because it has gone further than most other countries in insisting that all and not just some of its publicly funded qualifications in vocational education and training (VET) be based on CBT. Australian VET qualifications are derived from training packages, which are the equivalent of British NVQs. Governments introduced CBT to ensure that VET qualifications met the needs of industry and to ensure industry 'control' over VET (Goozee 2001). CBT putatively meets the needs of industry because qualifications are made up of units of competency that describe workplace tasks or roles, and learning outcomes are expressed as performances in the workplace. Learning *outcomes* are divorced from *processes* of learning and curriculum. Proponents of CBT insist that units of competency are not curriculum because they merely specify the outcomes of learning, and that this 'frees' teachers to develop creative and innovative 'delivery strategies' that meet the needs of 'clients'.

In contrast, this chapter argues that the structure and content of CBT acts as a mechanism for social power by privileging employer perspectives. It uses Australia as an illustrative case study to demonstrate that competency-based VET qualifications deny students access to the theoretical knowledge that underpins vocational practice. They result in unitary and unproblematic conceptions of work because students are not provided with the means to participate in theoretical debates shaping their field of practice. CBT is thus a form of 'silencing' because it excludes students from access to the means needed to envisage alternative futures within their field. The first part of this chapter draws on the work of Basil Bernstein, who was a key English sociologist of education from the 1970s till the end of the century, to distinguish between theoretical and everyday knowledge, and to argue for the centrality of theoretical knowledge in vocational qualifications. The second part of the chapter considers whether CBT shapes curriculum. The final part illustrates the chapter's argument by comparing two qualifications in community development; one is based on CBT and it replaced the other, which was not based on CBT.

A Bernsteinian framework

Individuals need to draw on increasingly complex knowledge as a consequence of changes to society, work and technology. Bernstein (2000) argued that fair access to theoretical knowledge was important for democracy because it is the means society uses to conduct its 'conversation' about itself and about what it should be like. This is why theoretical knowledge is socially powerful knowledge. Access to theoretical knowledge is also increasingly important in work. Young (2006: 115) argues that while all jobs require context-specific knowledge, 'many jobs also require knowledge involving *theoretical* ideas shared by a community of specialists' located within the disciplines. Workers need to be able to use theoretical knowledge in different ways and in different contexts as their work grows in complexity and difficulty. This means that occupational progression is strongly related to educational progression, because education is the main way in which most people are provided with access to theoretical, disciplinary knowledge (Barnett 2006). It also means that all qualifications should provide students with the disciplinary knowledge they need to study at a higher level within their field in addition to immediate occupational outcomes.

Bernstein argued that theoretical knowledge differs from everyday knowledge because each is embedded in a different system of meaning. Theoretical knowledge is *general, principled* knowledge. It is organised as 'specialised symbolic structures of explicit knowledge' in which the integration of knowledge occurs through the integration of *meanings* and not through relevance to specific contexts (2000: 160). Students need access to the disciplinary system of meaning as a condition for using knowledge in contextually specific applications. For example, students need access to mathematics as a condition for understanding and applying particular formulas, and if they are to use these formulas in different contexts. In contrast, everyday knowledge is *particularised* knowledge, because its selection and usefulness is determined by the extent to which it is relevant in a particular context (Gamble 2006). This is the tacit, context-dependent knowledge of the workplace. Bernstein (2000: 157) explains that everyday knowledge is 'likely to be oral, local, context dependent and specific, tacit, multi-layered, and contradictory across but not within contexts'.

Theoretical knowledge organised through disciplinary frameworks is also strongly *classified* knowledge because the boundaries between it and everyday knowledge are clearly defined, as are the boundaries between different academic disciplines. This is because each of the academic disciplines has a specialised language and strong boundaries that insulates it from other disciplines. In contrast, everyday knowledge is weakly classified because its contextual relevance is of primary importance. In everyday knowledge, contextually specific applications of knowledge matter more than the boundaries insulating different academic disciplines and the way knowledge is structured within these boundaries. The way an academic discipline is structured has implications for the way in which it is translated for pedagogic transmission. Induction into a particular academic discipline requires induction into its system of meaning, which may have implications for the way knowledge is selected, sequenced, paced and evaluated. This is the 'how' of pedagogic practice, and Bernstein refers to this as the process of *framing*. The more hierarchical a body of knowledge (for example, physics) the more likely it is that pedagogy will need to be strongly sequenced because students need to understand what came before in order to understand what comes after (Muller 2006).

VET qualifications are more likely to be based on *applied* disciplinary knowledge compared to academic qualifications, because the applied disciplines consist of disciplinary knowledge that has been recontextualised for use in a vocational field of practice (Barnett 2006; Young 2006). VET qualifications also differ from academic qualifications because the purpose of academic qualifications is to induct students into a body of knowledge, whereas the purpose of vocational qualifications is to induct students into a field of practice and the theoretical knowledge that underpins practice as the basis for integrating and synthesising each. Vocational curriculum shares this feature with curriculum for the professions, so there is continuity between vocational and professional education. While the purpose of academic and vocational/professional education is different, both academic and vocational teachers need to ensure that curriculum provides students with the capacity to *recognise* different types of knowledge so that they can, for example, distinguish between physics and chemistry or sociology and micro-economics. It is essential that these boundaries are rendered visible so that students can recognise and *use* knowledge appropriately.

Vocational curriculum consequently needs to 'face both ways' and provide students with access to both types of knowledge – to the theoretical knowledge that underpins vocational practice within a field, and to the tacit, context-dependent knowledge of the workplace (Barnett 2006). Trying to collapse the distinction between each type of knowledge does violence to both. It also means that the distinction between an educational institution and the workplace as a site of learning is important. An exclusive focus on learning in the workplace denies students access to disciplinary systems of meaning because, generally speaking, students have access only to contextually specific applications of theoretical knowledge in the workplace, and not to the system of meaning in which theoretical knowledge is embedded. This is because knowledge in the workplace is weakly classified and selected on the basis of its relevance. Similarly, an exclusive focus on learning theoretical knowledge in an educational institution does not provide students with access to the tacit, context-dependent knowledge of the workplace. *Both* sites of learning are needed (Barnett 2006). The problem is that CBT faces only one way, to the workplace.

Does CBT constitute curriculum?

The introduction of training packages caused fierce debate within Australia, so much so that Schofield and McDonald (2004c) called for a 'new settlement' to underpin them in their high-level review of training packages in 2004. In response to the argument that units of competency in training packages strip underpinning knowledge, particularly disciplinary knowledge, from VET qualifications, CBT supporters argue that units of competency merely specify the outcomes of training and the criteria that are used to assess whether those outcomes have been achieved (ibid.). This is because learning *outcomes* have been divorced from *processes* of learning, leaving 'providers' and teachers free to develop a curriculum approach that most suits their 'clients'. The putative problem is that teachers have interpreted training packages as curriculum when they are meant to be nothing of the sort. For example, Schofield and McDonald (2004b: 2) say that 'Consistent with their outcomes-based orientation, Training Packages are silent on how teachers and trainers should or could design the curriculum to achieve these outcomes.' In theory, it should be possible to construct 'subjects' that draw various components from units of competency and recombine and reconstitute these around subjects, if it was thought appropriate to do so.

Units of competency describe workplace tasks or roles. They are broken down into elements of competency that specify demonstrable and assessable outcomes or actions. They also include performance criteria that specify the required level of performance for elements of competency. Each unit of competency also includes statements about required knowledge and skills, and a range statement that describes the contexts and conditions in which the performance criteria apply. Each includes an evidence guide that describes the underpinning knowledge and skills that need to be demonstrated (assessed) to prove competence (Department of Education Science and Training 2006: 117). The 'rules' surrounding training packages and units of competency are that while knowledge must be included, it should be in context, and should 'only be included if it refers to knowledge actually applied at work' (ibid.: 114). Performance criteria include 'the primary context and source of knowledge and the skills that need to be applied' (ibid.: 139). The *Training Package Development Handbook* (ibid.: 126) says that: 'Performance criteria must be expressed precisely to enable appropriate training and assessment.' Furthermore:

> Units of competency that integrate knowledge into the overall performance specification of the unit and the assessment process advice *should fully include all relevant knowledge as it is applied in a work role.* This supports integrated training and assessment strategies in most cases. A training organisation may nonetheless determine that it is efficient and a supportable learning or assessment strategy to aggregate common knowledge topics from a number of related units.
>
> (ibid.: 140, emphasis added)

This reveals the way knowledge is classified in training packages, and it is not on the basis of disciplinary knowledge. Knowledge is distinguished by the way in which it is applied *at work* and not by *systems of meaning*. While it is possible to aggregate common knowledge for the purposes of teaching, this is primarily as an efficiency measure and because it may be a 'supportable learning or assessment strategy'; however, the primary source of knowledge (and skill) are the performance criteria. Knowledge is derived from workplace standards, not disciplinary systems of meaning.

This collapses the distinction between theoretical and everyday knowledge by delocating theoretical knowledge from the system of meaning in which it is embedded and tying it to specific contexts (Bernstein 2000). It results in weak classification of knowledge because the boundary between the theoretical and everyday is not visible, and weak framing because it does not distinguish contexts of learning by privileging workplace learning, or by stipulating the sequencing of knowledge. It translates knowledge from being general and principled knowledge to particularised knowledge, because its selection and usefulness is determined by the extent to which it is relevant in a particular context. Students thus have access to knowledge in its particularised form, but are not provided with the means to relate it to its general and principled structure and system of meaning.

Training packages shape curriculum because they stipulate the nature of assessment, and this means that there are limits on the what and how of *learning*, because, as Bernstein (ibid.: 36) explains, 'Content is transformed into evaluation. Context is transformed into transmission.' Bernstein explains that *evaluation* condenses the meaning of discourses shaping pedagogic practice, because the evaluative rules 'regulate pedagogic practice at the classroom level, for they define the standards which must be reached' (ibid.: 115).

It is clear that training packages *do* shape teaching and learning, and that they constitute an important component of curriculum, because they specify *what* is to be taught and, in broad terms, *how* it should be assessed. The point of training packages was that they would reshape teaching and learning in VET so that it was more 'industry responsive'. They were meant to change 'the what and how' of learning. Schofield and McDonald (2004a: 2) say that training packages are more than industry-endorsed products that have replaced curriculum, because they encapsulate 'the rules of the VET game' and ensure that VET delivers what industry wants.

Community development diplomas before and after training packages

Table 16.1 shows the structure of the old associate diploma in community development that existed in the state of Victoria in Australia prior to the introduction of training packages, and the national training package diploma in community development that replaced it. It only includes core modules and units and not electives. Both programmes are normally two years' duration. The associate diploma module titles indicate that it is based on applied disciplinary knowledge relevant to community development, but that it is

Table 16.1 Structure of the 'new' Diploma of Community Services (Community Development) and 'old' Associate Diploma of Social Sciences (Community Development)

*'New' Diploma**	*'Old' Associate Diploma***
Undertake systems advocacy	Introduction to Community Development
Implement a community development strategy	Australian Society: A Sociological Introduction Part 1
Develop and implement a community development strategy	Political Economy and Community Development 1
Develop and implement community programs	Introduction to Study and Community Development
Develop community resources	Group and Personal Communication 1
Support community action	Fieldwork Tutorial 1
Support community leadership	Human Rights and Advocacy
Develop, implement and promote effective communication techniques	Australian Society: A Sociological Introduction Part 2
Respond holistically to client issues	Political Economy and Community Development 2
Meet statutory and organisational information requirements	Information Access
Develop new networks	Fieldwork Placement
Work with other services	Organisations, Change and Community Development
Implement and monitor OHS policies and procedures for a workplace	Research 1
Undertake research activities	Group and Personal Communication 2
Develop and implement policy	Social Policy
Manage research activities	Fieldwork Placement
	Social Action – Analysis of Theory and Practice
	Research 2
	Fieldwork Tutorial 2
	Practical Strategies for Social Change
	Fieldwork Placement

Notes
* Community Services and Health Industry Skills Council (2005a: 123–124).
** Office of Further and Training Education Victoria (1997: A2–A3).

strongly classified disciplinary knowledge nonetheless. Progression through the programme was strongly sequenced. For example, students could not undertake Social Policy unless they had completed or were concurrently enrolled in Australian Society: A Sociological Introduction Parts 1 and 2 and Political Economy and Community Development Parts 1 and 2. The programme incorporates 'practice'-based requirements through the fieldwork components, but also through modules that integrate theory and practice such as Practical Strategies for Social Change, which came towards the end of the programme and required students to participate in, analyse and theorise a social action campaign. Fieldwork tutorials preceded fieldwork practice, so the situated knowledge of the workplace was pedagogised for curriculum. The programme 'faced both ways' to disciplinary knowledge and the field of practice through the subjects that faced towards theory and practice respectively and through the subjects that integrated both.

In contrast, 'spaces' in the programme structure in the training package diploma are defined and distinguished in curriculum through their relationship to work tasks or roles. Knowledge is weakly classified because it does not distinguish disciplinary fields and nor does it distinguish 'everyday' knowledge from theoretical knowledge. Students enrol in units of competency rather than subjects such as sociology or social policy. There are no rules stipulating prerequisites or co-requisites for studying particular units of competency, although students' choice may be constrained to some extent by the way in which the educational institution chooses to offer units of competency.

Disciplinary knowledge is also weakly classified within units of competency. This is clear if we compare and contrast the unit of competency 'Develop and Implement Policy' in the training package Diploma (Community Services and Health Industry Skills Council (CSHISC) 2005b: 587–590), with the module 'Social Policy' in the Associate Diploma (Office of Further and Training Education 1997: A-85–A-88). The module descriptor for 'Social Policy' explains that it explores the 'context, development and implementation of social policy in Australia', which includes exploration of 'debates surrounding the role of the welfare state and other areas of contention'. It also includes the way in which the 'social, political and economic context impacts on social policy formulation, implementation and evaluation' as the basis for understanding contextual factors that then become 'the basis for conducting policy analysis as an instrument for empowerment and social change'. The summary of content includes the following topics:

- the state
- the welfare state
- definitions of social welfare
- models of social policy
- current social policy debates
- implementation/evaluation issues
- community development issues.

The assessment requires students to, among other things, 'analyse underlying assumptions, values and theory of policy formulation'. Students must analyse economic, social and political factors that influence policy development and evaluate 'current debates on social policy within a community development context'. Students are provided with access to general, principled knowledge as a means of understanding the particular, and they are invited to participate in 'society's conversation' by participating in debates within their field of practice. These debates involve competing understandings of society and the state, and competing conceptions about human rights (including social rights) and citizenship, particularly when the Social Policy module is considered relationally to other modules in the programme such as Human Rights and Advocacy, and the modules in sociology and political economy.

In contrast, the unit descriptor for 'Develop and implement policy' states that it is about 'Developing and applying policy initiatives in the workplace.' There are four elements of competency, which are:

1   research and consult with others to develop policies;
2   test draft policies;
3   develop policy materials;
4   implement and review policies.

There are 17 performance criteria related to the elements of competency. The essential knowledge that must be assessed through the performance criteria is as follows:

• principles and practices of policy development;
• relevant policy at national and state level;
• key stakeholders at local, national and state level;
• organisational consultation processes;
• evaluation and review processes;
• organisational business and corporate plans and philosophy;
• funding bodies and their requirements.

The 'essential skills' that must be demonstrated are:

• documentation and report writing;
• policy development;
• research and consultation;
• promotion.

The essential knowledge and skills show that students are introduced to conceptual and theoretical language as is illustrated by the requirement that they demonstrate knowledge of 'Principles and practices of policy development'. However, this language is delocated from the theoretical, relational shaping of the concepts within the discipline of social policy. 'Principles and practices of policy development' is so ambiguous that it could be interpreted in many ways, including ignoring the way such issues are explored in the theoretical literature that shape policy studies. This can give the impression that the principles and practices of policy development have been settled, rather than subject to contest and debate because different understandings of society and citizenship are invoked. It may well be that teachers interpret this essential knowledge as requiring induction into the field of social policy and its debates, but that this interpretation *will* be used cannot be assured as it is widely open to interpretation. The notion that units of competency can be interpreted in unproblematic and uniform ways resulting in commensurable outcomes wherever the programme is delivered is clearly not supported. Learning *processes* cannot be distinguished from learning *outcomes*.

There is no differentiation between the *level* and *type* of knowledge that is required in 'Develop and implement policy'. Broad principles and theories (where they can be identified) are not distinguished from applied concepts such as 'Evaluation and review processes' or from contextualised knowledge such as 'Key stakeholders at local, national and state level'. Nor is theoretical knowledge distinguished from situated knowledge such as 'Organisational consultation processes'. Indeed, 'Organisational consultation processes' could be interpreted as requiring access to social policy concepts and theories around organisations, or it could be interpreted as knowing how one's own organisation does things, because that is the way they are done.

The focus in the elements of competency is on *procedural* tasks. Students are not required to analyse and critique as part of the elements of competency, and the elements of competency and performance criteria are tied to the specific. For example, the performance criteria associated with the first element of competency 'Research and consult with others to develop policies' requires:

1.1 Existing organisational, government and other policies relevant to the issue are evaluated to determine their currency and relevance for the organisation and its clients
1.2 Appropriate research and consultation which will contribute to policy development is undertaken and documented in accordance with organisational policies and procedures
1.3 Relevant stakeholders are consulted throughout the policy development process to ensure relevance and acceptance of the product
1.4 Appropriate mechanisms are provided to facilitate open constructive discussion about policy issues and their possible resolution
1.5 Policies are developed which reflect the culture, values and objectives of the organisation
1.6 Resourcing implications of implementation and review mechanisms are included in policies.

(CSHISC 2005b: 587)

The range statement says that 'Appropriate research may include':

• state, national or local level;
• written or oral sources of information.

The complexity of policy research is absent, as are the 'recognition rules' students need to distinguish between and evaluate formal and informal approaches to research, and between different kinds of information. This absence is not remedied by the compulsory unit 'Manage research activities' (CSHISC 2005b: 591–596). The elements of competency and performance criteria in this unit of competency are similarly tied to the specific, and the most conceptual statement is one performance criterion, which requires that 'Issues related to ethics, validity and reliability are incorporated in research designs'. This does not provide students with access to the debates around research and research paradigms. This is an important absence, because debates about research paradigms are part of broader debates within social science about the nature of society and individuals, and this is one reason why research is so contested in these disciplines.

The titles of the units in the diploma are presented as neutral or uncontested descriptions of workplace tasks or roles. However, *within* units of competency, individuals and groups are described as clients or consumers. For example, the elements of competency within the unit 'Undertake systems advocacy' are as follows:

1   Obtain, analyse and document information relevant to the needs of clients as a community of interest within the general community
2   Work with consumers, service users, services and other stakeholders to develop strategies to address identified needs
3   Advocate for and facilitate the implementation of strategies developed to address the needs of clients with specific needs

(CSHISC 2005b: 91)

The key debates within community development surrounding the nature of social change, power relations and the human actor are absent. The essential knowledge in this unit of competency includes the requirement that students demonstrate knowledge about the 'Structural, political and other social factors which operate to maintain discrimination against clients, consumers and service users'. Students are required to demonstrate knowledge of issues that are relevant to client groups, how these are contextualised by policy, an understanding of the balance between the rights of the community and clients, as well as specific knowledge to do with legislation, policy and stakeholders (CSHISC 2005b: 94). However, none of this is framed in terms of *debates* around these issues, and the fact that individuals are designated as clients, consumers and service users demonstrates that the human actor is defined through a consumer (i.e. market) relation, and that the underpinning philosophy is human capital theory. The range statement lists the strategies that students may be expected to implement in a community development context and this list includes public meetings but it does not include demonstrations or protests, strategies that are permissible within a pluralist theoretical framework, let alone more radical perspectives.

Students are excluded from controversies and debates through the designation of 'spaces' in the structure of the training package diploma as unproblematic descriptions of workplace tasks or roles, when they are part of the contests that shape the community development field. Similarly, the insistence on 'clients' within units of competency is presented as an unproblematic description of the relationship between community development workers and those with whom they work, yet the conceptual basis of this relationship as a market relation between consumers and service providers (and hence the diploma) is not made explicit. The conceptual basis is taken for granted and rendered invisible as a consequence. This constitutes a process of silencing, with the consequence that students are denied 'access to the forms of knowledge that permit alternative possibilities to be thought' (Beck and Young 2005: 193).

Community development students need access to competing accounts of the human actor and their relationship to society and the way these shape practice (often implicitly and tacitly) as a precondition for developing a critical approach to practice in their field. They do not need to be, and cannot be, philosophers or sociologists, because the purpose of their programme is to prepare them for a field of practice, but they do need access to the applied disciplinary knowledge drawn from these disciplines as the basis of practice in their field if they are to participate in shaping their field. The content and the structure of the Diploma of Community Services (Community Development) reinforce each other to result in students' exclusion from key debates in their field.

Conclusion

CBT qualifications consist of units of competency that must be based on workplace tasks or roles. Knowledge within units of competency is tied to workplace tasks and roles and only included if actually applied at work. This collapses the distinction between theoretical and everyday knowledge through privileging the everyday. It delocates theoretical knowledge from the system of meaning in which it is embedded and transforms it from general, principled knowledge to particularised knowledge. The way in which units of competency are distinguished from each other results in knowledge that is weakly classified and framed because learning outcomes are defined as workplace tasks or roles. This is reinforced within units of competency through the specification of underpinning knowledge, which does not distinguish between abstract, applied, contextual and situated knowledge.

The weak classification and framing of knowledge means that students are not provided with the means to recognise and distinguish knowledge and its boundaries. They are not provided with the means for distinguishing between theoretical and everyday knowledge. Students are not introduced to a disciplinary style of reasoning that they can use to consider the theoretical basis of their practice. They are not able to participate in debates shaping their field and this results in unitary and unproblematic conceptions of work because work cannot be problematised. They are also denied access to knowledge they can use in other contexts, including as the basis for their participation in society's conversation more broadly.

References

Allais, Stephanie Matseleng (2007) 'Why the South African NQF failed: Lessons for countries wanting to introduce national qualifications frameworks', *European Journal of Education* 42, 523–547.

Barnett, Michael (2006) 'Vocational knowledge and vocational pedagogy', in M. Young and J. Gamble (eds), *Knowledge, Curriculum and Qualifications for South African Further Education*, Cape Town: Human Sciences Research Council, pp. 143–157.

Beck, John and Young, Michael (2005) 'The assault on the professions and the restructuring of academic and professional identities: A Bernsteinian analysis', *British Journal of Sociology of Education* 26, 183–197.

Bernstein, Basil (2000) *Pedagogy, Symbolic Control and Identity* (2nd edn), Oxford: Rowman & Littlefield Publishers.

Community Services and Health Industry Skills Council (2005a) 'CHC02 Community Services Training Package Volume 2 of 4 National Competency Standards', Australian Training Products Ltd, Melbourne.

—— (2005b) 'CHC02 Community Services Training Package Volume 3 of 4 National Competency Standards', Australian Training Products Ltd, Melbourne.

Department of Education Science and Training (2006) *Training Package Development Handbook*, November, Canberra: Department of Education Science and Training.

Gamble, Jeanne (2006) 'Theory and practice in the vocational curriculum', in M. Young and J. Gamble (eds), *Knowledge, Curriculum and Qualifications for South African Further Education*, Cape Town: Human Sciences Research Council, pp. 87–103.

Goozee, Gillian (2001) *The Development of TAFE in Australia* (3rd edn), Adelaide: National Centre for Vocational Education Research.

Misko, Josie (2006) *Vocational Education and Training in Australia, the United Kingdom and Germany*, Adelaide: National Centre for Vocational Education Research.

Muller, Johan (2006) 'Differentiation and progression in the curriculum', in M. Young and J. Gamble (eds), *Knowledge, Curriculum and Qualifications for South African Further Education*, Cape Town: Human Sciences Research Council, pp. 66–86.

Office of Further and Training Education Victoria (1997) *Associate Diploma of Social Science (Community Development)*, Victoria, Melbourne: Office of Further and Training Education.

Schofield, Kaye and McDonald, Rod (2004a) *High Level Review of Training Packages Working Paper 2: Training packages today*, Brisbane: Australian National Training Authority.

—— (2004b) *High Level Review of Training Packages Working Paper 7: Supporting quality teaching, learning and assessment*, Brisbane: Australian National Training Authority.

—— (2004c) *Moving on ... Report of the High Level Review of Training Packages*, April, Brisbane: Australian National Training Authority.

Young, Michael (2006) 'Conceptualising vocational knowledge: Some theoretical considerations', in M. Young and J. Gamble (eds), *Knowledge, Curriculum and Qualifications for South African Further Education*, Cape Town: Human Sciences Research Council, pp. 104–124.

Chapter 17

'Well, if the government won't do it, we bloody well will!'

Third age activism and participatory action learning

Garnet Grosjean, Sheila Pither, Art Kube and Sylvia MacLeay

Introduction

English sociologist and historian, Peter Laslett, in his 1989 book *A Fresh Map of Life: The emergence of the third age*, coined the latter term to characterize that period of our lifespan when work takes on less importance, and non-vocational endeavours, friendships and life's closure occupy more of our attention. Over the past two decades, there have been significant changes in how citizens of the third age view their societal role. Rather than the stereotype image of 'going gently into that good night...' today's elders are actively participating in promoting their own well-being. Instead of waiting passively for government policy to address their needs, they are taking an active role in the policy-making process.

This chapter reports on the development of a pilot workshop for facilitators, which evolved into a train-the-trainer programme. These activities are part of an action research project conducted by co-investigators from provincial universities, and the Council of Senior Citizens' Organizations of British Columbia (COSCO). COSCO's roots reach back to the early 1950s, when a group of retired employees from Canadian Pacific Railway, Canadian National Railway and British Columbia Railway came together to provide an effective voice in the battle for decent pensions and social benefits. Some 30 years later, in 1981, the organization was formally registered under the Provincial Societies Act.

COSCO's Constitution and Bylaws mandate it to: (a) assemble, coordinate and advance proposals and resolutions concerned with the welfare of elder citizens, and submit them to the appropriate government bodies; and (b) advance the social and physical welfare of all elder citizens in the province of British Columbia. Over the years COSCO has grown to become an umbrella organization for seniors' organizations, and now has 42 affiliate members representing approximately 42,000 seniors. COSCO has become the voice for seniors' concerns at all levels of government; especially, it provides a unified opposition to the downloading of health care costs on to seniors.

COSCO is led by a retired labour activist; its executive is made up of a range of retired trades people and professionals. This leadership team chose to push back against cuts to seniors' health care by recruiting researchers and academics to assist them to develop and implement a plan of action to change government policies. As committed lifelong learners, the leadership team chose participatory action learning as the appropriate way to structure a response that would encourage the state to recognize the needs of seniors in all areas of health and well-being. A three-year demonstration project – Health and Safety Learning: for seniors by seniors – was developed and is in the process of being implemented.

The demonstration project comprises a series of health literacy transfer modules, and a programme of training groups of volunteer facilitators, themselves seniors, to deliver the modules in their own communities. The ultimate goal of the project is to establish learning communities throughout British Columbia that will foster an improved quality of life and independent living for older adults well into their advanced years. At the end of the demonstration period the model will be adapted for use across Canada.

Researchers from the adult education departments of the University of British Columbia and Simon Fraser University, as well as partner groups of health and safety experts, assisted with the design of educational materials appropriate to the learning capacity and literacy levels of workshop participants. The project confronts the important role of learning in maintaining the health, quality of life and longevity of older adults, and in preparing individuals to take on new roles in their community and society. In the following we provide the conceptual framework for the study, and discuss the choice of participatory action learning (PAL) as our methodological approach. The chapter describes the initial fieldwork and provides preliminary results from the early training workshops.

Conceptualizing the third age

The number of older persons has tripled over the last 50 years and, according to the United Nations, will more than triple again over the next 50 years. By the year 2050, projections indicate that more than one in five persons throughout the world will be 60 years or older. Seniors (aged 65 years or older) are one of the fastest-growing population groups in Canada, according to Statistics Canada (2001a). In 2000, there were an estimated 3.8 million Canadians aged 65 and over, up 62 per cent from 2.4 million in 1981. In fact, the senior population has grown twice as fast as the overall population since the early 1980s. As a result, more than one out of every eight Canadians is now a senior. In 2000, they represented 13 per cent of the population, up from 10 per cent in 1981 and 8 per cent in 1971.

Statistics Canada (2001b), further reports that although the Canadian population has aged rapidly in the past several decades, the senior component of the population is still relatively small compared with other major industrialized countries. In the late 1990s, for example, 12 per cent of all Canadians were aged 65 and older, compared with 13 per cent in the Netherlands, 14 per cent in the United States, 15 per cent in France, Japan and Switzerland, 16 per cent in the United Kingdom and Germany, and 17 per cent in Sweden and Italy.

This situation will change in the next several decades, however, because the number of Canadians nearing the age of 65 is larger than in these other countries. While Canadian seniors currently comprise a smaller share of the total population than in the United States, for example, by 2051 at least 25 per cent of the Canadian population will be seniors, compared with only 20 per cent of Americans. These predictions signal the need for enriching the lives of older Canadians as they become an increasingly significant demographic group. Lifelong learning is central in constructing fruitful adult roles as parents, workers, volunteers, grandparents, caregivers and active learners.

In his path-breaking book, Laslett provided a useful four-stage heuristic for considering the different ages/stages of people's lives. The first age refers to the early socialization that takes place in childhood. The second age consists of adult maturity, development of careers, earning a living through engagement in work and child rearing. The third age, the focus of this chapter, is a time when individuals begin to relinquish the responsibilities of the second age (mainly participation in the workplace), and seek other forms of self-fulfilment and autonomy. There are few studies on learning in the third age, and little information is to be found on the transition from the second to the third age. Closer consideration of this transition is needed to understand the impact of ageing on learning. The fourth age, the final stage of life where individuals may become increasingly dependent on others to maintain life, is the topic of the gerontological literature and does not concern us here.

Transitions to the third age

The third age is the time of life when people have usually completed conventional work and child-rearing responsibilities but still have several decades of active living ahead of them. While the onset of the third age is chronologically different for each person, this age is qualitatively distinct from the ages that precede and follow it: second age of full-time employment or parenthood on the one hand, and the fourth age of greater dependency on the other.

Transitions are formal turning points or events: complex processes of 'becoming somebody else', which combine both identity and agency in decision making about life choices. Navigating the transition from old to new identities and roles (e.g. from employed to retired) must be managed within the norms and expectations of a particular society or context. All transitions involve social, emotional and cognitive changes at points of transfer, which generate stress, fear and threats to self-confidence and self-esteem, even when successfully navigated. For the socially or economically disadvantaged further erosion can occur if the transition is not effectively managed.

The differential opportunities available to older adults depend on variables such as social class, gender, race/ethnicity and geographical location. These variables are shaped by ambivalence about whether seniors are a 'burden' or an 'asset' to society. Many Eastern cultures believe that wisdom comes with age. They respect elders as repositories of knowledge where opinions should be sought and endorsed. Western cultures, on the other hand, often adopt an economic perspective. When the economy is robust seniors are seen as assets that can contribute to prosperity through part-time or volunteer work. When the economy is poor, however, seniors tend to be viewed as economic burdens. As 'non-productive' citizens, they may command little respect.

Nevertheless, in the West transition to the third age provides increasing freedom for many seniors. While some may experience it as a time of poverty, isolation and reduced self-esteem, the majority of older adults are fit and healthy, with a desire to participate fully in the community and maintain control of their lives. For this group, community-based learning provides a pathway to an 'active' retirement.

Ageing and learning

As we grow older our bodies undergo age-related changes. At the same time, mental acuity can begin to decline as a result of physiological changes in the brain. Researchers suggest that overall brain mass shrinks modestly in some people between the ages of 60 and 70 years. There is also some evidence that neurotransmitters, the chemicals that relay messages from neuron to neuron in the brain, become less available and may play a role in declining memory among older adults. Learning requires more time and repetition; multitasking becomes more difficult, forgetfulness more common. The ability to think abstractly declines, as does the ability to maintain concentration over time.

But, the outlook is not completely negative. While the struggles to remember a name, a date or a place are known as 'senior's moments', recent research indicates that these 'slips of the mind' manifest as early as 20 years of age, and continue in a relatively linear fashion right into old age. Further, studies show that the effects of age-related brain function can be moderated by stimulation from active learning in the form of educational or leisure activities and professional pursuits. Engaging in active learning also provides a means for active engagement in the community, another strategy for delaying cognitive and social losses. Technology can be used to enhance learning, independence and social participation. Research shows that seniors are neither afraid of nor opposed to the use of technology. The design of technological products and services, however, needs to consider the particular learning needs of older adults. In our Health and Safety Learning project we train seniors to use technology to deliver subsequent training workshops to seniors' groups in different areas of the province.

Learning and community

The connection between learning and community has a long history in adult education and is supported by theory and research. A deeper understanding of the ways that adult learning and community are intertwined is now required. Particularly in the case of seniors, we need to understand the qualities that communities must possess to support best seniors' continued learning and thereby enhance their quality of life. Beattie *et al.* (2003) argue that community-based organizations that serve older adults are in a unique position to bridge the gap between the research and practice of healthy ageing. By developing a network of individuals in the health care sector, community organizations and the academy, organizations like COSCO create opportunities to enhance the health and well-being of seniors.

Many seniors must deal with circumstances and challenges that limit their individual quality of life. With people living longer it becomes increasingly important to overcome limitations and find ways to enhance quality of life through community involvement. We think of this as 'ageing in place' within a broader 'learning community' of seniors. In learning communities, seniors work together to define what is important to them, and develop the networks that are crucial for resilient participation in society. Such networks are an integral part of PAL.

What is participatory action learning?

PAL emerges from the same traditions as critical action research (CAR) and participatory action research (PAR). Beginning with the early work of Kurt Lewin in the 1940s (cf. Lewin 1946), action research was successfully revived as a methodological approach to social and educational research in the 1970s, 1990s and again in the early years of the twenty-first century. A concise definition of action research can be found in O'Brien (2001: 3): put simply, action research is 'learning by doing' – a group of people identify a problem, do something to resolve it, see how successful their efforts are and if not satisfied, try again.

CAR dates back to the emancipatory goals of the Frankfurt School of critical theory. CAR's goal is to enhance local problem-solving abilities through widening discourse, dialogue and respect for different kinds of knowledge (Adorno and Horkheimer 1972; Marcuse 1964). Carr and Kemmis (1986) stipulate that social research is intrinsically connected to social action and social movements. As such, CAR is a concrete and practical expression of the desire to change the social world for the better. Change is accomplished by improving shared social practices, and by sharing understandings of these social practices and the situations in which they are carried out. CAR is emancipatory in the sense that it is activist: it aims at creating a form of collaborative learning by shared action.

As a methodological approach or framework for social science research, PAR is similarly based on objectives of emancipation and social change. PAR is grounded in the life circumstances of communities and social groups. Its basic methodological feature is dialogue. Comstock and Fox (1993) argue that PAR is of direct and immediate benefit to the community of study because it involves that community in every step of the research process,

from problem formulation to interpretation of findings. Because it is an educational experience for all involved, individual and group learning takes
place. Learning develops as a dialectical process over time. PAR increases
community awareness of social problems and encourages commitment to
their solution.

Like PAR, the PAL approach comprises iterative cycles of community-
level action and reflection that places power in the hands of the beneficiaries.
Its aim is to bring about change within the communities where it is embedded. The learning process does not lend itself to formalized methods because
solutions are ill-defined at the outset and require learning through action.
The approach is best suited to social or political change processes in which
ongoing action and scrutiny enable actors to confront and respond to context-specific barriers to change as they emerge. As will be seen below, PAL's
methods were well suited to COSCO's needs in the Health and Safety Learning (HSL) project.

Developing an action framework

The beginning of any action research project must involve agreement on the
aims and objectives of the project or study. The HSL project began with a
meeting between executive members of COSCO, and representatives from the
adult education departments of two British Columbia universities. The preliminary meeting was to enable COSCO representatives to discuss their ideas
for a project to assist senior citizens in the province of British Columbia, and
to request assistance from university professors in structuring and carrying it
out. There was strong agreement by the end of the meeting that this was
a community project worthy of everyone's involvement. This first meeting
resulted in a joint plan of action to implement a demonstration project –
Health and Safety Learning – for seniors by seniors. We formed an advisory
group and began to recruit others to assist us, including retired civil servants
from relevant provincial ministries.

A first order of business was to apply for funding to launch the project. A
preliminary budget was prepared to outline the project's financial requirements and set targets for fund raising. Because of their experience in
applying for research grants, the group's academics took the lead in preparing applications to specific funding agencies. Within three months of
coming together, $79,000 had been raised to launch the project. Applica-
tions for matching funds have recently been submitted.

While awaiting the outcome of the grant submissions the advisory group
met to design a plan of action for implementation. The plan was elegant in
its simplicity: enough funds would be raised to train a cadre of facilitators
who would spread out across the province to deliver workshops on various
health and safety issues affecting seniors. Participants would be mobilized to
press government for changes in health policies that would enhance the lives
of older citizens. Once the model was proven successful in British Columbia,
facilitators would be trained in every province and territory in Canada creat-

ing a national seniors' lobby for positive changes to government policies that affect seniors' health and welfare.

It was agreed that a PAL approach was appropriate for the project. While PAL is similar to PAR it was felt that the word 'research' suggested an academic emphasis that made some of the group feel as if they were objects of study. As we all would be learning from each other and from the process we were engaged in, the group felt that 'learning' should be reflected in the title; the word 'project' rather than 'study' was adopted to describe this collaborative venture. The group also emphasized that we were training activists rather than recruiting traditional volunteers.

Once the overall vision of the project was decided, manageable objectives were set for designing materials for the workshops and training facilitators to deliver them. Three major components of content were established: information, awareness and commitment. People of every age require access to appropriate oral and written *information* tailored to their literacy levels. Mere provision of information, however, does not ensure the adoption of practices with a positive effect on an individual's health and safety. Therefore, COSCO's workshops would seek to increase participants' *awareness* of opportunities in their community. Finally, COSCO's volunteers would be trained to assist individuals to *commit* to improving their quality of life in order to maintain an independent lifestyle for as long as possible.

New knowledge and behavioural change would occur only if the workshop materials could be readily understood by participants. The final design criterion was that written materials and audio-visual aids must be appropriate to the learning capacity and literacy levels of workshop participants.

The workshops

Preliminary research into seniors' health and welfare issues identified a number of topic areas suitable for workshop treatment. The topic of 'falls' was chosen for the first workshops. Falls are the leading cause of fatal and non-fatal injuries to seniors: one out of three seniors falls each year; 40 per cent of residential care admissions are fall related; 84 per cent of injury-related hospitalizations are due to falls; seniors who fall are more likely to fall again (Vancouver Coastal Health 2005). The older you are, the more likely you are to fall and be seriously injured.

Falls not only cause injury, they represent a large financial burden to the Canadian health care system. Health care for seniors who have fallen is estimated to amount to $1 billion per year. Once it was agreed that the first workshop to be developed would focus on preventing injuries suffered from falls, we developed an engaging and informative PowerPoint presentation appropriate to the learning capacity and literacy levels of our target group.

The next task was to recruit and train facilitators to deliver the workshop to seniors' groups in the local area. An initial meeting was held with a group of potential recruits where the project was explained in detail and the responsibility of facilitators made clear. Those who chose to commit were invited back for a training session on how to use the audio-visual equipment, how to anticipate questions and on the role of a facilitator. Interestingly, these volunteers showed little reluctance to learn how to use computer technology and the PowerPoint program, even if they had little or no previous experience. This willingness may reflect commitment to their role, and our assurance of support with the technology in their initial presentations. As part of the evaluation of the facilitator workshops it became obvious that facilitator training should be provided in each region of the province. Regional facilitators would be trained by individuals who received training from COSCO. There was now a demand to design a longer 'train the trainer' programme of at least one week to prepare a province-wide group of seniors to train facilitators to present the workshops in their own communities. This became the second stage of the project as we developed the train the trainer programmes.

In preparation for the train the trainer programme, the advisory group prepared a Facilitators Handbook (including information derived from the initial presentations), and a Train the Trainer Manual. Two intensive one-week training sessions for 22 seniors were held in Vancouver in late 2007.

Train the trainer participant selection

In selecting participants for the train the trainer programme we chose to capitalize on the training of existing community leaders, rather than identifying and grooming potential leaders from 'outside' the community. Modest finances and limited time dictated this choice. Training leaders already in place would also help to strengthen local resources and reduce the costs of training. Participants for the initial train the trainer programmes were selected as a convenience sample (Merriam 1998; Patton 2001) from those individuals known as active volunteers in each of the regions of the province. Representatives from retired teachers' associations and similar professions were targeted. Computer literacy was not an essential criterion, but familiarity with the use of e-mail was preferred.

The first train the trainer programme for local participants from the Greater Vancouver area was conducted from 20 October to 2 November 2007, and the second, for participants from across the province, was held from 19 to 23 November 2007. There were eight participants in the first workshop and 14 in the second.

Evaluation of the training programmes

An important aspect of any action research project is to ensure that there are adequate provisions for evaluating its success. As the train the trainer programmes were the second stage in the larger health and safety learning initiative, their success was gauged through participant evaluations. Evaluation procedures were developed and tested with the participants in the first group. They included onsite observations of participants, daily evaluation of activities and materials by participants and a summative evaluation by participants at the end of the programme. Prior to the second group the evaluation instruments were reviewed and refined where needed (mainly in the use of plain language in the evaluation forms).

Approximately four months after these initial programmes, an online participant follow-up survey was conducted with all participants. Of the 22 participants in the groups, 17 completed the survey, a response rate of 77 per cent. Overall, respondents reported favourable impressions of the programmes. They indicated a range of features they liked best, including the underlying concept of seniors working with seniors, well-organized material, high-quality facilitation, interaction with peers, friendly atmosphere and learning to use computer and projector equipment. For example, participants were asked to rate their achievement on a set of learning outcomes, on a 5-point Likert-like scale where 1 = not effective and 5 = very effective. The average ratings for all the learning outcomes were high, ranging from 3.50 for 'Be able to operate and troubleshoot the equipment used to deliver presentations' to 4.69 for 'Be aware of the overall goals of this COSCO initiative'.

Participants were asked to rate their own levels of knowledge, commitment and confidence by comparing their status before and after the programme: 'Level of knowledge around health and safety learning for seniors' rose from 3.47 to 4.47. The largest shift in average ratings was for commitment to the initiative: 'Level of commitment to improving quality of life for seniors' increased from 3.18 to 4.53, and 'Level of confidence as a community-based facilitator' from 3.29 to 4.06. As well, 63 per cent of respondents were still in touch with each other four months after the programme, and 60 per cent had connected with community groups and professional health and safety practitioners as a result of participating in the programme.

Survey respondents were asked to reflect on what barriers older adults might face with respect to learning about life-prolonging health and safety measures. The main barriers mentioned were lack of information, financial constraints, lack of societal respect towards elders, harsh weather conditions in rural areas leading to isolation, unwillingness to learn anything new, denial about the affects of ageing, the need for periodic reinforcement of new material, access to transportation, physical challenges, fear of the unknown, desire to be self-sufficient, inadequate political will to improve health conditions for seniors and lack of familiarity with new technology.

Recommendations

Analysis of responses to the evaluation of the train the trainer programmes allows us to make some recommendations on how to improve and expand them as an integral part of the Health and Safety Learning initiative:

1   Continue to revise and update the modules in line with formative feedback and the need to customize material for various audiences. Encourage interactive presentations based on adult education principles.

2   Continue to support the facilitators with peer coaching and presentation packages (handouts, CD-ROM discs with presentation information, updating of the facilitators' training manual, provision of equipment and simplified instructions for use).
3   Consider including material and discussion space on political activism in future workshops.
4   Continue to track outputs of the initiative in order to develop a strong, evidence-based set of policy recommendations for health and safety training for seniors.

Evaluation of the Health and Safety Initiative

The COSCO advisory group proposed several research questions that together form a framework for evaluating the health and safety project's overall contributions:

- What have we learned about the perceived and actual barriers experienced by older adults in relation to learning about health and safety issues?
- Will the health promotion and accident prevention practices of participants change as a result of their participation in the seniors' workshops? In what ways?
- What evidence is there that the liaison with partner groups and professional health and safety practitioners is strengthened as a result of their participation in the project?
- What impact can the project have on future government health care planning?
- What information will be judged to be the most vital for participants to have?
- Will the project result in an attitudinal shift from an emphasis on acute care to an emphasis on prevention? Amongst which groups will this shift occur?
- How can the programme be adapted for use in different Canadian locales?

Overall, the success of COSCO's health and safety initiative will be judged by its ability to achieve three objectives: (1) create a change in seniors' behaviour (safer, more confident seniors in their own homes, decreased burden on the health care system), rather than passively conveying information on seniors' health and safety; (2) assist in the development of active health and safety support communities/networks among seniors throughout the province; and (3) mobilize seniors to become more active in their demands on government and policy makers (inspire and motivate seniors' advocates), thereby effecting significant changes in health care policy for seniors.

COSCO will continue to conduct formative and summary evaluations of each subsequent component of the project. These evaluations will be useful when considering the future extension of the programme across Canada.

Summary

The population of seniors in Canada is increasing at a rate almost double that of other age groups. These predictions signal the need for enriching the lives of older individuals as they become an increasingly significant demographic group. Lifelong learning is central in constructing fruitful adult roles as parents, workers, volunteers, grandparents, caregivers and active learners. Recognizing this need COSCO, a community action group, proposed that ways must be found to challenge current government health policy in order to improve the lives of seniors in British Columbia. An advisory group of volunteers from academic institutions, health care providers and seniors' groups was established to devise and implement a project to address seniors' concerns about health care. The goal of the project – Health and Safety Learning: for seniors by seniors – is to establish learning communities that will assist older adults in maintaining an improved quality of life and independent living well into their advanced years. The purpose of the project is to confront the important role of learning in maintaining the health, quality of life and longevity of older adults, and in providing opportunities for individuals to take on new roles in their community and society.

To promote the Health and Safety Learning Project, COSCO developed a vision to empower increasing numbers of seniors to take charge of their health and safety. The organization has recruited a group of motivated project leaders who can inspire others to contribute actively to this initiative, as well as expand it over time. It has assessed the need for relevant content to increase seniors' awareness of available resources, enlisted support from health authorities and academic partners in the planning and delivery of workshops, and successfully raised the required funding from granting agencies to enable the association to launch a programme of health and safety learning for seniors in British Columbia.

In conclusion, with the proportion of older adults increasing at a faster rate than younger cohorts, elders will have a significant impact on the shape of future societies. Perceptions of ageing are becoming more positive, as numbers increase. But as the ageing curve moves out it becomes important to find practical ways to enable seniors to maintain their quality of life throughout the third age, and beyond. Active community-based learning, as a strategy of lifelong learning, provides the practical tools required. It is inspired by the insight that 'you don't stop learning when you grow old; you grow old when you stop learning'.

References

Adorno, T. and Horkheimer, M. (1972) *Dialectic of Enlightenment* (trans. J. Cummings), New York: Herder and Herder.

Beattie, B.L., Whitelaw, N., Metter, M. and Turner, D. (2003) 'A vision for older adults and health promotion', *American Journal of Health Promotion* 18, 200–204.

Carr, W. and Kemmis, S. (1986) *Becoming Critical: Education, knowledge, and action research*, London: Falmer.

Comstock, D. and Fox, R. (1993) 'Participatory research as critical theory: The North Bonneville, USA, experience', in P. Park, M. Brydon-Miller, B. Hall and T. Jackson (eds), *Voices of Change:*

Participatory research in the United States and Canada, Westport, CT: Bergin and Garvey, pp. 103–124.

Laslett, P. (1989) *A Fresh Map of Life: The emergence of the third age*, London: Weidenfeld and Nicolson.

Lewin, K. (1946) 'Action research and minority problems', *Journal of Social Issues* 2, 34–46.

Marcuse, Herbert (1964) *One-Dimensional Man*, Boston, MA: Beacon Press.

Merriam, S.B. (1998) *Qualitative Research and Case Study Applications in Education*, San Francisco, CA: Jossey-Bass.

O'Brien, R. (2001) 'Um exame da abordagem metodológica da pesquisa ação' [An overview of the methodological approach of action research], in Roberto Richardson (ed.), *Teoria e Prática da Pesquisa Ação {Theory and Practice of Action Research}*, João Pessoa, Brazil: Universidade Federal da Paraíba. (English version: online, available at: www.web.ca/~robrien/papers/arfinal.html (accessed 20 January 2002).)

Patton, M.Q. (2001) *Qualitative Research and Evaluation Methods*, Thousand Oaks, CA: Sage.

Statistics Canada (2001a) *Canada's Seniors No. 1: A growing population*. Online, available at: www.hc-sc.gc.ca/seniors-aines/pubs/factoids/2001/no01_e.htm (accessed 15 January 2007).

Statistics Canada (2001b) *Canada's Seniors No. 5: The international perspective*. Online, available at: www.hc-sc.gc.ca/seniors-aines/pubs/factoids/2001/no05_e.htm (accessed 15 January 2007).

Vancouver Coastal Health (2005) *Health Link Archives*. Online, available at: www.vch.ca/enewsletter/files/2005-11-01/falls_prevention_stay_in_the_game.html (accessed 15 January 2007).

Chapter 18

Conclusion – researching transitions

Trends and prospects

Jim Gallacher, Robert Ingram and John Field

The contributions to this book indicate the complexity of the idea of transitions, when explored in the context of lifelong learning. While, as Ecclestone and others have noted, this has now become a major issue in policy in countries throughout the world, as well as being the focus for practice and research, the concept is used to cover many different activities and it is viewed as being important for many different reasons. As in so many other discussions concerning lifelong learning there are also competing agendas. Grace points to the predominance of economistic agendas that drive forward much of the policy with respect to lifelong learning, while he, and other contributors, emphasise the need to place a continuing emphasis on other agendas including social justice and personal development. Transitions can also refer to issues of the structures that facilitate and support transitions, as well as the processes for the people involved. They can also refer to transitions between different types of learning. In this brief concluding chapter we do not attempt to summarise the issues dealt with in the preceding chapters, nor to provide a comprehensive overview of the issues. Instead we focus on some issues that have been identified, and which we would suggest could be the focus of further research. We also seek to identify some issues that are relatively neglected in this collection, and in the wider research literature.

Transitions and stratification

An issue that is explored in a number of the chapters in this book, and most explicitly by Bathmaker and Thomas, is the one of stratification. While there is increasing interest in providing learners with opportunities for transitions of many different kinds, there is also increasing interest in the question of the extent to which opportunities for access to different kinds of education, learning or training are equally open to all. While Bathmaker and Thomas' research focuses on dual sector institutions in England, they refer to a wider literature, which is documenting and exploring the idea of differentiation and stratification in higher education. This can significantly limit the opportunities for progression for many students making the transition from one educational sector to another. Grubb, in his chapter, outlines the opportunities that community colleges in the USA can provide for adult learners, and there is considerable evidence that further education colleges have similar functions in the UK, as Moodie's chapter indicates. However, Moodie also discusses the extent to which opportunities for students who wish to progress may be limited. Research of this kind indicates an important area of work that could usefully be developed to explore the ways in which opportunities for transition can be constrained.

When considering constraints of this kind there is a need to consider issues of structure and process. Structural issues can be associated with the ways in which institutions operate, and the opportunities that they do or do not provide. Further research here is required into the nature and extent of the constraints that exist, and their consequences for learners. There is also a need to consider how the wider social structural issues constrain the lives of many learners. These issues are explored in a number of chapters within this book. Perhaps one of the most interesting in this respect, because it is a largely neglected area, is the contribution by Quinn and her colleagues on the issues faced by young people in jobs without training. This chapter brings out the complex ways in which the position of these young people in the social structure influences their opportunities for employment and for learning, and the opportunities for transition between different types of work and learning. It also explores the ways in which the perceptions of professionals, such as careers advisers, can shape the official responses to young people in these situations. Further work of this kind is required, both to explore the complexity of these issues, and the opportunities to identify innovative ways to address them.

Some emerging issues

A number of chapters in this book have highlighted areas of research that have in the past been relatively neglected, but are now emerging as issues of importance. One of these, which is increasingly recognised as being of considerable importance, is the issue of the under-representation of men in many areas of education. There is now widespread evidence of this form of under-representation, and while community-based learning is a very successful way of re-engaging many women, there is much less evidence of its success in this respect with men. Golding's chapter on the role of men's sheds in rural Australia is of considerable interest in this respect. An important aspect of this work is that it brings out the importance of activities that would not normally be defined as learning, in that they are not part of any formal learning structures, but they provide valued opportunities for the men involved to make transitions from their working lives, and the activities that have engaged them there, to a new range of activities, which are in many ways familiar to them, but provide new learning opportunities as well. It is clear that many of these men would never engage in formal learning activities, but these sheds are providing ways of breaking down these barriers. This chapter also very helpfully begins to explore some of the relationships between formal, informal and nonformal learning opportunities. These issues are also taken up, in a very different context, in the chapter by Chappell *et al.* on learning at work through 'integrated development practices'. These are development activities that provide learning opportunities for workers, although they are not characterised as formal learning or training activities. At a time when work-based learning, and learning through work is increasingly seen as being of considerable importance, it is valuable to see a discussion of this kind that emphasises the informal and nonformal learning opportunities. Research that can explore further the nature of these learning opportunities, and the processes through which people are able to engage with them, will be of considerable value.

The need for longitudinal studies

The final issue we would like to identify in this short concluding chapter is the need for more longitudinal studies of transitions. It is notable that many of the chapters in this book report on qualitative research, and in many cases the research involves relatively small samples, and there is little of a longitudinal nature. While qualitative research of this kind is often very valuable, and provides very useful insights into the experiences of learners, there is considerable need for larger-scale more quantitative studies that can provide data on the wider patterns of transition that exist as people move through different learning and working activities. It has often been difficult to obtain funding for studies of this kind, and while there are a number of cohort studies in the UK and elsewhere, there are few that have focused on the tracking of adults as they move through different stages of their working and learning lives. Studies of this kind could add greatly to our existing knowledge and understanding. In the meantime, we take great pleasure in presenting this collection as a way of continuing and stimulating the debate.

Index

rational planning 57–9
recruiting universities 136–7
recursive methodology 52–62
reflective learning model 43, 48
reflexive modernity 52
reflexive practice 113–14
responsibilisation, role of structure 59–62
responsible learners 50–63

San Francisco City College 96, 98
Scotland, higher education 134, 135–7, 139–40, 142–3
Scottish Vocational Qualifications 201
scripted life-stories 80–1
sectioned time 42–3
segmented HE systems 137–8, 139–40, 142–3
selectivity, HE admissions 135–40
self-awareness 21–2
self-fragmented narratives 192–4
service delivery, older men 73–4
shed-based workshops 65, 66, 68, 70–1, 73
short-term job training 99–101
situated learning 69, 114, 177, 180, 207, 211
skills acquisition, HE students 157, 158
skills transitions 53
slow time 41, 45
social capital 23, 33, 59–60, 62, 119
Social Exclusion Unit 11
social influences, student life cycle 146–59
social issues 30–2, 35, 37
social justice model 43, 48
social narratives 52–62
social transitions 12–13
socialisation 155–6
socially constructed identity 15
socio-cultural practice 114–16
SOMUL (Social and Organisational Mediation of University Learning) project 146–59
strategic repositioning 124–5
stratification 225–6
stratified HE systems 134–6, 142–3
street wise, young people as 195
structural changes, FE/HE 125–8
structure: combining with agency/identity 16–18, 178; role in responsibilisation 60–2
structures, navigation of 11–12
student experience, valuing impact of 154–6
student life cycles 146–59
student transitions in HE 123–31
subject choice 147–9, 150–4
subject engagement 155–7
Sure Start 82–3
systems, navigation of 11–12

teaching effectiveness, community colleges 102–3
Technology Enhanced Learning (TEL) Programme 161–71

theoretical knowledge 201–11
therapeutic approaches 21–2
Third Age: conceptualising 214–15; transitions to 215–16
time depth 42, 46–7
time factor, final-year students 156–7
time horizons, impact of 46
time management 47
time vision theories 41–3, 45–6
train the trainer programme 220–2
training, young people's lack of 189–99
training packages: community development diplomas 205–11; knowledge classification in 204–5
transfer, measures to improve 140–2
transition: challenges/critical questions 22–4; easing/supporting 19–20; emerging issues 226–7; in a liquid age 1–2; managing 18–22; meanings of 11–18, 147; possibilities/problems 97–101; researching 3–5; trends and prospects 225–7
Transition Practices Model 113–18
transparency, community colleges 101

'underfoot' syndrome 71–2
unemployment 189–90, 192
unified HE systems 134–5, 136–7
United Nations Educational, Social and Cultural Organisation (UNESCO) 29, 52
units of competency 204, 205–11
Universities and Colleges Admissions Service (UCAS) 130
University of Southern Queensland 107
US, community colleges 93–104; higher education 137–41, 142–3

vertical transitions 11
victims, young people as 195
visibility, community colleges 101
vocational education and training: competency-based 201–11; US 100–1
voluntary fire organisations 65, 68, 70

Western Australia Department of Education and Training 65–6
work-based learning 196–7
work-related socialisation 155–6
working lives and time vision theories 45–6
workload, final-year students 156–7
workplace learning contexts 111–12
workplace training: Canada 36; UK 56, 60–2
workshops, HSL project 219–20

young people: participation in work/training 189–99; transitions research 4